OECD Economic Surveys:
Poland
2020

This document, as well as any data and map included herein, are without prejudice to the status of or sovereignty over any territory, to the delimitation of international frontiers and boundaries and to the name of any territory, city or area.

The statistical data for Israel are supplied by and under the responsibility of the relevant Israeli authorities. The use of such data by the OECD is without prejudice to the status of the Golan Heights, East Jerusalem and Israeli settlements in the West Bank under the terms of international law.

Please cite this publication as:
OECD (2020), *OECD Economic Surveys: Poland 2020*, OECD Publishing, Paris, *https://doi.org/10.1787/0e32d909-en*.

ISBN 978-92-64-63259-2 (print)
ISBN 978-92-64-53919-8 (pdf)

OECD Economic Surveys
ISSN 0376-6438 (print)
ISSN 1609-7513 (online)

OECD Economic Surveys: Poland
ISSN 1995-3542 (print)
ISSN 1999-060X (online)

Table of contents

Executive Summary   9

1 Key Policy Insights   14

    Ensuring continued convergence with higher living standards   14
    The economy requires continued policy support   20
      The economy weakened substantially   20
      A comprehensive fiscal package has cushioned the initial crisis impact   21
      Monetary policy has been appropriately accommodative   26
      Risks to financial stability have increased and require close monitoring   28
    Boosting the recovery while containing medium-term spending pressures   30
      The crisis legacy will compound long-term challenges   30
      Ageing will put significant pressures on the quality of pension, health and long-term care   33
      Improving the tax system   37
      Illustrating the fiscal effects of government's and OECD-recommended reforms   40
    Improving productivity, employment and well-being   41
      Enhancing labour market inclusiveness   41
      Greening growth is essential for well-being   52
      Preventing corruption and economic crimes   55
    References   58

Annex A. Progress on structural reforms   62

2 Boosting SMEs' internationalisation   63

    Poland's internationalisation has been remarkable but unequal   64
    A bird's eye view of Poland's internationalisation and SMEs' landscape   68
      Polish exports concentrate on medium and low-tech goods   68
      Small size and low productivity hinder SME internationalisation   71
    Boosting SMEs' internationalisation through a better business environment   76
      Easing further administrative costs for potential exporters   76
      Easing tax compliance and ensuring sound public support for SMEs   79
      Increasing SMEs innovation, its diffusion and productivity   82
      Trade facilitation has improved   83
      Developing local clusters and SMEs' consortia could boost internationalisation   84
    Increasing skills to foster integration in global value chains   87
      Raising skills through better life-long training   87
      Supporting better management skills for SMEs   92
      Facilitating the immigration of skilled workers   93
    Harnessing the benefits of digitalisation to support SMEs' exports   94
      Developing high-quality digital infrastructure   96
      Preparing SMEs for the digital transition   99
      Encouraging the use of ICTs by SMEs   101
    Improving transport infrastructure to boost internationalisation   105
      The capacity and quality of transport infrastructure need to be enhanced   105
      Maintenance and upgrading investments are needed to improve the quality of infrastructure   107
      Investment in transport should better reflect environmental concerns   108
      Developing multi-modal transport links to improve logistics' performance   109
      Improving the governance of infrastructure   110
      Supporting the tourism sector and its more equal regional development   110
    References   114

Tables

Table 1. The recovery remains uncertain 10
Table 1.1. Macroeconomic indicators and projections 22
Table 1.2. Low-probability events that could lead to major changes in the outlook 24
Table 1.3. Government structural fiscal plans from 2018 to 2025 and OECD's recommendations 40
Table 1.4. Past OECD recommendations on fiscal policy and pensions 41
Table 1.5. Potential impact of some reforms proposed in this Survey on GDP 44
Table 1.6. Past OECD recommendations on labour market and migration policies 51
Table 1.7. Past OECD recommendations on environmental policies 55
Table 2.1. Tourism is concentrated in a few destinations 111

Figures

Figure 1. The long-term expansion stalled 10
Figure 2. The SMEs productivity gap is wide 11
Figure 3. Exposure to air pollution remains widespread 12
Figure 4. Demographic pressures are high 12
Figure 1.1. The catch-up with living standards in other OECD countries has continued 14
Figure 1.2. Poverty had fallen until the onset of the crisis 15
Figure 1.3. The COVID-19 crisis has dented economic prospects 15
Figure 1.4. The impact of population ageing is already visible 16
Figure 1.5. Regional disparities are high 17
Figure 1.6. The crisis could widen inequalities 17
Figure 1.7. New COVID-19 cases have increased rapidly over the autumn 20
Figure 1.8. Activity had bounced back after the initial Covid-19 sudden stop 21
Figure 1.9. Labour market adjustments are significant 23
Figure 1.10. Exchange rate variations have been limited and export performance has so far been robust 24
Figure 1.11. Poland's export structure is well diversified 26
Figure 1.12. Monetary policy has reacted forcefully to the crisis 27
Figure 1.13. Inflationary pressures have decreased 27
Figure 1.14. Evolution of macro-financial vulnerabilities 28
Figure 1.15. The risk of a credit crunch has increased 29
Figure 1.16. Banking sector's profitability and holding of sovereign bonds 30
Figure 1.17. The fiscal response to the crisis has been substantial 31
Figure 1.18. Spending commitments on some social programmes are rapidly increasing 32
Figure 1.19. Ageing will put further pressure on public debt 32
Figure 1.20. A steep decline in replacement rates is set to contain pension expenditures 34
Figure 1.21. Old-age work is low and declining 35
Figure 1.22. The health sector suffers from numerous weaknesses 36
Figure 1.23. Tax revenues are around the OECD average, but could be more redistributive 38
Figure 1.24. Tax-based carbon price signals are weak 39
Figure 1.25. Upskilling and automation are challenging issues 42
Figure 1.26. Educational outcomes have improved rapidly but there are significant skill gaps 43
Figure 1.27. Urban sprawl could reinforce employment access issues 45
Figure 1.28. Temporary contracts tend not to be a stepping-stone for career development 47
Figure 1.29. The minimum wage could increase substantially 48
Figure 1.30. The employment rate of women with young children has stagnated 49
Figure 1.31. The use of formal childcare is improving 50
Figure 1.32. Poland's energy and carbon intensities have declined but remain elevated 52
Figure 1.33. Significant investments are needed in the electricity sector 53
Figure 1.34. Air pollution levels are high and result in a high number of premature deaths 54
Figure 1.35. There is room to further limit the risks of corruption 55
Figure 2.1. Poland's internationalisation and export performance have been impressive 64
Figure 2.2. SMEs play a key role in the Economy 65
Figure 2.3. SMEs internationalisation has been heterogeneous 66
Figure 2.4. SMEs have been hard hit by the coronavirus crisis 67
Figure 2.5. Polish exports have been robust, and well diversified 68

Figure 2.6. The structure of Polish exports 69
Figure 2.7. Foreign multinationals and exports are tightly linked 70
Figure 2.8. Poland is specialised in low- and medium-tech exports 71
Figure 2.9. Smaller firms have low export intensity in manufacturing and services sectors 73
Figure 2.10. Micro-firms lag multiple forms of internationalisation 74
Figure 2.11. SMEs productivity is weak and young firms lack opportunities to grow 75
Figure 2.12. Micro-firms account for a high share of employment 75
Figure 2.13. SMEs' gaps have significant economic and social consequences 76
Figure 2.14. Selected features of the OECD product market regulation indicators 77
Figure 2.15. Some administrative procedures remain burdensome 78
Figure 2.16. Some services trade barriers remain important 78
Figure 2.17. Tax compliance costs remain elevated 79
Figure 2.18. Business and SMEs' support are heavily reliant on EU funds 80
Figure 2.19. SMEs lag R&D investment and innovation 82
Figure 2.20. Strengthening firms' cooperative linkages and clusters could support SMEs 84
Figure 2.21. The share of high-skilled adults and their contribution to GVCs is low 88
Figure 2.22. Shortages of skilled staff, demographic ageing and automation remain major issues 89
Figure 2.23. Training is low and insufficiently targeted, 2016 90
Figure 2.24. Public funding for training is low and small firms provide low access to training 92
Figure 2.25. Management skills appear lagging, notably for domestic firms 93
Figure 2.26. Poland's digital transition has been relatively lagging 95
Figure 2.27. SMEs lag in the adoption of more sophisticated digital technologies 96
Figure 2.28. Barriers to the deployment of digital infrastructure are elevated 97
Figure 2.29. The quality of Poland's digital network needs to improve further 98
Figure 2.30. Participation in e-commerce is low 100
Figure 2.31. SMEs' e-commerce export participation is low 100
Figure 2.32. Awareness of digital security by SMEs is weak 102
Figure 2.33. Poles lack advanced digital skills 103
Figure 2.34. Polish SMEs offer too little ICT training 104
Figure 2.35. There is room to improve trade logistics 105
Figure 2.36. Investment in transport infrastructure is sizeable, but regional disparities in infrastructure are large 106
Figure 2.37. Increasing road maintenance spending would be a good move 107
Figure 2.38. Rail freight transport needs a boost 108
Figure 2.39. Airport traffic expanded fast before the coronavirus crisis 109
Figure 2.40. International tourism was lagging before the coronavirus crisis 112

Follow OECD Publications on:

 http://twitter.com/OECD_Pubs

http://www.facebook.com/OECDPublications

http://www.linkedin.com/groups/OECD-Publications-4645871

http://www.youtube.com/oecdilibrary

http://www.oecd.org/oecddirect/

This book has...

StatLinks 📊

A service that delivers Excel® files from the printed page!

Look for the *StatLinks* 📊 at the bottom of the tables or graphs in this book. To download the matching Excel® spreadsheet, just type the link into your Internet browser, starting with the *http://dx.doi.org* prefix, or click on the link from the e-book edition.

This *Survey* is published on the responsibility of the Economic and Development Review Committee of the OECD, which is charged with the examination of the economic situation of member countries.

The economic situation and policies of Poland were reviewed by the Committee on 17 September 2020. The draft report was then revised in the light of the discussions and given final approval as the agreed report of the whole Committee on 23 October 2020.

The Secretariat's draft report was prepared for the Committee by Antoine Goujard and Pierre Guérin under the supervision of Pierre Beynet. Sections of this *Survey* also benefitted from contributions by Paula Adamczyk, Priscilla Fialho and Alexandra Paciorek. Statistical research assistance was provided by Paula Adamczyk and Patrizio Sicari, and editorial assistance by Alexandra Guerrero.

The previous *Survey* of Poland was issued in March 2018.

Information about the latest as well as previous Surveys and more information about how *Surveys* are prepared is available at http://www.oecd.org/eco/surveys.

BASIC STATISTICS OF POLAND, 2019*
(Numbers in parentheses refer to the OECD average)**

LAND, PEOPLE AND ELECTORAL CYCLE					
Population (million, 2018)	38.0		Population density per km² (2018)	124.0	(37.8)
Under 15 (%, 2018)	15.1	(17.8)	Life expectancy at birth (years, 2018)	77.8	(80.2)
Over 65 (%, 2018)	17.5	(17.1)	Men (2018)	73.9	(77.6)
Foreign born (%, 2012)	1.8		Women (2018)	81.8	(82.8)
Latest 5-year average growth (%)	0.0	(0.6)	Latest general election	October-2019	

ECONOMY					
Gross domestic product (GDP)			Value added shares (%, 2018)		
In current prices (billion USD)	592.2		Agriculture, forestry and fishing	2.4	(2.5)
In current prices (billion PLN)	2 273.6		Industry including construction	32.7	(27.3)
Latest 5-year average real growth (%)	4.3	(2.2)	Services	64.9	(70.2)
Per capita (000 USD PPP, 2018)	31.8	(46.4)			

GENERAL GOVERNMENT					
Expenditure (OECD: 2018)	42.0	(40.3)	Gross financial debt (OECD: 2017) ***	63.6	(109.0)
Revenue (OECD: 2018)	41.3	(37.3)	Net financial debt (OECD: 2017)	37.0	(69.0)

EXTERNAL ACCOUNTS					
Exchange rate (PLN per USD)	3.84		Main exports (% of total merchandise exports)		
PPP exchange rate (USA = 1)	1.75		Machinery and transport equipment	38.0	
In per cent of GDP			Manufactured goods	18.2	
Exports of goods and services	55.8	(54.2)	Miscellaneous manufactured articles	17.1	
Imports of goods and services	50.5	(50.4)	Main imports (% of total merchandise imports)		
Current account balance	0.4	(0.3)	Machinery and transport equipment	36.2	
Net international investment position	-50.4		Manufactured goods	17.0	
			Miscellaneous manufactured articles	13.0	

LABOUR MARKET, SKILLS AND INNOVATION					
Employment rate (aged 15 and over, %)	54.4	(57.5)	Unemployment rate, Labour Force Survey (aged 15 and over, %)	3.3	(5.4)
Men	63.1	(65.6)	Youth (aged 15-24, %)	9.9	(11.7)
Women	46.4	(49.9)	Long-term unemployed (1 year and over, %)	0.7	(1.4)
Participation rate (aged 15 and over, %)	56.2	(61.1)	Tertiary educational attainment (aged 25-64, %, 2018)	30.9	(36.9)
Average hours worked per year	1,806	(1,726)	Gross domestic expenditure on R&D (% of GDP, 2017)	1.0	(2.6)

ENVIRONMENT					
Total primary energy supply per capita (toe, 2018)	2.8	(4.1)	CO2 emissions from fuel combustion per capita (tonnes, 2018)	8.1	(8.9)
Renewables (%, 2018)	8.2	(10.5)	Water abstractions per capita (1 000 m³, 2018)	0.3	
Exposure to air pollution (more than 10 g/m³ of PM 2.5, % of population, 2017)	99.9	(58.7)	Municipal waste per capita (tonnes, 2018)	0.3	(0.5)

SOCIETY					
Income inequality (Gini coefficient, 2017, OECD: 2016)	0.275	(0.310)	Education outcomes (PISA score, 2018)		
Relative poverty rate (%, 2017, OECD: 2016)	9.6	(11.6)	Reading	512	(487)
Median disposable household income (000 USD PPP, 2017, OECD: 2016)	17.7	(23.9)	Mathematics	516	(489)
Public and private spending (% of GDP)			Science	511	(489)
Health care	6.3	(8.8)	Share of women in parliament (%)	29.1	(30.7)
Pensions (2014, OECD: 2015)	11.2	(8.5)	Net official development assistance (% of GNI, 2017)	0.1	(0.4)
Education (% of GNI, 2018)	4.6	(4.5)			

* The year is indicated in parenthesis if it deviates from the year in the main title of this table.

** Where the OECD aggregate is not provided in the source database, a simple OECD average of latest available data is calculated where data exist for at least 80% of member countries.

*** National account definition. Public debt (Maastricht definition, as used in the main text) was at 45.7% of GDP in 2019.

Source: Calculations based on data extracted from databases of the following organisations: OECD, International Energy Agency, International Labour Organisation, International Monetary Fund, World Bank.

Executive Summary

The global crisis interrupted long-term socio-economic progress

The coronavirus (COVID-19) crisis has hit the economy and society hard. The pandemic occurred after a long expansion of living standards when unemployment and poverty rates had fallen to historically low levels (Figure 1). Early containment measures have limited contagion in the first part of 2020. Though production and consumption rebounded quickly after their easing until September, a new rise of infections led to renewed restrictions in October.

Despite extensive policy support, the recession will have long-lasting consequences (Table 1). Broad fiscal measures and unprecedented monetary support cushioned the socio-economic impact of the pandemic. Growth and employment have hold up well at the beginning of 2020, notably compared to European peers. Yet, even if sanitary conditions improve progressively, GDP is projected to drop sharply, while further outbreaks would weaken economic outcomes.

Figure 1. The long-term expansion stalled
GDP volume, 2005Q1=100

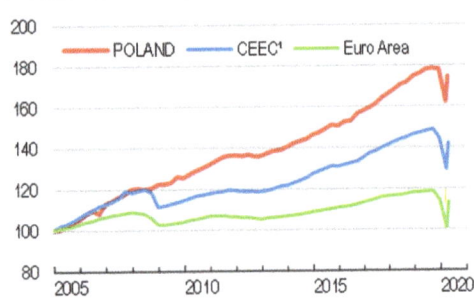

1. The average of Hungary and the Czech and Slovak Republics.
Source: OECD (2020), OECD Economic Outlook 108.

StatLink https://doi.org/10.1787/888934207880

Uncertainty is particularly high. More severe than expected coronavirus outbreaks or the delayed roll-out of an effective vaccine could hurt economic conditions. International trade tensions also remain high and could spread further.

The crisis legacy will compound long-term issues. Employment has declined and public debt has increased abruptly, while the low productivity of some workers, weak environmental outcomes and the shrinking working-age population remain key challenges.

In welcome moves, the government has vouched to increase healthcare spending and to boost investment, innovation and entrepreneurship.

Table 1. The recovery remains uncertain

	2019	2020	2021	2022
Gross domestic product	4.5	-3.5	2.9	3.8
Unemployment rate (%)	3.3	3.8	5.5	4.3
Fiscal balance (% of GDP)	-0.7	-10.8	-6.8	-4.8
Public debt (Maastricht, % of GDP)	45.7	56.5	62.0	63.6

Source: OECD Economic Outlook 108.

Macroeconomic policies should remain supportive

As economic conditions weakened rapidly, fiscal and monetary policy easing helped cushion the coronavirus shock.

The government adopted a comprehensive fiscal package, worth around 5.2% of GDP in 2020, to support the most affected households and firms. Temporary measures, combined with the spontaneous impact of the recession, will push the deficit to 11% of GDP in 2020. Maastricht debt will reach historically high levels. In addition, the Financial Shield programme supports small, medium and large companies. The discussed EU budget and the planned EU recovery package are also set to support the economy. As high uncertainty and weak global conditions will dent the recovery, the fiscal stance should remain supportive. Frontloading investment, notably in healthcare and infrastructure, would boost short- and long-term prospects, while supporting the transition to a more sustainable economy. Once the recovery is firmly underway, the authorities should pursue fiscal consolidation to reduce public debt.

Monetary policy responded quickly and forcefully. The Central Bank reduced its policy rate to 0.1%, and introduced unprecedented quantitative easing. The authorities also eased firm financing, extended liquidity support and decreased capital requirements for banks. In the case of a further weakening, monetary policy could expand asset purchases further or consider negative nominal rates, especially as inflationary pressures have receded on the back of depressed total demand.

Tax reforms should support the recovery. The labour tax wedge shows little progressivity, tax breaks remain numerous and property taxes are relatively low. The tax wedge for low-skilled workers could be lowered to boost job creation. When the recovery is firmly underway, Poland could build on its past successes to further increase tax compliance and revenue collection to finance such measures. Reducing inefficient tax expenditures and strengthening property taxes, notably on vacant properties and building lots, would raise revenues and housing supply.

Boosting productivity and inclusiveness

Strengthening the recovery to sustain the catch-up of living standards is a challenge. The reforms proposed in this *Survey* – targeted at improving productivity, skills and employment outcomes – could have a substantial impact, lifting GDP by 5.6% after 10 years.

The productivity of many workers and small and medium-sized enterprises (SMEs) is low (Figure 2). The pandemic has disproportionally affected weaker regions, smaller firms and disadvantaged workers. The development of higher-technology sectors is also increasing the demand for non-routine tasks and higher skills, and many workers are at risk of being left behind.

Figure 2. The SMEs productivity gap is wide
Relative value added per employee, large firms=100

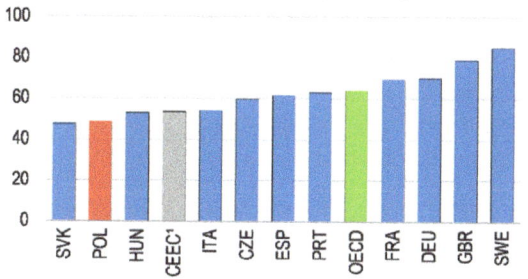

1. The average of Hungary and the Czech and Slovak Republics. Source: OECD (2020), OECD Structural Business Statistics (database).

StatLink ᴹˢᴸ https://doi.org/10.1787/888934207899

Improving the business environment would boost the growth and internationalisation of numerous small-firms. Tax-compliance costs remain high, while regulatory and tax changes are frequent. Tax expenditures and derogatory regulative measures for small firms lower these

costs, but they run the risk of creating fiscal and regulatory "cliff edges" hindering firm expansion. Continuing to foster the use of digital tools by the tax administration and smoothing tax and administrative thresholds would support firm growth. Ensuring effective consultations and evaluations in the design of taxes and regulations would also support firm growth and investment. Finally, fostering judicial independence is key for business confidence, notably from foreign investors, which would require limiting the potential involvement from the executive branch in procedures applicable to judges.

Digital and transport infrastructure are still a bottleneck for innovation and resource allocation. Absorption of EU funds for large transport infrastructure has reduced infrastructure gaps, though it focused on new roads. A stronger focus on local public transport and the maintenance of the local roads would reduce congestion, pollution and trade costs. The development of high-speed broadband and data hubs, for example in the health sector, would also boost productivity. Establishing an independent evaluation body for ex-ante cost-benefit analyses would ensure better management of large local projects. Tasking this institution in collecting data on projects' ex-post performance would provide more evidence for spending prioritisation.

Ensuring the supply of the right skills would boost job creation and productivity. The test scores of 15-year olds have made impressive progress, but lagging adult basic skills (except for younger workers) limit employment opportunities. Small firms have lacked engagement in upskilling strategies, hampering the diffusion of new technologies and their productivity and internationalisation. The planned integrated skills strategy should provide stronger guidance for SMEs looking for employees and encourage the creation of SMEs' consortia for training. Evaluating and scaling-up effective training and consulting programmes for digital technology diffusion in SMEs would help to boost worker reallocation and productivity.

Higher job quality is key to an inclusive recovery. The 2020-21 minimum-wage rises could eventually weigh on the labour-market recovery and increase some atypical forms of employment. Strengthening incentives for permanent contracts, including through labour law enforcement, will be essential for low-wage workers and SMEs. Rapidly developing a well-designed international migration strategy would also increase employment opportunities for migrant workers.

Strengthened active labour market policies and a more efficient housing market would support access to jobs. Unemployed and low-skilled workers make little use of training, and information about training quality should be developed. The new schemes to develop the rental market should go hand in hand with increased mobility vouchers for low-income workers. Strengthening urban planning would avoid further urban sprawl and the associated risks of concentrating poverty and negative consequences on congestion and pollution.

Ensuring sustainable growth

Air pollution and population ageing are pressing concerns. Greening investment and containing demographic pressures are essential to support the recovery and sustainable growth.

The use of poor quality coal and biomass in the housing sector, together with low energy efficiency, produces substantial urban air pollution (Figure 3). This, together with an old car fleet and mostly coal-fired electricity generation capacity, contributes to climate change and poses health hazards that have a negative impact on productivity.

Strengthened environmental policies would improve health and environmental outcomes. The "Clean Air programme" that targets energy efficiency in the housing sector and efforts to develop electric mobility and reduce the dependence of the energy mix on coal are welcome. Once the economy is on a clear recovery path, increasing the tax rates on energy use while boosting social transfers for the poorest households would be positive. Adopting a clear strategy together with higher and more homogeneous price signals, notably taxes on cars and carbon emissions, should be a priority to ease the transition towards a less carbon intensive energy mix. This should include relevant support for low-income households.

Figure 3. Exposure to air pollution remains widespread
% of population exposed to more than 15 micrograms/m³ of PM2.5

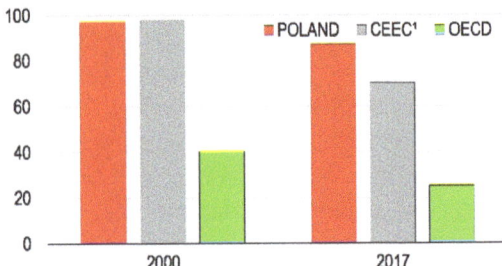

1. The average of Hungary and the Czech and Slovak Republics.
Source: OECD (2020), OECD Environment Statistics (database).

StatLink https://doi.org/10.1787/888934207918

Ageing will weigh on labour supply and public finances. The old-age dependency ratio is rising (Figure 4). The ongoing increase in healthcare spending and the foreseen decline of pension replacement rates will boost social expenditures in the long term, while public debt is historically high.

Figure 4. Demographic pressures are high
Ratio of 65 and over to 15-64 population, %

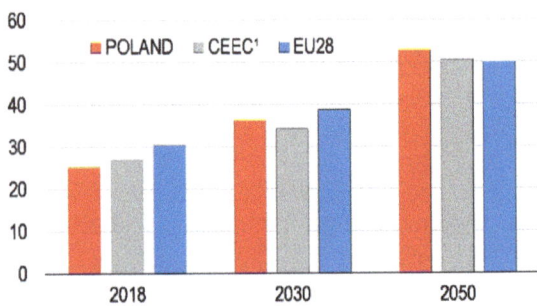

1. The average of Hungary and the Czech and Slovak Republics.
Source: Eurostat (2019), Baseline population projections.

StatLink https://doi.org/10.1787/888934207937

Increasing the efficiency of health-related spending and promoting longer working lives is essential to free up public resources in the longer term. Beyond pandemic related expenditures, the planned increase in health spending should focus on prevention and coordinated care to reduce the high prevalence of risky behaviours and costly hospital admissions. Incentives to expand working lives and policies to improve the employability of old-age workers are also needed to encourage old-age employment and boost long-term growth.

MAIN FINDINGS	KEY RECOMMENDATIONS
Macroeconomic and financial policies	
Fiscal and monetary policy have responded quickly and effectively to the crisis. Yet, uncertainty about the pace of the recovery and potential new coronavirus outbreaks remains high.	If economic conditions weaken rapidly, ease fiscal and monetary policies further, by ensuring that additional fiscal spending supports the most affected households and firms and considering further asset purchases.
Widespread uncertainty could hold back the recovery.	Bring forward green and digital investment to kick-start the recovery.
Poland's healthcare system had low funding over the long term. Further coronavirus outbreaks could put the system under heavy strains.	Expand intensive care capacity and ensure a successful testing, tracing and isolation strategy.
The coronavirus crisis has increased public debt, while ageing and other spending pressures weigh on long-term fiscal sustainability.	When the recovery is firmly underway, pursue fiscal consolidation to decrease the public debt-to-GDP ratio.
Ensuring an inclusive recovery	
The crisis and its legacy will potentially imply large-scale reallocation of workers. Too many adults, notably older ones, have weak basic skills. Lifelong training opportunities are low for unemployed, low-skill and older workers.	Strengthen lifelong learning opportunities notably for low-skilled workers, with a special focus on developing digital skills.
Labour costs on standard contracts are relatively high and the tax wedge lacks progressivity. Low-skilled workers suffer from weak career prospects.	Envisage an income-tax-credit and/or subsidise social security contributions for low-income workers.
Enrolment of young children in child-care facilities remains low, despite recent progress.	Continue to expand the supply of childcare and long-term care facilities, targeting low-income households and disadvantaged areas.
Strengthening green and sustainable growth	
The health care system lacks efficiency and access is uneven. The government has announced a significant increase in spending by 2024.	Use the planned increase in health spending to strengthen primary care and prevention.
Stimulus measures need to be aligned with long-term environmental goals. Yet, regulatory uncertainty has hold back investment in the energy sector.	Implement stable climate-change policies aligned with European and international objectives.
The pricing of the environmental costs of fossil fuels is uneven in all sector of the economy. The transport sector is responsible for increasing greenhouse gas emissions and air pollution.	Once the economy recovers, increase road pricing and introduce CO_2-based vehicle taxation, together with redistribution targeted towards poorer households.
Reduced VAT rates and exemptions are widespread. Broadening the tax base would help lower tax rates on labour.	Limit the use of reduced VAT rates and exemptions over the medium term.
Pension replacement rates are set to shrink and the effective retirement ages of men and women are lower than the OECD average.	Progressively align male and female statutory retirement ages and increase it in line with life expectancy gains in good health.
Potential involvements of the executive in disciplinary proceedings of judges may undermine judicial independence and investment.	Amend the disciplinary procedures applicable to judges, in particular by excluding the possibility for the executive to intervene in these proceedings.
Boosting productivity and SMEs' internationalisation	
Many small local firms are not integrated into national and international supply chains.	Scale up existing programmes for SMEs with a focus on training and showcase best practices based on thorough impact analyses.
The government improved tax compliance successfully, but tax procedures remain overly time consuming for SMEs.	Reduce the use of special tax provisions (e.g. exemptions, special rates). Involve stakeholders further in the design of taxes and regulations through early consultation procedures. Conduct systematic ex-ante and ex-post evaluations of regulations.
Access to high-quality infrastructure remains uneven across regions. Infrastructure needs remain high, notably on transport, energy and digital technologies.	Strengthen the role of ex ante cost-benefit analyses in the selection of infrastructure projects, for instance by establishing an independent evaluation body.
Digitalisation remains uneven. The use of big data is constrained which may limit productivity gains and evidence-based policymaking, in particular in the healthcare sector.	Develop data hubs providing companies and public services with access to large databases, notably in the healthcare sector, while ensuring digital security and privacy.

1 Key Policy Insights

Ensuring continued convergence with higher living standards

Poland has experienced strong economic growth over the past two decades. It has been very successful in integrating into global trade, not least thanks to its increasing role as an outsourcing destination for business services. The catch-up with average living standards in other OECD countries and regional peers has continued (Figure 1.1). Until the outbreak of the coronavirus, rising household incomes had contributed to more inclusive economic development, while poverty rates, inequality and the unemployment rate had declined (Figure 1.2).

Figure 1.1. The catch-up with living standards in other OECD countries has continued

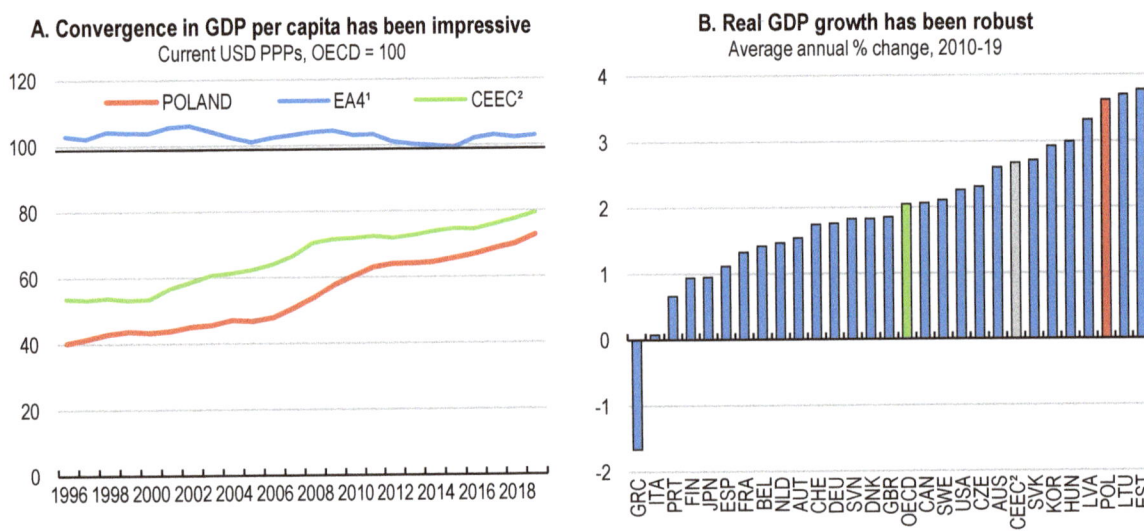

A. Convergence in GDP per capita has been impressive
Current USD PPPs, OECD = 100

B. Real GDP growth has been robust
Average annual % change, 2010-19

1. EA4 is the average of Germany, France, Italy and Spain.
2. CEEC is the average of Hungary and the Czech and Slovak Republics.
Source: OECD (2019), OECD National Accounts and OECD Economic Outlook: Statistics and Projections (databases).
StatLink https://doi.org/10.1787/888934207956

The coronavirus pandemic threatens these achievements made over the past decades. Though the initial shock has been lower than in many OECD countries, the economy is projected to see a marked contraction in economic activity in 2020 before partially recovering in 2021 (Figure 1.3). As confinement measures were lifted in May 2020, many businesses reopened and most workers returned to work, and consumption and production are rebounding from their low confinement levels. Yet, the pace of the recovery remains very uncertain: unemployment has risen slightly, renewed sanitary restrictions have been imposed in the autumn, uncertainty is high and global demand is still depressed.

Figure 1.2. Poverty had fallen until the onset of the crisis

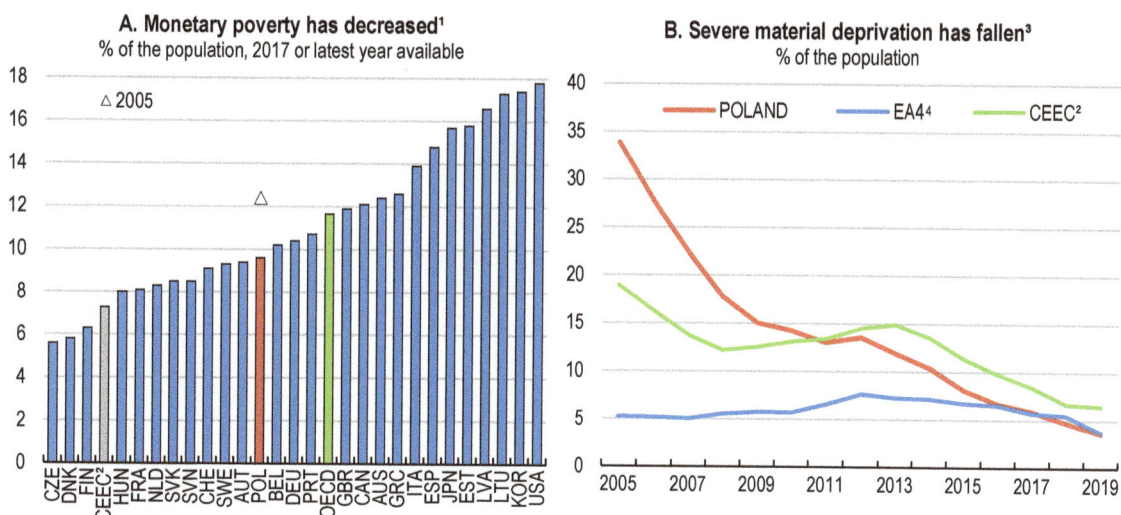

A. Monetary poverty has decreased[1]
% of the population, 2017 or latest year available

B. Severe material deprivation has fallen[3]
% of the population

1. Poverty rate after taxes and transfers, Poverty line 50% of median equivalised disposable income.
2. CEEC is the average of Hungary and the Czech and Slovak Republics.
3. Severe material deprivation rate is defined as the enforced inability to pay for at least four items that are considered by most people to be desirable or even necessary to lead an adequate life.
4. EA4 is the average of Germany, France, Italy and Spain.
Source: OECD (2019), OECD Income Distribution Statistics (database); Eurostat (2019), "Severe material deprivation rate by age and sex", Eurostat Database.

StatLink 📊 https://doi.org/10.1787/888934207975

Figure 1.3. The COVID-19 crisis has dented economic prospects

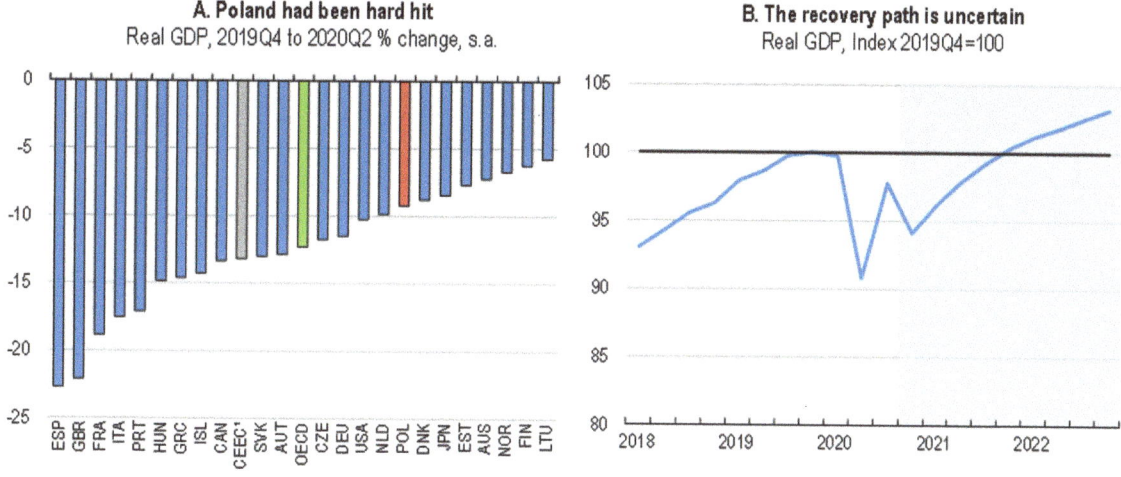

A. Poland had been hard hit
Real GDP, 2019Q4 to 2020Q2 % change, s.a.

B. The recovery path is uncertain
Real GDP, Index 2019Q4=100

1. CEEC is the average of Hungary and the Czech and Slovak Republics.
Source: OECD (2019), OECD National Accounts and OECD Economic Outlook: Statistics and Projections (databases).

StatLink 📊 https://doi.org/10.1787/888934207994

Policy support should remain available while the economy is still operating well below capacity. The shock will dent prospects for some industries, and many workers risk losing attachment to employers and facing difficulties in finding new jobs. The measures announced by the government and at the European Union level (Box 1.1) should also be used as an opportunity to ensure more sustainable and inclusive growth in the longer term. Poland faces pressing environmental issues, with high greenhouse gas (GHG) emissions and air pollution. Persistent air pollution hurts people's health, including by making individuals more

16 |

vulnerable to acute respiratory illnesses like the coronavirus. More generally, Poland scores below the OECD average in terms of health status, housing adequacy, and labour productivity per employee, the latter being 23% below the OECD average in 2018, despite its fast growth. The country also faces significant demographic pressures owing to low fertility and past negative net migration rates, as well as a still significant gender participation and employment gaps, which will weigh on GDP growth and challenges the current labour-intensive growth model. This, together with the legacy of the coronavirus pandemic, will reduce Poland's ability to finance pension and health-related spending in the longer term (Figure 1.4).

While government interventions have shielded most families from the brunt of the shock (Box 1.2, OECD, 2020a), the pandemic could raise inequalities. In particular, the high share of temporary and self-employed workers could suffer from the ongoing labour-market adjustments (Figure 1.6, Panel A). About 14% of temporary workers work on freelancing type of contracts and are not fully covered by workers' rights and some contracts may not be covered by social security benefits. At the same time, many micro- and smaller firms have weak productivity and connections to local, national and international markets, which translates in low wages and job quality (Chapter 2). These firms may have less resilience and flexibility in dealing with the costs of the pandemic and changes in work processes, such as suppliers and export markets shocks, as well as the shift to teleworking and prevention measures due to the pandemic (OECD, 2020b).

Figure 1.4. The impact of population ageing is already visible

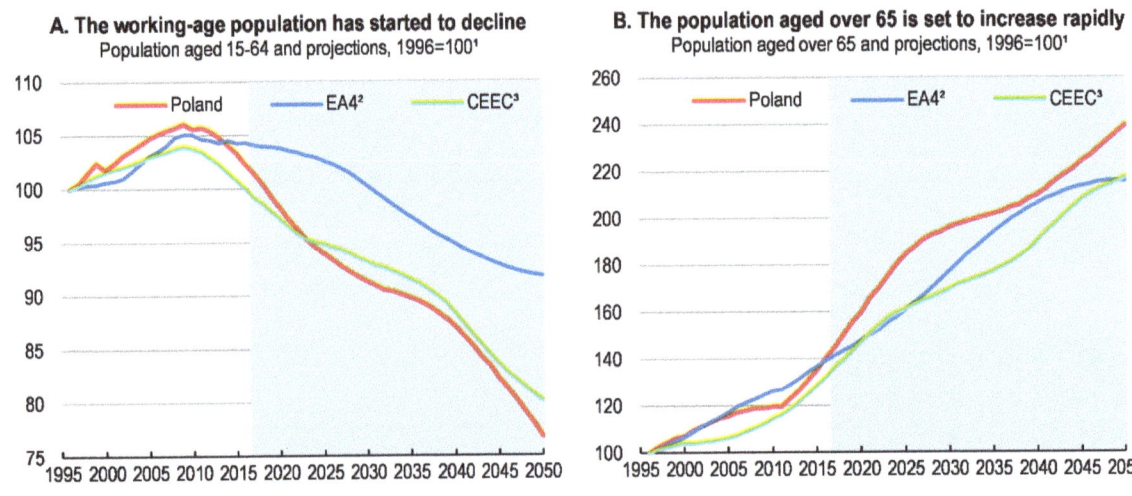

1. Eurostat baseline projections including migrations.
2. EA4 is the average of Germany, France, Italy and Spain.
3. CEEC is the average of Hungary and the Czech and Slovak Republics.
Source: Eurostat (2019), "Demography and Population Projections", Eurostat Database.

StatLink 🖳 https://doi.org/10.1787/888934208013

Disparities between regions could grow further. Disparities had already widened over 2011-16 (OECD, 2018a). Disposable income per household is 20% below the national average in some regions and 20% above in the capital (Statistics Poland, 2019a), and regional well-being indicators show significant gaps, despite some recent progress (Figure 1.5). Many small cities and rural areas still struggle with the outmigration of young people, and access to high quality public services such as healthcare, education or public transport (EC, 2019a). Following the coronavirus outbreak, in April 2020, the change in average paid employment ranged from -5.2% to +0.7% year on year (Statistics Poland, 2020), the most recent declines being much more pronounced in weaker regions (Figure 1.6, Panel B).

In this context, the key messages of this Economic Survey are:

- There is high uncertainty about economic growth. Macroeconomic policies need to support the recovery and should be ready to act in case of further waves of contagion or unexpected downturn.

- To sustain the recovery and more inclusive growth, policies should help job prospects of disadvantaged groups, and improve the links between SMEs and national and international markets.

- More sustainable growth should be supported by policies focusing on innovation, the greening of infrastructure and increasing employment opportunities for women and older workers.

Figure 1.5. Regional disparities are high

Regional well-being, regional ranking, 2017[1]

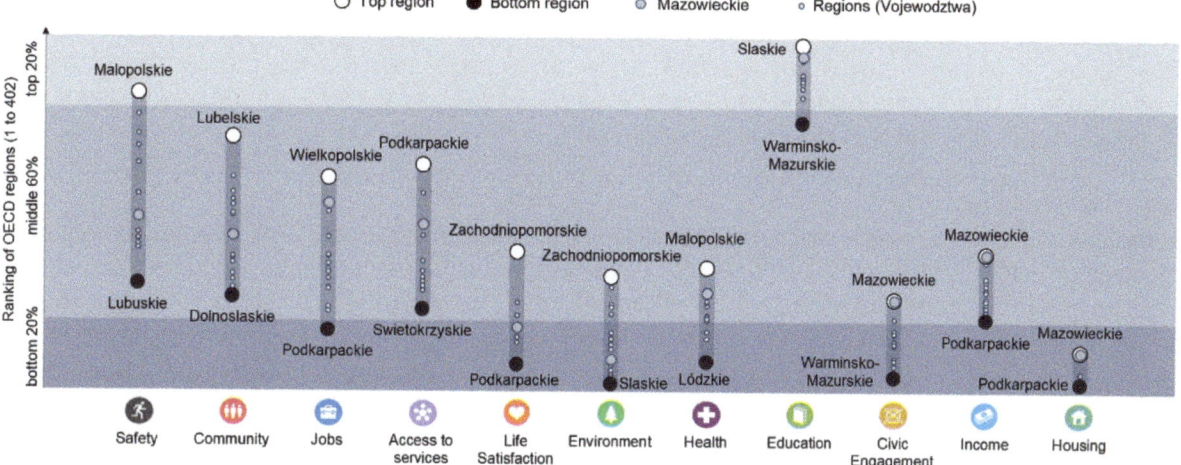

1. Relative ranking of the regions (refers to Poland's 17 voivodeships – NUTS2-) with the best and worst outcomes in the 11 well-being dimensions, with respect to all 395 OECD regions. The eleven dimensions are ranked according to the size of regional disparities in the country.
Source: OECD (2019), OECD Regional Well-Being Database.

StatLink https://doi.org/10.1787/888934208032

Figure 1.6. The crisis could widen inequalities

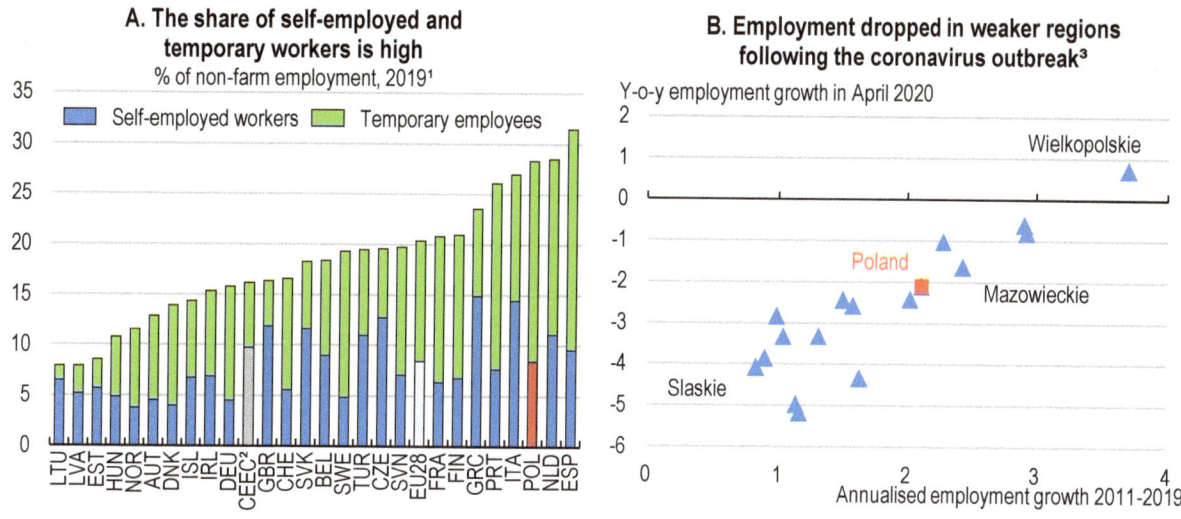

1. 2019 or average of the four latest available countries. Share of self-employment and temporary contracts among 15-64 employed workers, excluding agriculture, forestry and fishing.
2. CEEC is the average of Hungary and the Czech and Slovak Republics.
3. Regions refers to Poland's 17 voivodeships (NUTS 2).
Source: Eurostat (2019), "Employment, Labour Force Statistics series", Eurostat Database; OECD calculations based on Statistics Poland (2020), Average paid employment in enterprise sector (short-term data).

StatLink https://doi.org/10.1787/888934208051

Box 1.1. Measures adopted to contain the coronavirus outbreak and support the economy

Confinement measures

Following the first coronavirus cases in early March, the government took rapid action to ban mass events, close schools and universities and move to online education, promote remote working, and progressively close large public venues. International air and rail passenger traffic was suspended and borders reinstated. On March 24, a strict lockdown was implemented. Leaving home was only allowed unless necessary to buy food and medicine, to consult a doctor or to go to work. In October, the authorities have applied renewed restrictions to curb the rebound of infections. The wearing of face masks in public places has been made mandatory, most schools have moved to distance learning, gyms and eat-in restaurants have closed again, while public gatherings, the number of customers in retail shops and cultural events have been limited.

Health care measures

As the March lockdown was progressively eased, the government made the wearing of masks mandatory in public spaces, unless a minimum two meters distance could be respected. The authorities unlocked more than EUR 23 million (PLN 98 million) for hospitals at a very early stage of the epidemic and an additional EUR 2.3 billion (PLN 10.1 billion) package for the healthcare sector was announced later on. Pharmacists were allowed to issue prescriptions directly and extra funds were made available for personal protection equipment to rescue and fire services, the police and the railway sector.

Fiscal measures

The government implemented a fiscal package as early as March 19. The package was revised three times since, with additional measures to support the economy. The new crisis fund in the State development Bank (BGK) is set to finance fiscal measures of around EUR 22.7 billion (PLN 100 billion) in 2020. In addition, EUR 2.8 billion (PLN 12.2 billion) have been earmarked to support local-government investment.

Income support for individuals

Parents whose children were affected by the closures of schools and early childcare facilities could apply for a care allowance. Firms could apply for a wage subsidy if experiencing difficulties, conditional on not dismissing workers for the duration of the benefit. Self-employed and workers on freelancing civil-law contracts could also apply for a subsidy up to 80% of the statutory minimum wage, exempted of social security contributions and taxes. The government also introduced a solidarity benefit of PLN 1400 per month, for up to three months, for workers who lost their job after March 15 and increased the monthly minimum unemployment benefits by 36% to EUR 272 (PLN 1,200) from September 2020.

Public subsidies, loans, loan guarantees and capital injections to businesses

The government announced the Financial Shield, an unprecedented loan and subsidies scheme worth EUR 22.7 million (PLN 100 billion) for firms to maintain liquidity and protect jobs. The programme managed by the Polish Development Fund (PFR) is dedicated to small, medium and large firms. The loans were awarded for three years, with zero interests, and repayments will only start in the second year. If firms keep their employees for the entire loan duration, up to 60% of the value of the support may be disbursed as a grant instead.

The State Development Bank (BGK) also increased its loan guarantees de minimis programme for firms by EUR 4.5 billion (PLN 20 billion) initially, and an additional EUR 91 million (PLN 400 million) in EU funds was redirected for further loan guarantees at the end of April. For small firms, the guarantee coverage was extended from 60 to 80% of the loans and a new liquidity guarantee fund in BGK was created for loans taken by medium and large enterprises.

The Polish Development Fund (PFR) increased its investments and financing operations on preferential conditions. The government also announced that further capital injections would be financed by drawing on available EU regional funds.

Taxes and social security contributions deferrals

Self-employed and micro-firms experiencing an important drop in revenues could apply for the deferral of taxes and the temporary cancellation of the payment of social security contributions. The measure was later extended to firms with between 10 and 49 employees.

Monetary policy and prudential regulation

Monetary policy has been exceptionally accommodative. The National Bank of Poland (NBP) reduced its policy interest rate three times, from 1.5% in early March to 0.1% at the end of May. In addition, the central bank introduced repo operations to provide liquidity to the banking sector and announced it would purchase Polish Treasury securities and government guaranteed debt securities in the secondary market. The NBP introduced a programme to provide funding for bank lending to non-financial private enterprises similar to the ECB's TLTRO.

Macro prudential regulation was eased. Reserve requirements were lowered from 3.5% to 0.5%, while the interest on mandatory reserves was set at the level of the policy rate (currently 0.1%). Following recommendations from the Financial Stability Committee, banks were released from the obligation to maintain the systemic risk buffer, and allowed to reduce the risk weight from 100% to 50% for some secured exposures on commercial real estate, which considerably increased their available capital. The Polish Financial Supervision Authority (KNF) introduced some flexibility in the classification of exposures and allowed banks to operate below the combined buffer requirement and the Loan-to-Capital ratio.

The "Next Generation EU" plan

The "Next Generation EU" recovery plan agreed among EU leaders in July 2020 reaches EUR 750 billion. After approval by the European Parliament and the Council of the legislative proposals that will create the financial instruments necessary to make "Next Generation EU" operational, the plan is expected to start being implemented from 1 January 2021. It will be financed through borrowing by the Commission on financial markets and repayments will take place over 2028-58. This plan is completed by the 2021-27 EU budget – which would itself reach EUR 1,074.3 billion – to a total of EUR 1,824.3 billion over 2021-27.

The "Next Generation EU" plan creates new financial instruments and is frontloaded over the coming years. The new Recovery and Resilience Facility concentrates most funds (EUR 672.5 billion, of which 312.5 in the form of grants and 360 in the form of loans) to help finance investment and reforms over 2021-23. In particular, grants of the Recovery and Resilience Facility are set to reach around EUR 23.1 billion for Poland (around 4.4% of 2019 GDP over six years). According to the foreseen allocation, the EUR-30-billion "Just Transition Fund" to support the transition towards a climate neutral economy could increase this amount to a total of around EUR 29.1 billion for Poland (5.5% of 2019 GDP) (EC, 2020).

Source: OECD (2020), COVID-19 Tracker; OECD (2020), Economic Outlook, June 2020 – World Economy on a Tightrope from Collapse to Recovery, OECD Publishing, Paris; EC (2020), The Pillars of the Next Generation EU, https://ec.europa.eu/info/sites/info/files/3pillars_factsheet_0.pdf

The economy requires continued policy support

The economy weakened substantially

Following the first positive cases in early March, Poland's daily new COVID-19 infections surged until the beginning of April (Figure 1.7). On 8 March, in the wake of the first confirmed cases, the authorities took rapid action to promote remote working, banned mass events, suspended schools and universities and progressively closed all cultural, accommodation, food and entertainment venues, together with shopping centres (Box 1.1). In mid-March, international air and rail passenger traffic came to a halt and border controls were reinstated. A few days later, the government declared a state of epidemic emergency and implemented tighter confinement measures. The swift introduction of these measures helped limit the extent of the contagion. However, new cases have again increased rapidly in the autumn and the authorities imposed renewed sanitary restrictions.

Industrial production and retail sales dropped sharply in April to below levels observed during the global financial crisis (Figure 1.8). The end of the two months lockdown in May allows activity to resume. Industrial production and retail sales have improved markedly. Accommodation, food services and the transportation sectors have been hit particularly hard. Mobility to retail shops and restaurants decreased by 28% compared to a normal period and retail sales in enterprises employing up to 9 persons dropped by 23% year-on-year in April. Exports and imports, that had been resilient during the first quarter, have also dropped sharply and bounced back thereafter. Business confidence remains relatively low in most sectors, notably services, and the recent resurgence of the pandemic has hurt confidence: domestic demand and mobility indicators started falling again with the renewed restrictions.

Figure 1.7. New COVID-19 cases have increased rapidly over the autumn

Daily new cases, per million of population

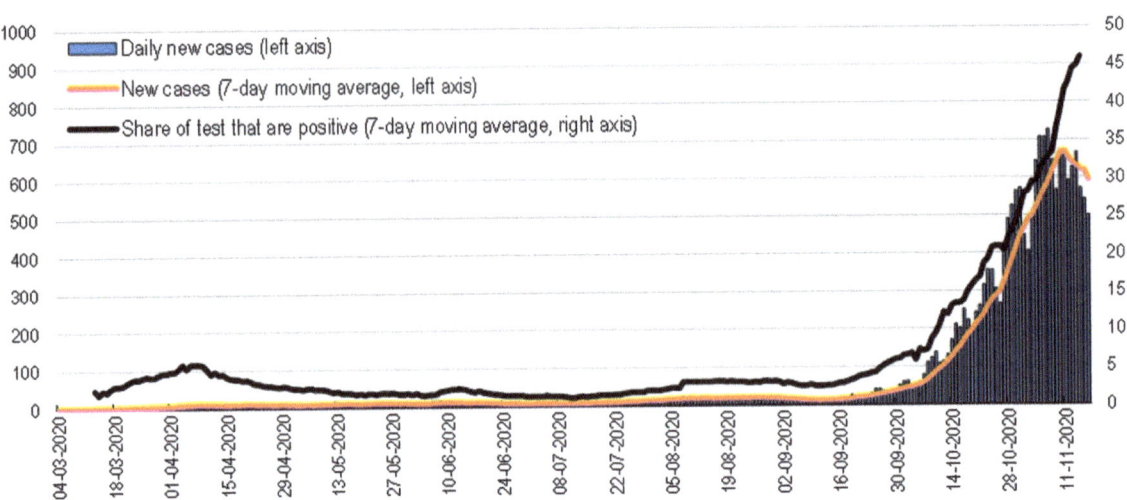

Source: Our World in Data, ourworldindata.org; OECD calculations based on John Hopkins University Centre for Systems Science and Engineering (JHU CCSE) database, and Statistics Poland (2020), Population Statistics.

StatLink 🔗 https://doi.org/10.1787/888934208070

Figure 1.8. Activity had bounced back after the initial Covid-19 sudden stop

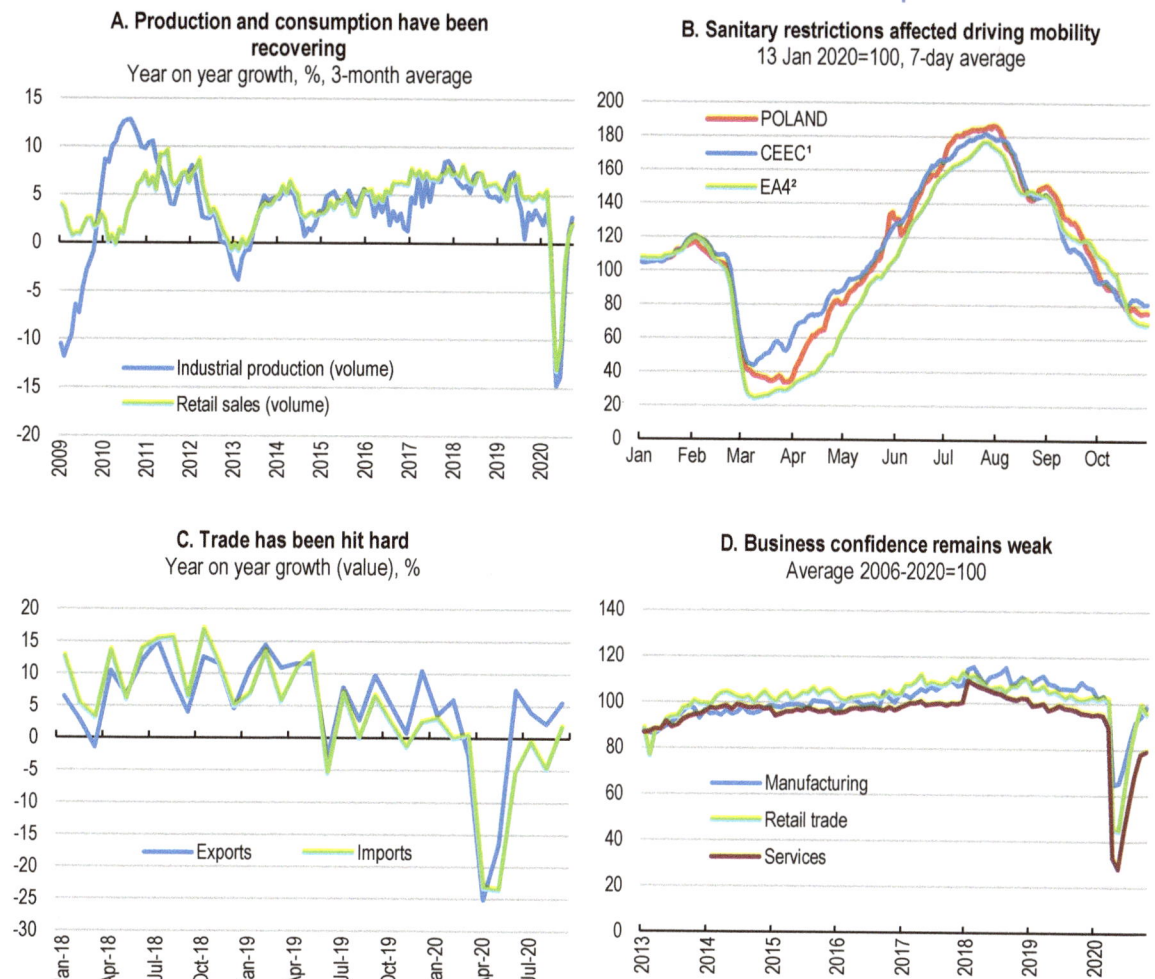

1. CEEC is the average of Hungary and the Czech and Slovak Republics.
2. EA4 is the average of Germany, France, Italy and Spain.
Source: Statistics Poland (2020), Short-term monthly indicators and Business confidence indicators; Apple (2020), Mobility trends reports.

StatLink https://doi.org/10.1787/888934208089

A comprehensive fiscal package has cushioned the initial crisis impact

Fiscal policy reacted forcefully to the coronavirus crisis. The authorities have announced an anti-crisis package that foresees discretionary measures worth about 5.2% of GDP in 2020 (PLN 112.2 billion) in addition to the action of automatic stabilisers and the Financial Shield (Box 1.1). In a welcome move, this package aimed at preserving jobs by sustaining business liquidity, boosting healthcare spending and encouraging infrastructure investment during the recovery. The measures extended income support to numerous self-employed and temporary workers. To avoid widening inequalities due to the pandemic, the government enhanced transfers to local authorities and postponed loan repayments, for up to three months, for individuals having lost their job or main source of income. It also introduced a 3-month solidarity allowance payable to the most disadvantaged jobseekers and raised permanently unemployment benefits. A subsidised micro-loan facility supports the cash-flows of the smallest firms, while a loan guarantee scheme cover loans up to PLN 100 billion (4.4% of GDP) for all firms with no tax arrears, in proportion to their size.

Postponed consumption and delayed investment decisions supported the initial recovery, but another outbreak and the associated sanitary restrictions, the expected rise in unemployment and uncertainties around the extent of global value chain destructions are denting household and business confidence. GDP growth will be limited to 2.9% in 2021, after a deep recession in 2020. In case of further epidemic outbreaks, associated with renewed containment measures, the recovery would further weaken. In addition, the slower euro area recovery, as well as a more pronounced deterioration of the outlook for the global automotive industry and business services, will reduce export prospects.

Table 1.1. Macroeconomic indicators and projections

Poland	2017	2018	2019	2020	2021	2022
	Current prices PLN billion	Percentage changes, volume (2015 prices)				
GDP at market prices	1 989.8	5.4	4.5	-3.5	2.9	3.8
Private consumption	1 166.8	4.5	3.9	-4.5	1.7	4.5
Government consumption	351.9	3.5	6.2	3.1	3.6	1.8
Gross fixed capital formation	348.7	9.4	7.2	-7.4	-1.6	8.2
Final domestic demand	1 867.4	5.2	5.0	-3.6	1.4	4.6
Stockbuilding[1]	47.5	0.4	-1.3	-1.3	-0.4	0.0
Total domestic demand	1 914.9	5.6	3.5	-5.0	1.0	4.6
Exports of goods and services	1 077.7	6.9	5.1	-7.0	7.9	11.3
Imports of goods and services	1 002.7	7.4	3.3	-9.6	8.4	14.4
Net exports[1]	75.0	0.0	1.1	1.0	0.3	-0.7
Memorandum items						
GDP deflator	–	1.2	3.1	3.8	-0.3	2.3
Consumer price index	–	1.8	2.2	3.4	2.3	2.6
Core inflation index[2]	–	0.8	1.9	3.9	3.3	2.6
Unemployment rate (% of labour force)	–	3.9	3.3	3.8	5.5	4.3
Household saving ratio, net (% of disposable income)	–	-1.0	1.9	13.7	12.8	9.7
General government financial balance (% of GDP)	–	-0.2	-0.7	-10.8	-6.8	-4.8
General government debt, Maastricht definition (% of GDP)	–	48.8	45.7	56.5	62.0	63.6
Current account balance (% of GDP)	–	-1.3	0.5	2.3	1.2	0.5

1. Contributions to changes in real GDP, actual amount in the first column.
2. Consumer price index excluding food and energy.
Source: OECD (2020), OECD Economic Outlook 108: Statistics and Projections (database).

Ongoing labour market adjustments will have long-lasting consequences for households and firms (Figure 1.9). The initial shock has been smoothed by government measures, the lowering of working hours and the take-up of unpaid leaves (Statistics Poland, 2020). The number of employees and hours worked have slowly decreased in part due to the effect of the short-time work scheme. The rebound in employment after the initial lockdown has only been partial, and many workers will not be able to retain attachments to employers. These adjustments are set to intensify with the expected weak recovery, the associated likely dismissals and bankruptcies, as well as the significant reallocation and reskilling needs. The unusually large share of workers on temporary contracts or self-employment could bear the main costs. Small and micro enterprises, with little financial reserves, are also particularly at risk. Following the initial outbreak, many of them decreased wages to reduce short-term losses and maintain liquidity without having to resort to redundancies and the renewed autumn's restrictions are set to weigh further on their financial situations.

Figure 1.9. Labour market adjustments are significant

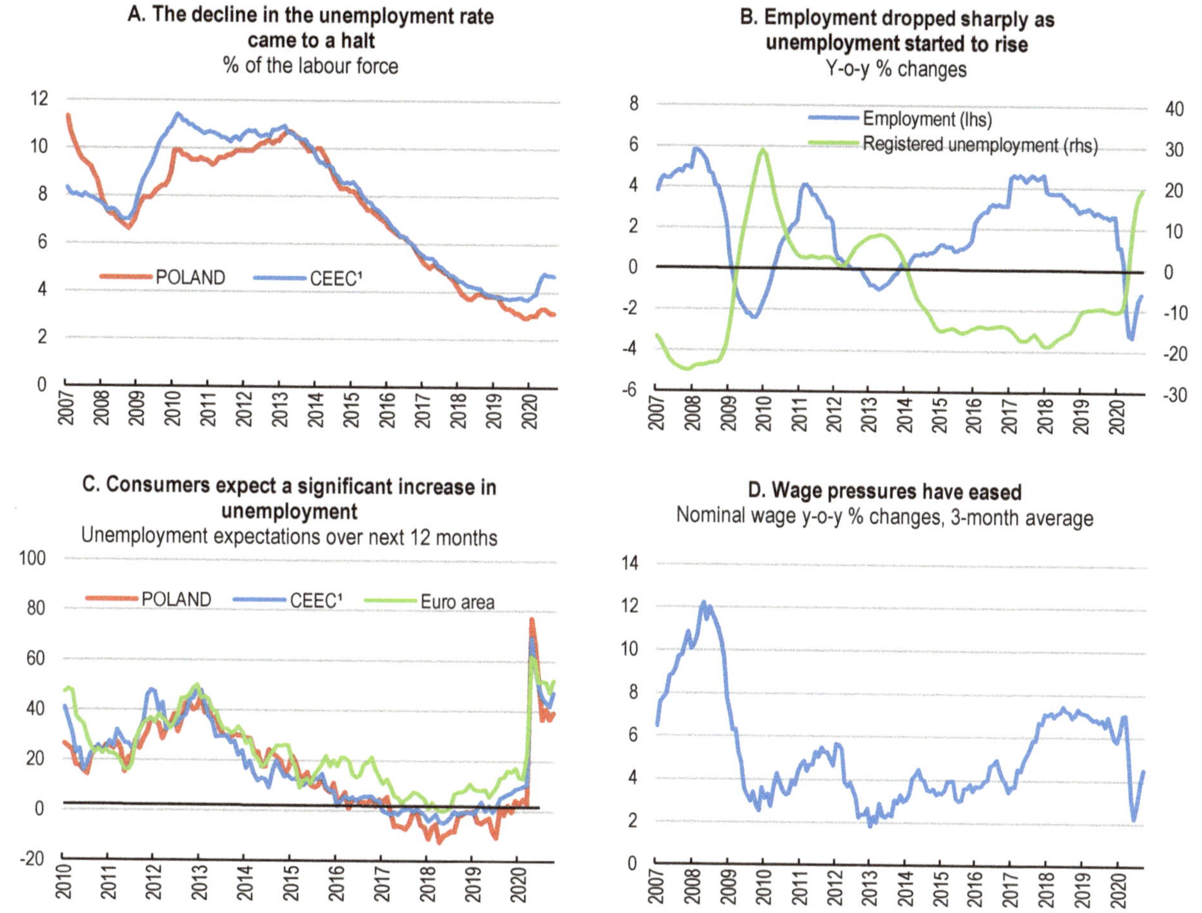

A. The decline in the unemployment rate came to a halt
% of the labour force

B. Employment dropped sharply as unemployment started to rise
Y-o-y % changes

C. Consumers expect a significant increase in unemployment
Unemployment expectations over next 12 months

D. Wage pressures have eased
Nominal wage y-o-y % changes, 3-month average

1. CEEC is the average of Hungary and the Czech and Slovak Republics.
2. Employment is the number of full-time equivalent jobs.
Source: Eurostat (2020), "Unemployment Statistics" (database); European Commission (2020), Business and Consumer Surveys (database); Statistics Poland (2020), Short-term monthly indicators.

StatLink https://doi.org/10.1787/888934208108

Exports are set to be relatively resilient to the depressed global economic conditions (Figure 1.10). Over recent years, Polish exporters resorted to diversification of trade ties to make up for the shrinking demand from the European Union or negative demand shocks from Russia and Ukraine. Poland's exports of goods are well diversified in terms of composition, although goods exports remain mostly specialised in low- and medium-tech products and directed towards other European countries (Figure 1.11 and Chapter 2). Yet, unlike the sharp currency depreciation experienced during the global financial crisis, the global pandemic shock and the recent monetary policy easing (see below) have not changed much exchange rate levels so far.

The short-term outlook is subject to particularly high uncertainty. New, longer and wider coronavirus outbreaks could hurt local and global economic conditions and be a drag on growth. Escalations of trade tensions risk further lowering the growth of exports and private investment. A further slowdown in the German car industry would also hurt exports and notably the automotive industry. Worsening perceptions about the evolution of judicial independence and the rule of law could also weaken business investment. On the upside, the large-scale roll-out of an effective vaccine commercialised already in 2021 could accelerate the pace of recovery by boosting external demand and investors' confidence. A faster-than-expected recovery of household confidence could boost private consumption. A number of large possible shocks could also alter the economic outlook significantly (Table 1.3).

Figure 1.10. Exchange rate variations have been limited and export performance has so far been robust

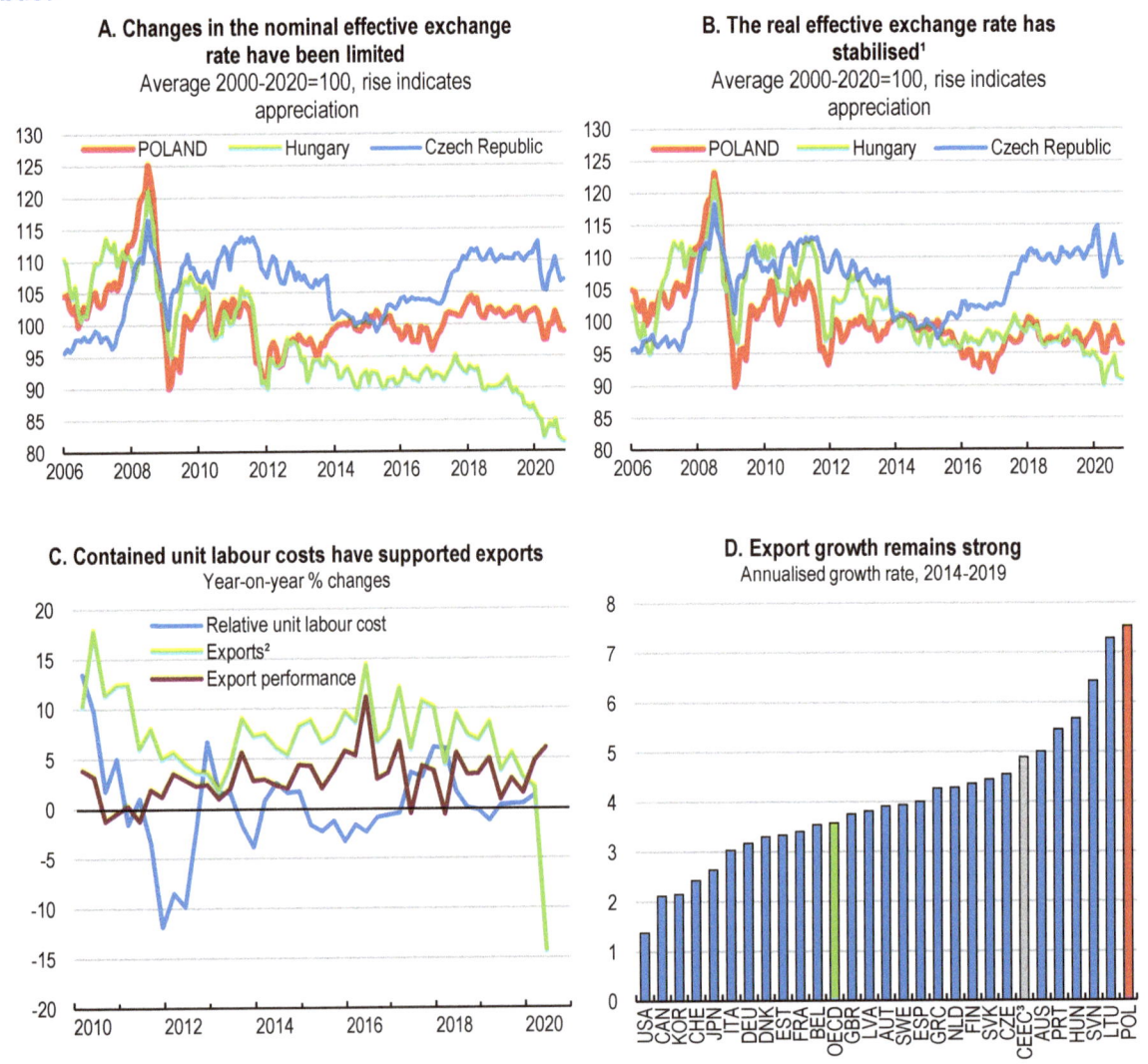

A. Changes in the nominal effective exchange rate have been limited
Average 2000-2020=100, rise indicates appreciation

B. The real effective exchange rate has stabilised[1]
Average 2000-2020=100, rise indicates appreciation

C. Contained unit labour costs have supported exports
Year-on-year % changes

D. Export growth remains strong
Annualised growth rate, 2014-2019

1. Based on relative consumer prices.
2. Goods and services, volume.
3. CEEC is the average of Hungary and the Czech and Slovak Republics.
Source: OECD (2019), OECD Economic Outlook: Statistics and Projections (database).

StatLink https://doi.org/10.1787/888934208127

Table 1.2. Low-probability events that could lead to major changes in the outlook

Shock	Possible impact
Long and globalised outbreaks of coronavirus	New, longer lasting and more intensive outbreaks could spread much more widely than assumed. This would hurt global growth prospects and demand in key export markets. This could also constrain Poland's productive capacity by reducing its labour supply and supply chains.
A rapid increase in the global risk premium	This would lead to higher domestic rates, and the zloty could depreciate, driving up interest payments and risks of fiscal policy slippages.
Rise of protectionism and tensions in international trade	Poland would be severely affected by a slowdown of its European partners in case of prolonged and heighted trade tensions. This would have adverse effects on exports and firm entry and undermine investors' confidence, harming productivity and potential growth.

Box 1.2. Key ongoing policies and reforms

Increasing social transfers: the July 2019 extension of the "500+" benefit granted an unconditional monthly benefit of PLN 500 (EUR 117) to every child aged 0-18. The "pension plus" scheme is a yearly one-off lump-sum pension payment amounting to PLN 1,100 gross in 2019 (EUR 249)and PLN 1,200 (EUR 281) in 2020.

Pension reforms: the Open Pension Funds (OFE) are set to be dismantled, and the funds transferred to private individual retirement accounts (IKE), or to the personal accounts at the Social Insurance Institution (ZUS). The authorities also set up voluntary Employee Capital Plans (PPK) in 2019. They aim at increasing long-term private savings and, in particular, may improve future pension adequacy.

Increasing tax expenditures for low-wage earners and younger workers: Since 2018, the tax-free income for PIT has increased, and the first tax rate has been reduced in October 2019 (from 18 to 17 percent). Young income taxpayers (up to PLN 85,528) have been exempted from the personal income tax in since August 2019 and tax deductible costs have more than doubled in October 2019.

Improving VAT compliance: Poland created a centralised data warehouse, merged tax administration, customs and fiscal control operations. It also improved modelling tools to better detect irregularities and facilitated information exchange with banks when suspicion of fraud.

The government has increased the minimum wage. An increase of 15.6% took place in January 2020 and another increase of 7.7% will take place in January 2021 (to PLN 2,800).

The 2018 "Clean Air" and the 2020 "My energy" programmes aim at reducing air pollution from residential heating, improving the energy performance of buildings and increasing the use of small-scale renewable installations. Grants and loans are available for investments such as stove, window and door replacements, property insulation, and installation of renewable energy systems. The 2020 "My energy" programme will co-finance up to 50% of individual photovoltaic installations.

Increasing public health expenditures: Before the COVID-19 outbreak, the government had plans to increase public health-care spending to 6.0% of GDP in 2024 from 4.5% in 2015. Additional spending already occurred in 2020 as a response to the ongoing crisis.

Increasing some specific taxes: a new levy on soft drinks and some alcoholic beverages, the so-called "sugar tax", and a tax on retail sales' turnover are to be introduced in 2021.

Initiatives supporting SMEs (Chapter 2): The 2018 Business constitution and "100 Changes for Enterprises" aim at reducing the administrative burden, notably for SMEs and foreign investors. In addition, in 2019 the authorities lowered the reduced corporate income tax rate for SMEs to 9%.

Integrated Skills Strategy: The general part of the Integrated Skills Strategy (ZSU) has been adopted in January 2019. The detailed part is being developed with the support from the OECD.

Judicial reforms: In the context of the general pension reform, the authorities lowered the retirement age of judges and allowed the Ministry of Justice to retain selected judges, among other measures. The European Court of Justice ruled the proposed reform to be unlawful (EC, 2019) and the government has subsequently amended the retirement age of judges. Another reform, potentially allowing to dismiss judges for their court rulings, has been criticised by the Polish Supreme Court (2020) and the Council of Europe (2020).

Source: EC (2019), European Commission statement on the judgment of the European Court of Justice on Poland's Ordinary Courts law, European Commission; Council of Europe (2020), Poland- Urgent Joint Opinion on the amendments to the Law on organisation on the Common Courts, the Law on the Supreme Court and other Laws, Opinion No. 977 / 2019, CDL-PI(2020)002-e; Polish Supreme Court (2020), 24 January 2020.

Figure 1.11. Poland's export structure is well diversified

Share of exports by sector and destination, 2019 or latest year available

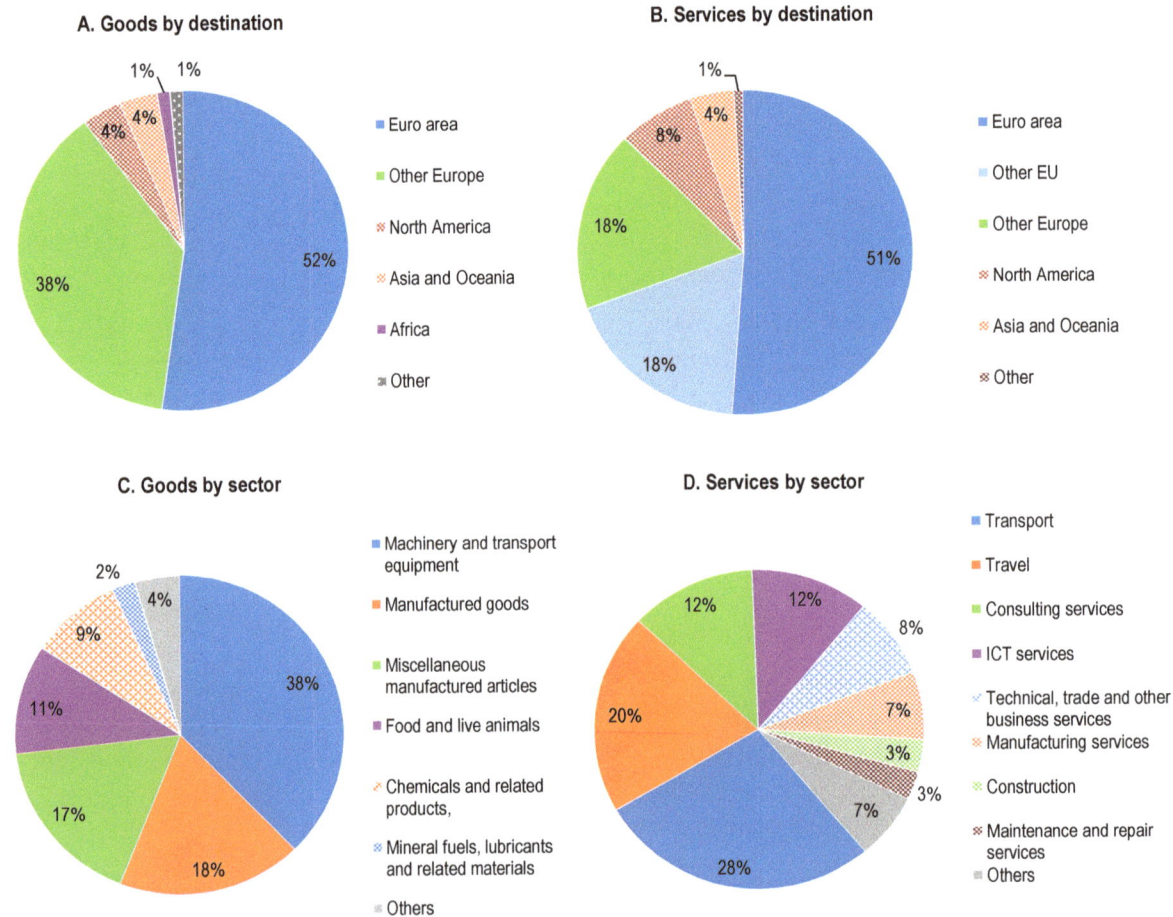

Note: Data on good exports refer to 2019, while data on services exports refer to 2018. In Panel C, Others include crude materials, beverages and tobacco, animal and vegetable oils, and commodities and transactions. In Panel D, Others include R&D services, financial services, insurance and pension, construction services, and cultural services.
Source: OECD International Trade Statistics.

StatLink https://doi.org/10.1787/888934208146

Monetary policy has been appropriately accommodative

Monetary policy has reacted forcefully and quickly to the emerging coronavirus crisis. The central bank cut its policy rate from 1.5% in early March to 0.1% at the end of May coupled with a narrowing of the interest rate corridor (Figure 1.12), strengthened banks' liquidity through reduced reserve requirements, started an asset purchase programme – including state-guaranteed debt securities – and introduced TLTRO-type refinancing. These measures eased monetary conditions and smoothed the financing of the fiscal anti-crisis measures, as the yields of government bonds have declined markedly (NBP, 2020a). Statements also made clear that the central bank will continue to purchase government securities and government-guaranteed debt securities in the secondary market and will offer bill discount credit aimed at refinancing loans granted to enterprises.

Headline inflation has sharply decelerated, driven by the reversal of earlier energy and food price hikes (Figure 1.13, Panel A). In October, headline inflation (as defined Statistics Poland) stood at 3.1% year on year, down by 1.6 percentage points since its February high. Decreasing oil prices and slowing food price growth have more than compensated increasing wholesale electricity prices, due to recurrent weaknesses in supply (OECD, 2016), and the end of the 2019-electricity price freeze for households in January 2020

(ERO, 2020). Yet, core inflation remains relatively high. This reflects lagged effects from administered price hikes, the mild zloty depreciation and the pass-through of the costs of new health-and-safety type procedures, as wage growth has sharply decelerated and unemployment has started to rise. OECD inflation and Central Bank's projections for inflation are set to remain within the Central Bank's tolerance band in 2021-21 (Figure 1.13, Panel B, NBP, 2020a and c). Wage growth is projected to ease further and the economy to recover slowly and at a very uncertain pace, as there are ongoing headwinds to activity from weak global growth, risks of more severe and longer-lasting coronavirus outbreaks and rising trade tensions.

Figure 1.12. Monetary policy has reacted forcefully to the crisis

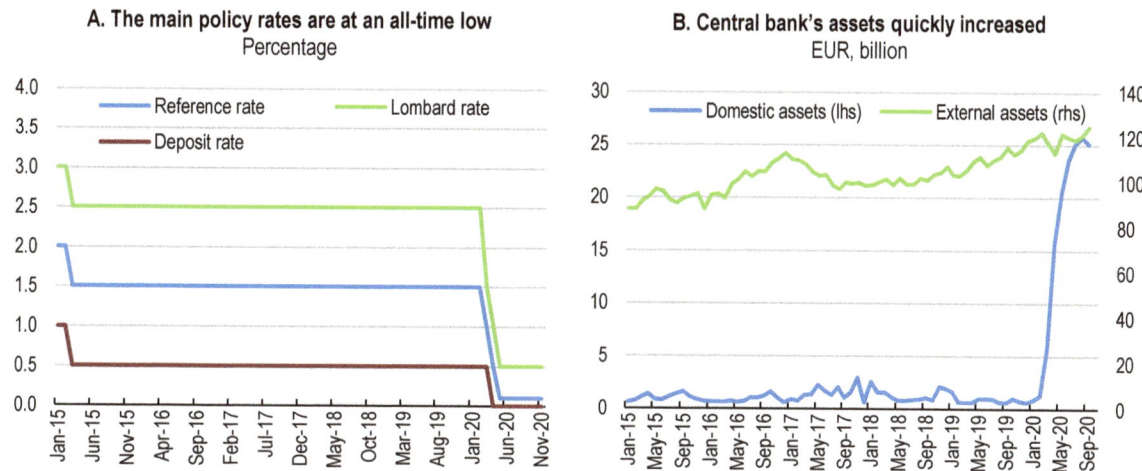

A. The main policy rates are at an all-time low
Percentage

B. Central bank's assets quickly increased
EUR, billion

Source: NBP (2020), Balance sheet of the National Bank of Poland – Assets - stocks in PLN million; Central bank interest rates; OECD (2020), Monthly Monetary and Financial Statistics (MEI) dataset.

StatLink https://doi.org/10.1787/888934208165

Figure 1.13. Inflationary pressures have decreased

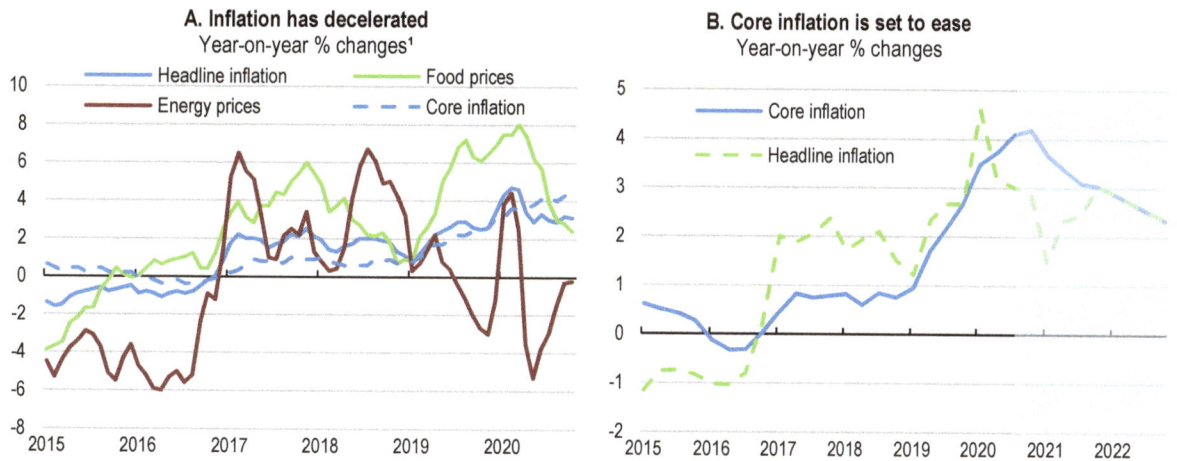

A. Inflation has decelerated
Year-on-year % changes[1]

B. Core inflation is set to ease
Year-on-year % changes

1. Harmonised indices.
Source: Eurostat (2019), "Harmonised index of consumer prices", Eurostat Database; OECD (2019), OECD Economic Outlook: Statistics and Projections (database).

StatLink https://doi.org/10.1787/888934208184

Under these circumstances, the current monetary stance appears appropriate. In responding to the coronavirus shock, monetary policymakers have enhanced and expanded their tools. Local currency bond yields fell significantly following the programme announcements, with little effect on exchange rates. The authorities have signalled that they are ready to keep interest rate at their historically low level for an extended period, and that they will continue to purchase government and government-guaranteed debt securities in the secondary market to strengthen the monetary policy transmission mechanism. Yet, monetary policy decisions should remain data-contingent and forward-looking, responding rapidly should economic conditions deteriorate (or improve) faster than expected. Given potentially limited room for manoeuvre, in case of an even more severe downturn, the authorities may consider adjusting large-scale asset purchases, including through the possibilities for expanding the range of eligible assets, and using of negative interest rates.

Risks to financial stability have increased and require close monitoring

The coronavirus crisis raised several financial risks. Before the crisis, the financial system stood in relatively good condition, despite the increase of some vulnerabilities (Figure 1.14). Yet, a long-lasting decrease of employment and fall in corporate revenues would lower households and firms' capacity to repay outstanding debts and translate into increased credit risk costs for banks (OECD, 2020a and 2020c). This risk is, however, reduced by massive fiscal support and monetary actions (Box 1.1). At the same time, high uncertainty and increasing risk aversion are having a negative impact on banks' propensity to grant new loans, which could further exacerbate the liquidity position of businesses and their solvency (Figure 1.15, Panel A; NBP, 2020b). Yet, according to banks' surveys, the decreased pace of new lending over 2020 has been caused rather by subdued demand than tightened credit standards.

Figure 1.14. Evolution of macro-financial vulnerabilities
Index scale of -1 to 1 from lowest to greatest potential vulnerability[1]

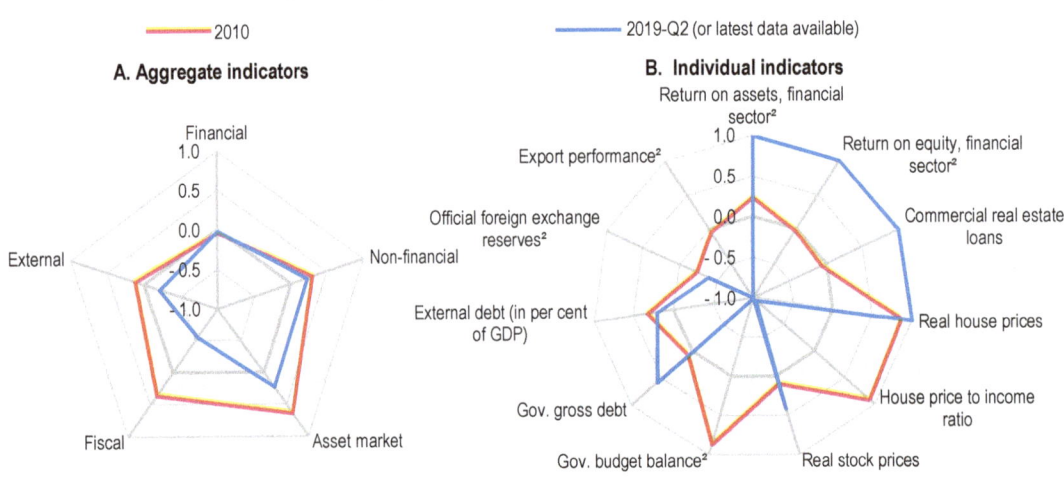

1. For each aggregate macro-financial dimension, displayed in Panel A, the vulnerability index is based on a simple average of all indicators from the OECD Resilience Database that are grouped under that dimension's heading. Indicator values are normalised to take values between – 1 and 1. They are positive when the last observation of the underlying time series is above its long-term average, indicating more vulnerability, and negative when the last observation is below its long-term average, indicating less vulnerability. Long-term averages are full-sample estimates calculated since 2000.
2. Inverted scales, higher values indicate higher potential vulnerabilities.
Source: Calculations based on OECD (2019), OECD Resilience Database, December.

StatLink [StatLink logo] https://doi.org/10.1787/888934208203

The healthy position of the banking sector before the crisis and regulatory measures averted problems with banks' liquidity and capital position so far. Despite historically low interest rates, macro-financial vulnerabilities had receded since 2010. The debt-service ratio of the non-financial corporate sector was low in international comparison (Figure 1.15, Panel B). Loan losses, the share of loans in arrears and impaired loans were decreasing (NBP, 2019). The banking system was also well capitalised and liquid (KNF, 2019; EBA, 2018). These accumulated buffers, as well as the release of the systemic risk buffer recommended by the Financial Stability Committee and the measures taken by the central bank to provide liquidity to the banking sector, such as lower reserve requirements, the introduction of repo transactions and structural market operations, have contained liquidity risk and the need to increase banks' capital.

Notwithstanding the good aggregate indicators, caution is warranted. Bank share prices have declined, impeding their ability to raise funds from external sources if needed. There is heterogeneity across banks, with some smaller institutions that are more sensitive to shocks having suffered losses that significantly reduce their available capital (NBP, 2020b). Though non-performing loans have remained broadly stable until September 2020, the coronavirus crisis has increased the risks of non-performing loans and banks should use their profits to increase their capital buffers, for example by not distributing dividends, as recommended by the regulator.

Figure 1.15. The risk of a credit crunch has increased

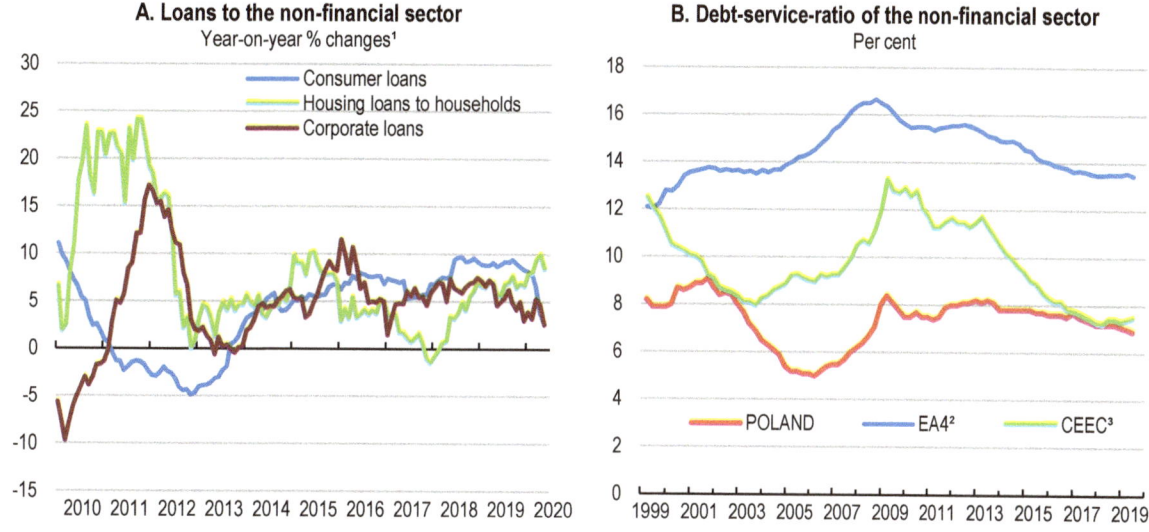

1. Growth rate on the total number of loans.
2. EA4 is the average of Germany, France, Italy and Spain.
3. CEEC is the average of Hungary and the Czech Republic.
Source: NBP (2020), Monetary and financial statistics (database); BIS (2019), Debt Service Ratios for the Private Non-financial Sector (database), Bank for International Settlements, Basel.

StatLink ᐧᐧᐧ https://doi.org/10.1787/888934208222

The crisis has worsened financial institutions' profitability. Polish banks were already affected by global downside pressures on profitability (EBA, 2019), as well as domestic factors related to the asset tax introduced in 2016 and increased contributions to the bank-guarantee fund (Figure 1.16, Panel A; NBP, 2019). As demand for banking services and investment products fell during the lockdown, non-interest margins dropped, while lower interest rates reduced banks' interest margin income. At the same time, higher provisions for credit risk lower banks' profitability further. Further medium-term risks stem from the declining stock of foreign-currency denominated mortgages, as the ongoing rise of customer challenges and court disputes could negatively affect banks' profitability if the conditions of particular foreign-currency denominated mortgages are deemed abusive (ECJ, 2019).

Sovereign-financial institution linkages have increased, exposing banks to potential negative feedback effects between the financial situation of the State and the banking sector. Before the pandemic, the state control of the financial system had already increased to around 40% of the sector' assets, following the purchases of stakes by the authorities in two large banks in 2017 and a 2019 reform strengthening state involvement in nominations to the Polish Financial Supervision Authority (KNF). Banks have also significantly increased their holdings of sovereign bonds (Figure 1.16, Panel B). The 2016 bank asset tax incentivises higher holdings of government securities as such assets are currently exempted. Replacing the current bank asset tax with a tax on profits and remuneration would be less distortive (IMF, 2019).

Strengthening the regulatory framework would support financial stability. The Polish Financial Supervision Authority (KNF) is in charge of the banking sector supervision and its resources have increased in 2019. Yet, its independence remains potentially constrained. The governing members of the KNF should be selected solely based on their expertise and experience. The KNF should also have responsibility for the oversight of its human resources' management, as well as for evaluating the supervisory effectiveness. In order to improve the effectiveness of early intervention in the case of troubled banks, the KNF should be able to execute bank insolvency assessments, without having to require an external third-party opinion (IMF, 2019).

Figure 1.16. Banking sector's profitability and holding of sovereign bonds

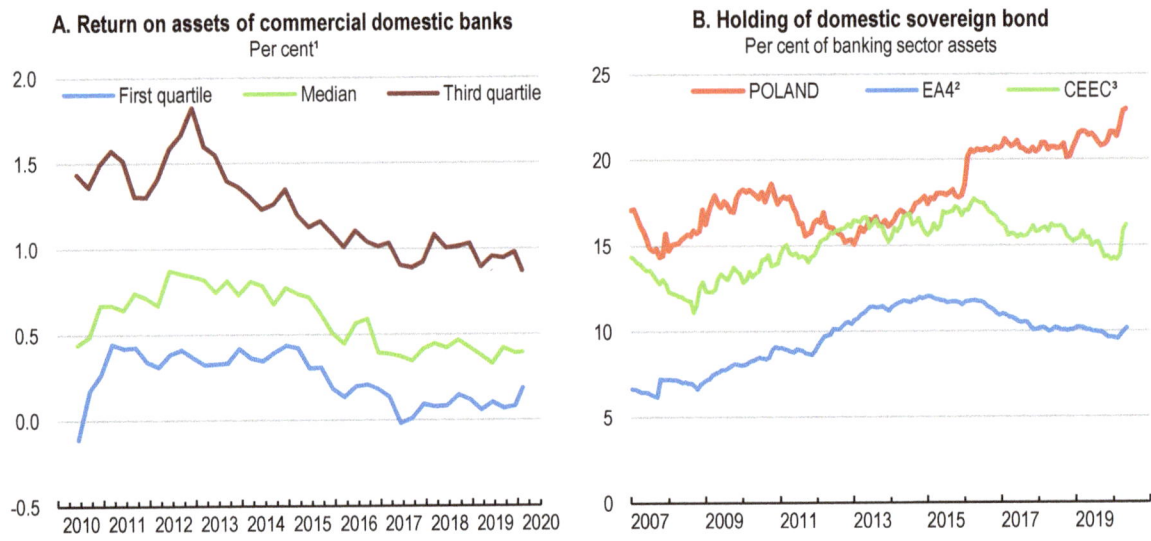

1. Annualised data.
2. EA4 is the average of Germany, France, Italy and Spain.
3. CEEC is the average of Hungary and the Czech Republic.
Source: NBP (2020), Financial Stability Report - June, National Bank of Poland, Warsaw; ECB (2019), Statistical Data Warehouse (database), European Central Bank, Frankfurt.

StatLink https://doi.org/10.1787/888934208241

Boosting the recovery while containing medium-term spending pressures

The crisis legacy will compound long-term challenges

Before the crisis, the fiscal position was strong in the short term (Figure 1.17). The fiscal deficit had been reduced significantly since 2010 and the public debt-to-GDP ratio was set to decline further from its 2016 peak, bringing it well below the European Union average in 2021. This achievement owed to strong growth, better tax collection (notably through the successful elimination of tax loopholes) and low spending growth till recently. Yet, even before the crisis, the authorities had been raising social expenditures (Figure 1.18 and Box 1.2). In particular, the 500+ child benefit programme introduced in April 2016 (and its later expansion) and the reversal of the minimum retirement age reform (to the levels of 2012) implemented in October 2017 increased medium-term financing needs. Both measures are expected to cost more than 2% of GDP annually. The new child benefits has doubled public support for families to about 3.8% of GDP, well above most other OECD countries (Figure 1.18, Panel A). The additional payment for pension and the reversal of the retirement age reform are set to push public pension spending to close to 12.0% of GDP in 2020 (Panel B).

In the current environment of very low interest rates, which could be long lasting, high public borrowing levels might be sustainable if they finance growth-enhancing investments. Yet, the sharp temporary increase in the deficit in the response to the coronavirus crisis will increase the need for controlling medium-term spending pressures (Figure 1.17). Compared to the OECD November 2019 projections, the crisis will push 2021 Maastricht debt up by 17 percentage points of GDP to 62% of GDP. Long-term sustainability challenges are also significant. There are a number of reasons to expect further pressure on the fiscal balance in the longer run. Firstly, health and long-term care costs are set to rise by around 1.4% of GDP by 2050 (EC, 2018a). Secondly, infrastructure needs will remain strong to allow a transition towards a greener and more efficient economy, as bottlenecks remain in energy and transport infrastructure.

Figure 1.17. The fiscal response to the crisis has been substantial

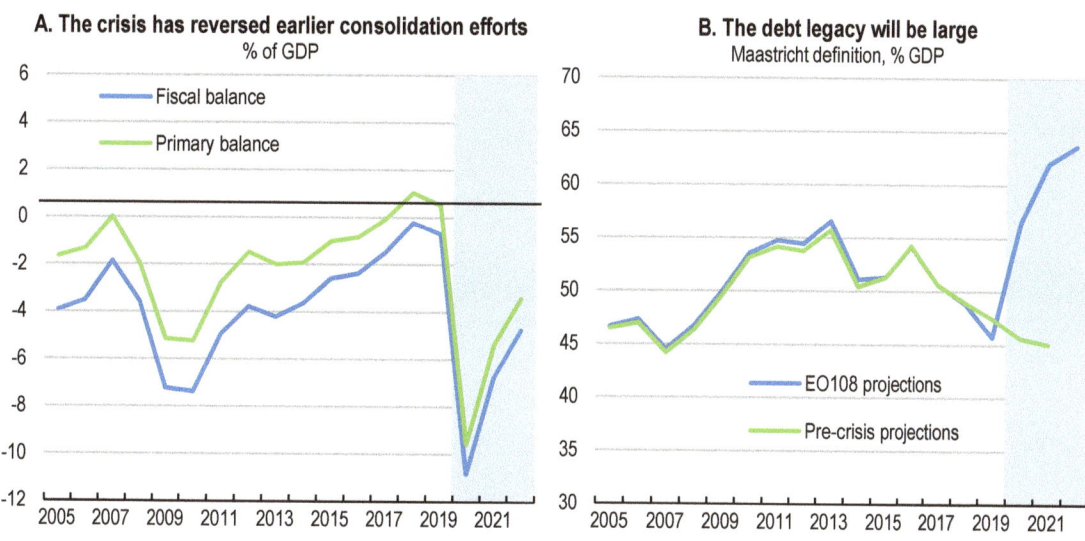

Source: OECD (2019 and 2020), OECD Economic Outlook: Statistics and Projections (database).

StatLink ▐▊▊▊ https://doi.org/10.1787/888934208260

According to illustrative OECD simulations that are surrounded by particularly high uncertainty, Poland's public debt – Maastricht definition – could increase to around 90% of GDP by 2050 if ageing costs and the legacy of a single coronavirus outbreak were not offset (Figure 1.19). Even taking into account Poland's spending rule, which imposes to remain close to Poland's Medium Term Objective of a structural balance of -1% of GDP, the offsetting consolidation efforts would not put public debt on a firmly declining path since ageing will progressively reduce the growth potential. In this scenario, due to the sharp increase in debt stock over 2020-21, the public debt would continue to increase to a level close to 74% of GDP in 2050.

Further strengthening the fiscal framework would help to ensure sustainability over the longer term. The current system requires public debt to be kept below 60% of GDP (national definition) according to the Constitution. In normal circumstances, the application of the 2013 spending rule should lead to a reduction of the deficit if one of the following three instances occur: the preventive net public debt-to-GDP thresholds – 43% and 48% – are crossed; the general government deficit exceeds 3% of GDP; or there are significant deviations from the medium-term budgetary objective. Since 2019, the budget process should also incorporate a medium-term (three years) perspective and provide guideline for future spending ceilings, which is welcome. The National Bank of Poland and the European Commission (through the Convergence Programme) issue opinions about the draft budget and the Supreme Audit Office (NIK) ensure ex-post control. Yet, Poland remains the only EU Member State without a fiscal council (EC, 2019a) and it would be helpful to have an independent institution make ex-ante assessment of the government's fiscal plans and conduct long-term fiscal sustainability analyses (OECD, 2016).

32 |

Figure 1.18. Spending commitments on some social programmes are rapidly increasing

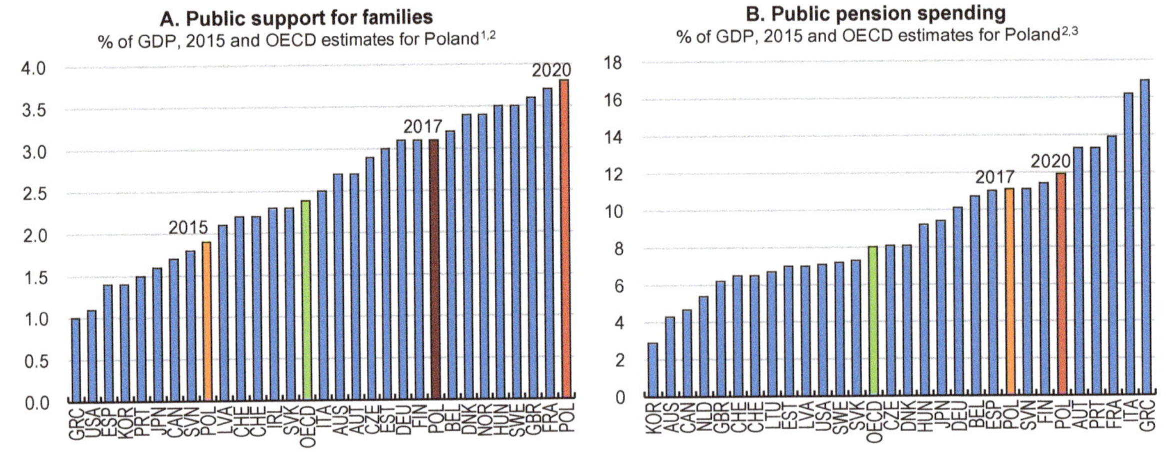

A. Public support for families
% of GDP, 2015 and OECD estimates for Poland[1,2]

B. Public pension spending
% of GDP, 2015 and OECD estimates for Poland[2,3]

1. Poland's public spending on family benefits of 2015, augmented with the costs of the family 500+ child benefits introduced in 2016 with mean testing and its full-year extension in 2020. The full-year costs associated with the 2018 Good Start programme and the 2019 Mother 4 plus scheme are also taken into account in the 2020 estimate. Other changes are not taken into account.
2. The 2020 GDP figures are based on the OECD pre-crisis projections (November 2019 Economic Outlook).
3. The 2020 estimate takes into account the pension plus scheme and the 2019 hike in minimum pension and indexation. The 2016 reversal of the retirement age increase is expected to cost 0.1% of GDP in 2020. Other changes are not taken into account.
Source: OECD calculations based on OECD (2020), OECD Family Statistics and OECD National account (databases); OECD (2019), Pension at a Glance, OECD Publishing, Paris; and Republic of Poland (2019), Convergence Programme – 2019 Update, Warsaw.

StatLink https://doi.org/10.1787/888934208279

Figure 1.19. Ageing will put further pressure on public debt

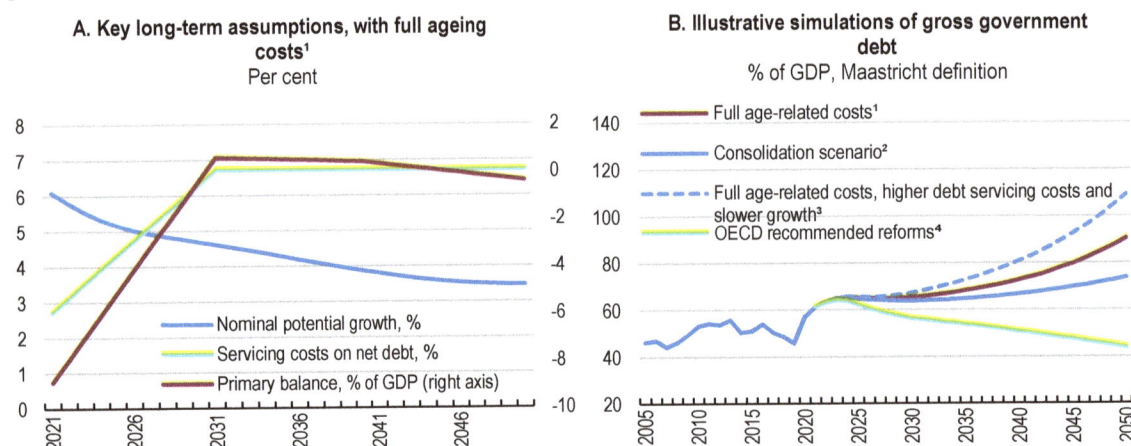

A. Key long-term assumptions, with full ageing costs[1]
Per cent

B. Illustrative simulations of gross government debt
% of GDP, Maastricht definition

1. The key long-term assumptions build on Table 1.1 for 2019-21. They assume a long-term potential growth declining from 3.0% in 2021 to 1% in 2050 in line with OECD (2018). The GDP deflator and the debt servicing costs are set at 2.5% after 2026, and 6.7% of net debt after 2031. The primary balance converges from -0.3% of GDP in 2021 to +1.0% in 2031, consistently with Poland's Medium Term Objective and fiscal rules. Yet, total ageing-related public expenditures (pensions, long-term care, health and education) are not compensated. These add 1.4 percentage points of GDP to annual government spending in 2050 (EC, 2018) and the primary balance is negative at -0.4% of GDP in 2050. Government gross financial assets are kept constant as a share of GDP.
2. The consolidation scenario assumes that the primary balance remains constant at +1.0% of GDP after 2031.
3. The net debt servicing costs increases to 7.7% in 2031 and remains stable thereafter. Compared to the key assumptions, potential growth declines faster and by an additional 0.25 percentage points in 2050.
4. The "OECD-recommended reforms" scenario adds the estimated effects of the reforms recommended in this Survey (Box 1.3) and the expected effects of some of the key recommendations as described in Table 1.6. The primary balance improves faster to 1.25% of GDP in 2026. Potential GDP improves by 5.6% after 10 years compared to the baseline scenario.
Source: OECD calculations based on OECD (2019), OECD Economic Outlook: Statistics and Projections (database), November; OECD (2018), Long-term baseline projections; and EC (2018), "The 2018 Ageing Report - Economic and budgetary projections for the 28 EU Member States (2016-2070)", European Commission, Directorate-General for Economic and Financial Affairs.

StatLink https://doi.org/10.1787/888934208298

Additional risks could weigh on the debt burden. General government contingent liabilities are substantial. They reached nearly 43% of GDP in 2018 (MF, 2019) and they have increased with the coronavirus crisis. Poland's government guarantees and liabilities related to Public Private Partnerships are low in international comparison (Eurostat, 2020a). Yet, the liabilities of the numerous state-owned enterprises in the financial and non-financial sectors are large. Monitoring of state-owned enterprises and strengthening their governance should be aligned with OECD best practices (EC, 2019a; OECD, 2020d).

Ageing will put significant pressures on the quality of pension, health and long-term care

Before the coronavirus crisis, the financial sustainability of the pension system appeared assured, based on long-term projections. Yet, it would be at the expense of a gradual decline in the level of pension compared to working wages over the longer term. This poses a risk of old-age poverty and many Poles are for this reason concerned by financial security in old age. They also feel that they do not have access to good quality long-term care and healthcare (OECD, 2019a). Reforms need to be implemented that go beyond the sole financial sustainability concerns to ensure efficient and adequate expenditures in the pension, health and long-term care sectors.

Reforms are needed to reduce risks of old-age poverty and boost employment

Public expenditures on pensions appear broadly under control over the longer term. Despite one-off increases in 2019-20, public pension spending is set to remain close to the European Union average at about 11% of GDP (Figure 1.20, Panel A). Public expenditures on pensions would remain broadly stable until 2050 according to European Commission's projections (EC, 2018a). The financial sustainability of the pension system has been ensured by high standard contribution rates and a steep decrease in replacement rates (Panel B) driven by the transition to pensions based on lifetime contributions and the indexation of future pension mostly on prices (rather than the wage bill). This would offset the rapid population ageing. Yet, in the absence of further improvements in labour market outcomes and longer contributory periods, replacement rates are expected to become among the lowest in the OECD.

The recent introduction of an auto-enrolment private occupational savings scheme (PPK) could somehow improve this bleak prospect. The net household saving rate has declined over the long term to around -1.0% of disposable income in 2018. PPKs could increase future pension prospects by adding another component to the pension system if they succeeds to rebuild confidence in private pensions, which was undermined by the reversals of the mandatory funded scheme (OFE) (OECD, 2019b). From July 2019, large companies must enrol their employees into PPK with a standard contribution of 3½ percent of their gross wage financed through employer (2 percent) and employee (1.5 percent) contributions. The State also finances top-ups. Smaller companies followed from 2020 and public entities and the smallest firms are set to be covered in 2021. The participation of employees in large companies was 40%. The authorities expect to cover 75% of employees and inject into capital markets about 0.7% of GDP annually (EC, 2019a). Moreover, in 2019, the authorities increased the minimum pension (after a first hike in 2017), pension indexation and the coverage of women with more than four children through unconditional cash transfers (RSU). One-off benefit for all pensioners in 2019 and 2020 at the level of 0.5% of GDP annually, the so-called pension plus scheme (Box 1.2), are also boosting retirees' incomes.

Employment rates for workers close to retirement (54-64) and the combination of work and pension have made rapid progress, but old-age poverty risks are still set to increase over the longer term, notably for women. While the average effective retirement ages both for men and for women has increased until 2018, they remain relatively low and the employment rates of 60-64 women and 65-69 men have decreased since 2018 (Figure 1.21). This is likely the consequence of reversing the 2013 retirement age reform to 60 for women and 65 for men in late 2017, as life expectancy at 50 years old has increased by 20 months over 2010-18 (Eurostat, 2020b). Indeed, in many studies, the statutory pension age is a powerful focal point that tends to have a strong effect on retirement decisions beyond any financial incentive effects (Cribb et al., 2016). Combined with the high share of temporary contracts and self-employed with low contributions and associated pensions (OECD, 2019b and below), these risk raising old age poverty and the share of pensioners who have no more than a minimum pension. Women, whose pension eligibility depends on a particularly low statutory retirement age, tend to benefit from lower replacement rates and are the most at risk (Bledowski et al., 2017; Tyrowicz and Brandt, 2017): their average age at labour market exit today is among the lowest in the OECD.

Figure 1.20. A steep decline in replacement rates is set to contain pension expenditures

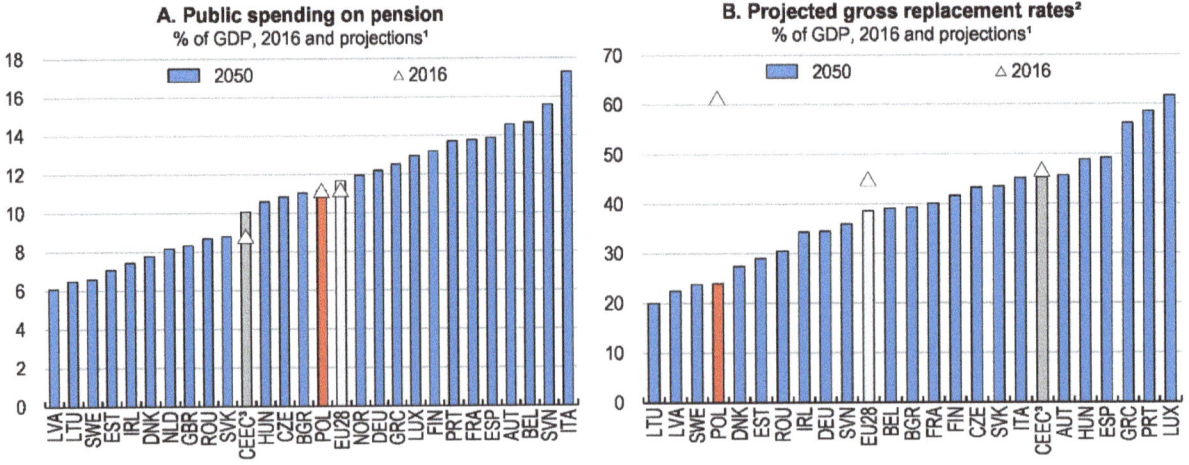

1. European Commission projections (2018).
2. Gross replacement rates are measured as the very first pension benefit relative to the last wage before retirement.
3. CEEC is the average of Hungary and the Czech and Slovak Republics.
Source: European Commission (2018), "The 2018 Ageing Report - Economic and budgetary projections for the 28 EU Member States (2016-2070)", Directorate-General for Economic and Financial Affairs.

StatLink https://doi.org/10.1787/888934208317

A continued increase in the effective retirement age, in line with progress with life expectancy in good health, and improved working opportunities for women and older workers are crucial for labour market participation and the level of pensions. The pension system provides increased benefits for those postponing retirement beyond the statutory retirement age. Moreover, yearly letters and counsellors in regional offices inform and advise workers about their pension situation and the potential benefits of delaying their retirement. Yet, harmonising employment protection for all age groups to avoid disincentives to hiring older workers, who are currently better protected, could raise their employment prospects (OECD, 2015). Raising and equalising the statutory retirement ages for men and women and linking it to healthy life expectancy, as in many other OECD countries, such as Denmark or Portugal, would also help to take into account improvements of health conditions of older workers and accelerate the increase in effective retirement age. Efforts to strengthen job-search assistance and training programmes, and to reduce discrimination for older workers will also be needed.

Existing preferential pension schemes imply fiscal costs and reduce the mobility of workers between sectors. Special pension expenditures affect more than 22% of current pensioners and amount to 2.6% of GDP (EC, 2018a). In particular, the special social insurance system for farmers (KRUS) based on flat contributions and subsidised at a cost of around 0.8% of GDP, is hampering labour mobility and contributing to hidden unemployment in agriculture, though the share of those working in agriculture has decreased. Although they may be partly justified by hazardous working conditions, the special pension rules of for miners appear substantially more generous than the general rules. Similarly, survivor pension schemes could be reviewed to increase incentives to work at older age and reduce their costs. Indeed, the ratio of the deceased partner's pension awarded to the survivor, at 85%, is among the highest in the OECD, and greater than the estimated ratio needed to sustain the surviving spouse's living standards (OECD, 2018d). Progressively scaling back these programmes would allow to boost employment and inclusiveness.

Figure 1.21. Old-age work is low and declining

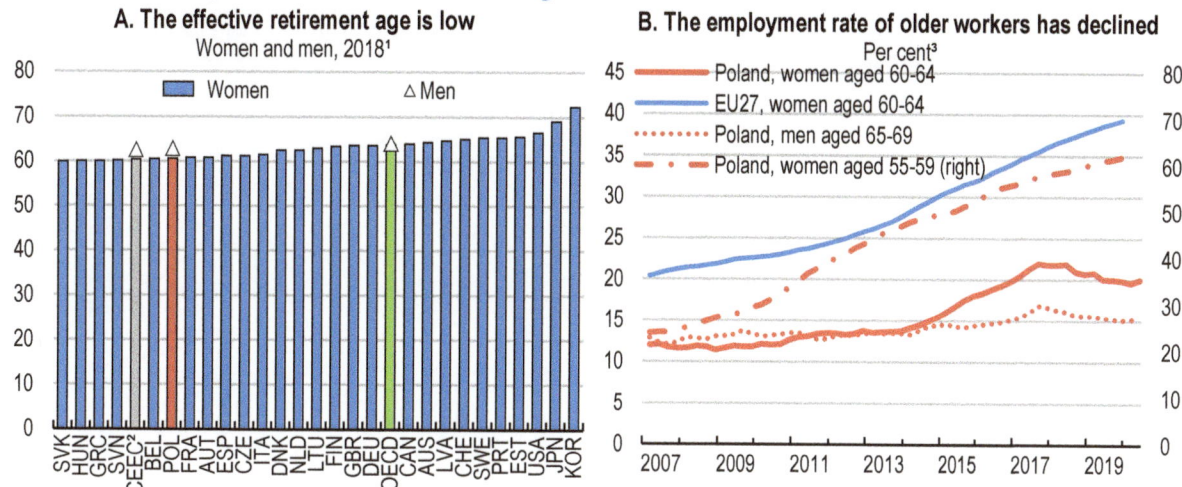

1. The average effective age of retirement is calculated as a weighted average of (net) withdrawals from the labour market at different ages over a 5-year period for workers initially aged 40 and over. In order to abstract from compositional effects in the age structure of the population, labour force withdrawals are estimated based on changes in labour force participation rates rather than labour force levels. These changes are calculated for each (synthetic) cohort divided into 5-year age groups.
2. CEEC is the average of Hungary and the Czech and Slovak Republics.
3. 4-quarter moving averages.
Source: OECD (2019), Pensions at a Glance 2019: OECD and G20 Indicators, OECD Publishing, Paris; Eurostat (2020), "Labour Force Survey Statistics", Eurostat Database.

StatLink 🔗 https://doi.org/10.1787/888934208336

Containing the necessary increase in health and long-term care spending

Though early containment measures curbed the contagion of the pandemic, the healthcare system suffers from several weaknesses. Spending on healthcare is relatively low. At 6.3% of GDP in 2018 (among which 71.8% financed through mandatory public schemes, i.e. 4.5% of GDP being publicly funded), it is only around 50% of the OECD average in per capita terms (Figure 1.22, Panel A). This leads to relatively poor health outcomes: amenable mortality, i.e. mortality that could have been avoided through appropriate health care interventions, is above the EU average (OECD/EOHS, 2019). As such, the planned increase in public health financing to a minimum of 6% of GDP by 2024 is welcome. To prepare for a potential second coronavirus outbreak, the priority should be to ensure sufficient resources to boost intensive care capacity and allow for successful mass testing and isolation. Ageing will also add pressure to the health care system in the longer term, as its efficiency is suffering in particular from a high dependency on hospital care. Its coordination could be improved through a more efficient referral system and shorter waiting lists.

Strengthening primary care would avoid an excessive reliance on costly hospitalisations. The number of physicists is low, notably for generalists and avoidable hospital admissions are high (Figure 1.22, Panels C and D). The lack of general practitioners and nurses also effectively limit access to healthcare, notably for poor people living in rural areas. It is partly caused by inadequate remuneration. The general practitioner annual salary in 2016 was by far the lowest among OECD countries with available data. The same problem applies to nurses, whose salaries are second lowest only to Hungarian nurses. To deal with this problem, the authorities have introduced a national long-term policy on nursing and midwifery in 2019, thereby significantly increasing the number of schools for nurses, and raising the wages of nurses and midwives. Yet, developing, as planned, an integrated healthcare strategy to allocate the forthcoming increase in public spending could go a long way to address these issues, if it gives more prominence to primary care, prevention and e-health services.

Figure 1.22. The health sector suffers from numerous weaknesses

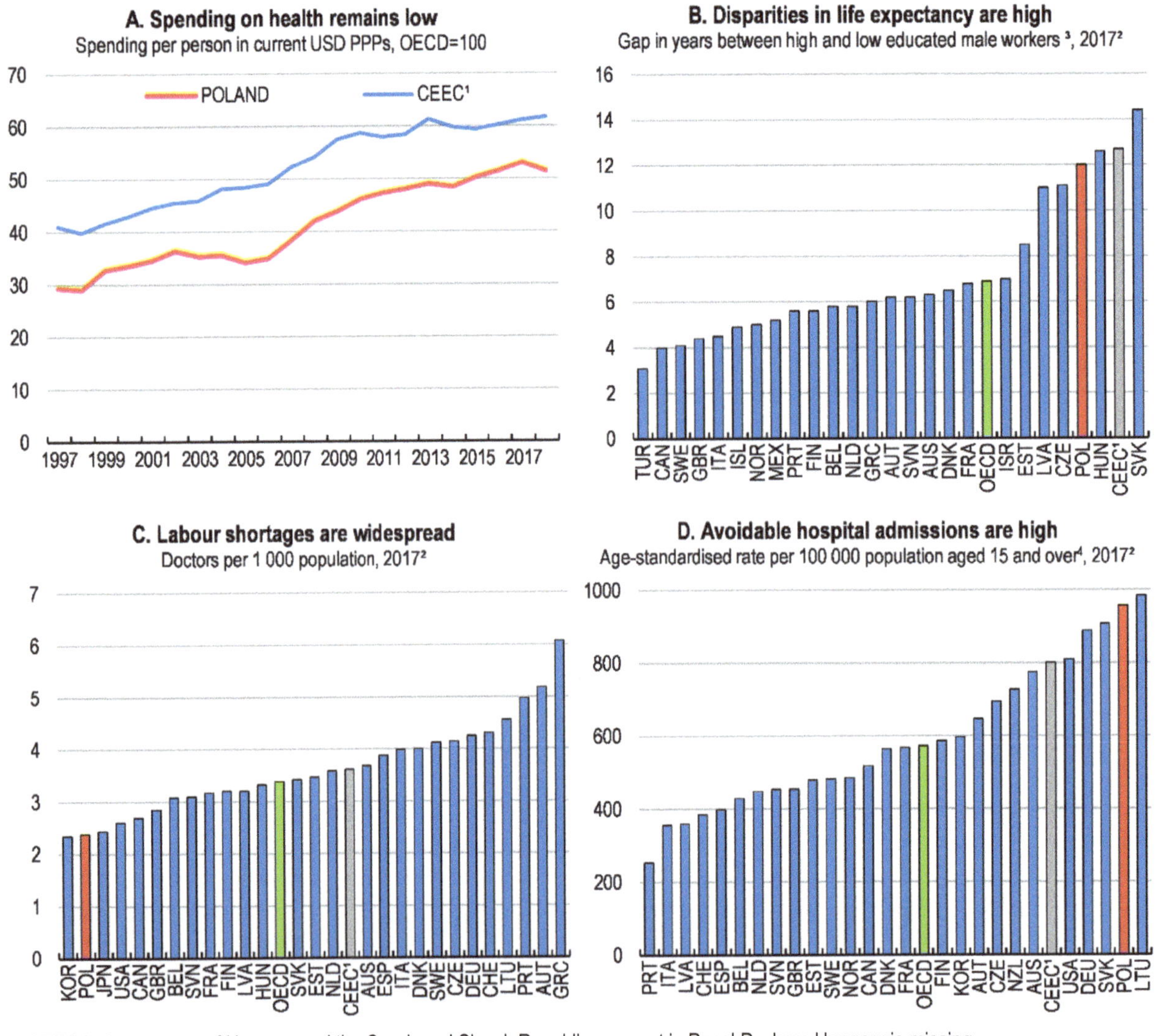

A. Spending on health remains low
Spending per person in current USD PPPs, OECD=100

B. Disparities in life expectancy are high
Gap in years between high and low educated male workers [3], 2017[2]

C. Labour shortages are widespread
Doctors per 1 000 population, 2017[2]

D. Avoidable hospital admissions are high
Age-standardised rate per 100 000 population aged 15 and over[4], 2017[2]

1. CEEC is the average of Hungary and the Czech and Slovak Republics, except in Panel D where Hungary is missing.
2. Or latest available year.
3. Gap in life expectancy at age 30 between highest and lowest educational level, by sex.
4. Sum of avoidable admissions for asthma, COPD, congestive heart failure and diabetes.
Source: OECD (2020), OECD Health Statistics (database).

StatLink https://doi.org/10.1787/888934208355

Equity is also a pressing concern. Differences in life expectancy by educational attainment are high (Figure 1.22, Panel B). Behavioural risk factors, including dietary risks, tobacco smoking, alcohol consumption and low physical activity, account for almost half of all deaths in Poland (OECD/EOHS, 2019), and the costs of air pollution are substantial (see below). Most of these risk factors are more common among people with lower education or income (Wojtyniak and Goryński, 2018). Preventive care accounts for only 2.3% of total spending, and could do much to close these gaps. Further attention needs to be paid to policy tools such as food and health standards, marketing bans or fiscal instruments such as taxes or subsidies. The 2017 creation of a national centre to promote healthy nutrition and physical activity in the population and the 2020 tax hikes on tobacco and alcohol use, as well as additional charge for sugar-sweetened beverages, are welcome moves. There is also a need for further information campaigns to promote good diet practices and strengthen vaccination rates, notably for people over aged 65.

Improving the tax system

Tax reform should support the recovery and inclusiveness and, once the economy is back to a firmly growing path, help to finance increasing spending needs and improve environmental outcomes. In the short term, lower tax rates on labour, notably for low- and middle-income households, would help to strengthen the employment recovery and social cohesion. Over the longer term and insofar as it is necessary, raising additional revenues should be done in the most inclusive and the least growth distortionary manner possible. A streamlining of the large tax expenditures would help in this regard. Indeed, the tax-to-GDP ratio is already in line with the OECD average (Figure 1.23, Panel A) and the tax wedge is relatively high, suggesting that efficiency gains and careful implementation are crucial to limit the necessary raise in some spending items. The government plans to continue to finance higher spending mainly by reducing tax fraud and boosting tax compliance, together with an increase in consumption taxes (Table 1.4). Indeed, efforts to improve VAT compliance have been very successful so far, as the losses due to tax evasion may have been reduced by about 25% in 2017. Yet, this was also partly linked to the favourable economic cycle (EC, 2019a).

Improving the redistribution of the tax system

There is room to make personal income tax fairer and decrease the tax wedge for low-income workers to boost inclusiveness and employment (Figure 1.23, Panel B). The contribution of the progressive personal income tax to overall revenues is low in international comparison (OECD, 2018c). The 2017 introduction of a degressive non-refundable tax credit helped to raise the system's overall progressivity (EC, 2018e). The government also lowered the first tax rate and exempted some young workers (those aged under 26 and with gross labour income below PLN 85 528 annually, around EUR 19 992) from the personal income tax in August 2019, and increased tax deductible costs for employees in October 2019 (Box 1.2). The 2017 personal income tax credit and the lowering of the bottom tax rate are welcome. Yet, the targeting of the youth created substantial age-based threshold, which could lead to higher employee screening and lower tax compliance.

Several measures could raise the progressivity of income and property taxes without endangering growth prospects. Firstly, there is room to strengthen the personal income tax credit. The full amount is available only to very low-income families (in 2019 the threshold was 13% of the average gross wage). Thus, it mostly affects single part-time workers and low-income families subject to joint taxation (Browne et al., 2019). Secondly, there are four regimes for paying taxes and social-security contributions for self-employed workers. The main one is based on shares of the (projected) average wage, notably for health and unemployment insurance contributions. Some of them pay social contributions based only on the minimum wage and a flat-rate personal income tax. These low costs compared to workers on permanent contracts runs risks for job quality of low-skilled workers (see below). Thirdly, once the economy is on a firm growth path, higher property taxes, which contribute relatively little to overall revenues, would be a complement to such reforms (Figure 1.23, Panel C). This could be done by establishing market-value-based property taxes (rather than based on area), by taxing capital gains on investment properties and by increasing taxes on vacant land and properties in urban areas. Such measures would improve inclusiveness, as housing tax revenue fell relatively evenly over the income distribution (Boone et al., 2019), and make the tax system more neutral vis-à-vis other types of investment and thus improve resource allocation (OECD, 2018f).

Once the recovery is firmly underway, the high number of reduced VAT rates and exemptions will require careful examination (Figure 1.23, Panel D). Poland applies reduced VAT rates to a number of goods and services, such as food, confectioned food and hygiene products, newspapers and books, restaurant and hotel services, water supply, housing repairs and some transport services (CASE/IAS, 2019; OECD, 2018vat). In a welcome step, the authorities are simplifying the system of reduced rates to limit uncertainty about their application. Yet, limiting the reliance on reduced rates could allow for lowering the relatively high statutory rate of 23%, while still increasing tax revenues. These would also allow for a more inclusive structure of taxation. Indeed, reduced rates often benefit higher-income households or firm owners, sometimes disproportionately, for example in the case of the reduced VAT rate on hotels and restaurants, as shown by VAT tax cuts on restaurants in France (Benzarti and Carloni, 2019). Lower-income households could be more efficiently reached through the personal income tax system or targeted social transfers, which have increased but remain low in Poland.

Figure 1.23. Tax revenues are around the OECD average, but could be more redistributive

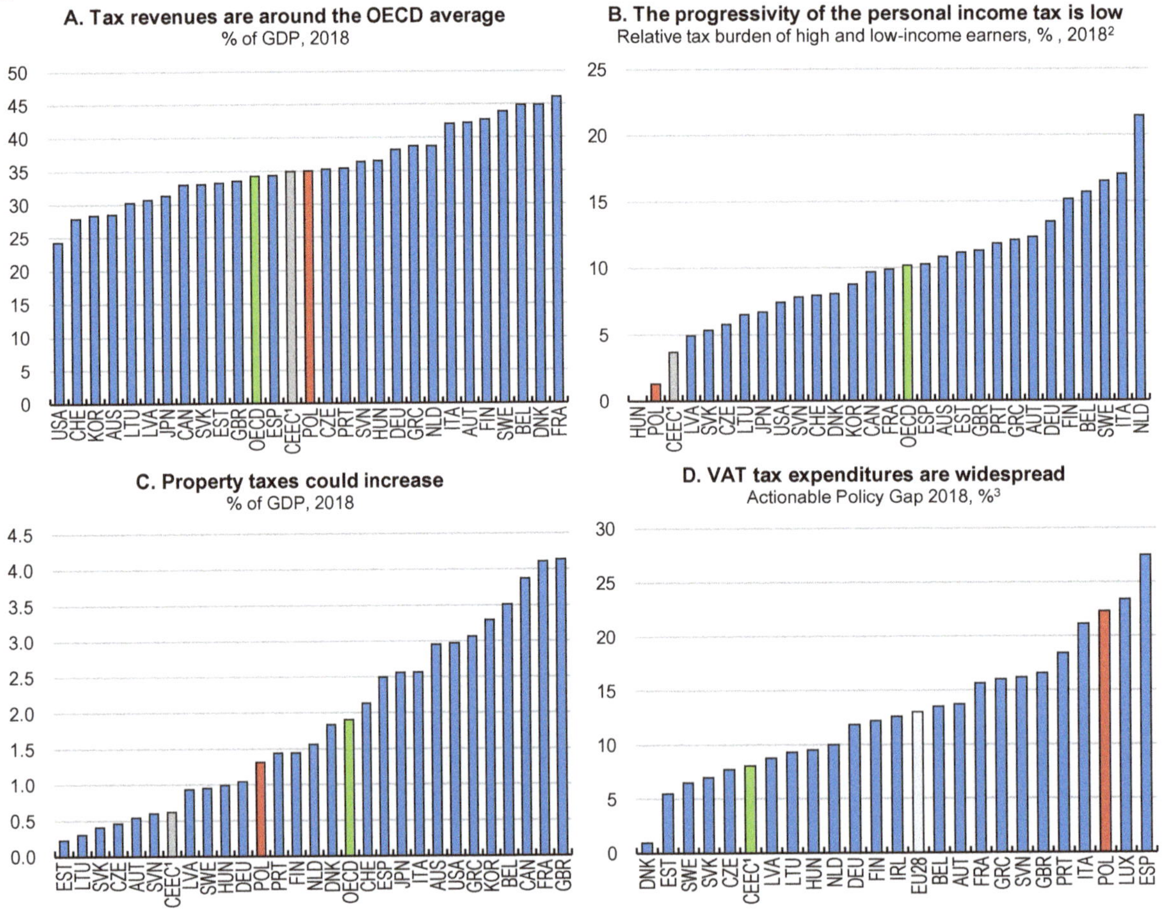

A. Tax revenues are around the OECD average
% of GDP, 2018

B. The progressivity of the personal income tax is low
Relative tax burden of high and low-income earners, % , 2018[2]

C. Property taxes could increase
% of GDP, 2018

D. VAT tax expenditures are widespread
Actionable Policy Gap 2018, %[3]

1. CEEC is the average of Hungary and the Czech and Slovak Republic.
2. Difference between the average income tax rate between a single persons at 67% and 167% of average wage.
3. % of theoretical VAT liabilities. The actionable VAT gap takes into account reduced rates and exemptions, but exclude exemptions on services that cannot be taxed in principle, such as imputed rents or the provision of public goods by the government (CASE/IAS, 2019).
Source: OECD (2020), OECD Tax Statistics and OECD Taxing Wages (databases); CASE/IAS (2019), Study and Reports on the VAT Gap in the EU-28 Member States: 2019 Final Report, Report TAXUD/2015/CC/131 for the Directorate General Taxation and Customs Union, Center for Social and Economic Research and Institute for Advanced Studies.

StatLink ᴍᴤᴸ https://doi.org/10.1787/888934208374

Strengthening environmental taxation

During the recovery, it is essential for stimulus measures and new investment to be aligned with ambitions on climate change, biodiversity and wider environmental protection (see below). Over the longer term, the phasing out of fossil fuel subsidies is a crucial step towards improving environmental and health outcomes. In 2015 only 15% of CO_2 emissions from energy use were priced above 30 EUR/tonne, which is the low-end estimate of carbon cost today (OECD, 2018b) and effective taxes on energy use are also low (OECD, 2019c). As in other OECD countries, tax rates on energy use are relatively higher in the road sector, but they are low or absent in the residential sector and the electricity excise tax rate is low. Major exemptions from energy taxes are in place, such as exemptions from tax on coal in the agriculture sector and for households' consumption or exemptions from coal and gas excise duty offered to some energy intensive industries (OECD, 2019c). The government should develop a strategy to phasing them out, while ensuring that any impact on energy poverty is alleviated.

Once the recovery is firmly underway, more effective carbon pricing would ease the energy transition (Figure 1.24). Around 48% of Poland's greenhouse gas (GHG) emissions were covered by EU-wide emissions trading system (ETS) with a price of allowances around 25 EUR/tCO2 in 2019. Yet, effective carbon taxes – i.e. the sum of explicit carbon taxes and fuel excise taxes, net of applicable exemptions, rate reductions and refunds – that complement the ETS system currently fail to provide broad-based carbon price signals (OECD, 2019c). Broadening the tax base would contribute to mitigation of GHGs emissions and air pollution, while raising revenues in the short-term that could be used to finance environmental projects. Though CO_2 emissions from road transport remain relatively low, transport emissions per inhabitant have more than doubled over 1997-2017. Poland is one of very few OECD countries without a specific CO_2-related vehicle tax. Moreover, diesel is taxed at a lower rate than petrol. Such taxes would need to be accompanied with transitory social measures to improve their acceptability. For the same reason, part of their proceeds could be used to subsidise low-income households when they purchase less polluting cars or heating systems, for example, as was done recently for electric car purchases.

Electricity retail prices should be allowed to increase. In 2019, Poland capped retail electricity prices through a cut in the tax rate on electricity and a decrease in transition fees and electricity tariffs. This cap applied to all electricity consumers in 2019H1 and was later restricted to households, SMEs, local authorities and hospitals. The authorities also compensated electricity trading companies for the difference with market values. This slowed down the transition to greener alternatives for households that were supported through additional programmes (Box 1.2). In a welcome move, the cap on electricity prices was removed in 2020, but the regulator refused high price hike for households in 2020 that could compensate for the increasing production costs and wholesale electricity prices. Before the crisis, plans were to combine the electricity price hike for households with mean-tested transfers towards poorer households in 2021. If well-designed, this could help achieve the environmental goals while avoiding to put an excessive burden on energy affordability for lower-income households (Flues and van Dender, 2017).

Figure 1.24. Tax-based carbon price signals are weak

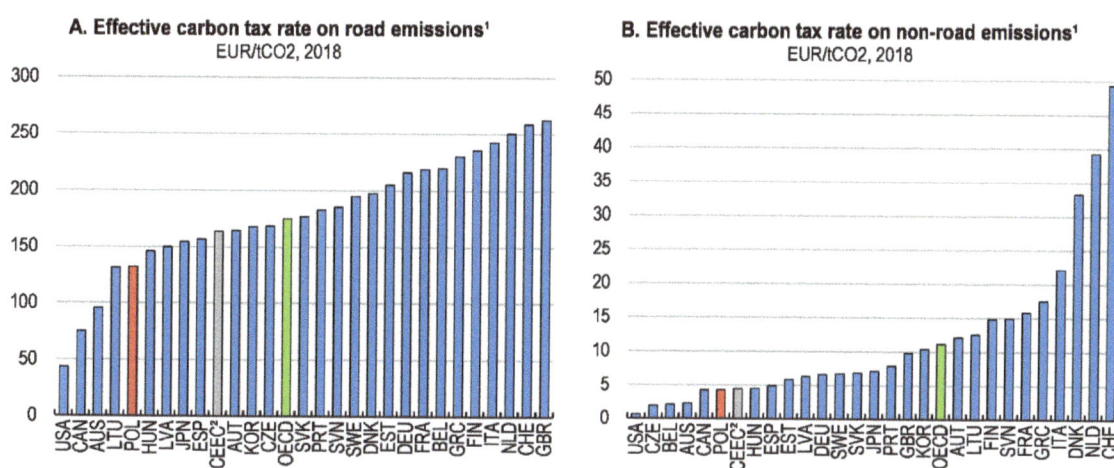

1. 2018 tax rates as applicable on 1 July 2018. CO2 emissions are calculated based on energy use data for 2016 from IEA (2018), World Energy Statistics and Balances. Emissions from the combustion of biofuels are included. Effective carbon taxes are not the only price-based climate policy instrument. The European Union's ETS, for instance, covers most emissions from electricity generation and in industry; allowance were traded at approximately EUR 25 in 2019. Carbon price signals are thus somewhat more widespread than the Figure suggests. The scale of the horizontal axis differs between Panel A and Panel B. In Chile, the average effective carbon tax on non-road emissions is due to the Green Tax.
2. CEEC is the average of Hungary and the Czech and Slovak Republics.
Source: OECD (2019), Taxing Energy Use 2019: Using Taxes For Climate Action, OECD publishing, Paris.

StatLink 🖳 https://doi.org/10.1787/888934208393

Illustrating the fiscal effects of government's and OECD-recommended reforms

The proposed tax and spending reforms give the government a choice of options to improve the structure of public spending and revenues in the medium run. These options would also make room to boost growth-enhancing investment, for example, public expenditures on R&D. This is quantified in an illustrative manner in Table 1.4.

Table 1.3. Government structural fiscal plans from 2018 to 2025 and OECD's recommendations

Estimated effects on the 2025 fiscal deficit (% of 2025 GDP)[1]

Panel A. Key government spending plans until 2025	% of GDP
The 2019-20 extension of the child benefits programme (500+), independently of households' income level.	0.8
The 2018-19 strengthening of other childcare programmes (the 2018 Good Start programme and the 2019 Mother 4 plus).	0.1
Additional health-care spending: 1.3% of GDP.	1.3
Additional pension spending due to the reversing of the 2013 retirement-age increases.	0.5
Increase in R&D spending not financed by EU funds.	0.3
Panel B. Key government revenue plans until 2025	
Further improvement in tax compliance.	-1.5
The implementation of a tax on digital firms and the retail tax.	-0.1
New tax expenditures in personal income tax (new threshold, increased tax-free allowance, exemption for young taxpayers) introduced in 2020.	0.4
The 2020 increase of alcohol and tobacco taxes and the new sugar tax.	-0.15
The reform of the second pillar (OFEs) will bring higher social security contributions.	-0.1
Panel C. Total effect of government plans on the fiscal deficit	**1.55**
Panel D. OECD-recommended reforms	
Rebalancing long-term and childcare spending towards long-term care, the development of childcare facilities and lower-income families: 0% of GDP. An increase of spending on childcare and long-term care services of 1.4% of GDP could be financed by eliminating child tax credits and family benefits that existed before the introduction of the 500+ benefit programme, together worth 0.6% of GDP, and scaling back and reforming the 500+ extension, worth 0.8% of GDP. In net terms this would leave the level of spending unchanged by 2025.	0
Increasing training for the low-skilled and unemployed workers by 0.1% of GDP.	0.1
Increase in public spending on higher education and research: a 0.5% of GDP increase in public funding for universities would bring Poland's spending on tertiary education roughly into line with the United Kingdom and the Netherlands[2].	0.5
A reduction of the tax wedge for low-skilled workers equivalent to 0.4% of GDP.	0.4
Strengthening the progressivity of the personal income tax by increasing revenues by 0.6% of GDP (16% of the gap with the OECD average) and using these revenues to reduce general social security contributions for low-wage workers.	0
Reducing VAT revenue shortfalls due to reduced rates and exemptions: 0.8% of GDP[2].	-0.8
Increasing environmental and property taxes.	-0.85
Aligning the special pension regime for farmers and the specific rules applied to miners with the general regime. Gradually increase in the statutory retirement age to 67 for women and men phased in over 2020 to 2040.	-0.9
Panel E: Total effect of OECD proposals on the fiscal deficit	**-1.55**
Panel F. Total effect of government plans and OECD proposals on the fiscal deficit (=Panel C+Panel E)	**0**

1. Excluding temporary support measures in response to the coronavirus crisis. Positive numbers indicate a deterioration of the fiscal balance. Numbers may not add to totals because of rounding. Measures enacted before 2018 and that do not have a staggered impact on the deficit are not taken into account.
2. These recommendations are taken from the 2018 Survey.
Source: OECD calculations based on Republic of Poland (2019), Convergence Programme – 2019 Update, Warsaw and OECD (2018), OECD Economic Surveys: Poland 2018, OECD Publishing, Paris.

Table 1.4. Past OECD recommendations on fiscal policy and pensions

Main recent OECD recommendations	Actions taken since the 2018 Survey
Evaluate the effects of the pension reform, and make corrections such as aligning male and female retirement ages and indexing them to healthy life expectancy. Inform the public about the impact of working longer on pension income.	Yearly letters are sent to inform about future pensions and a network of local counsellors has been developed. Social campaigns and online pension calculators have been developed. The Council of Ministers adopted an official evaluation of the 2016 reform.
Strengthen environmentally related taxes, limit the use of reduced VAT rates and exemptions, and make the personal income tax (PIT) more progressive, e.g. by introducing a lower initial and more intermediate tax brackets and ending the preferential tax treatment of the self-employed.	Since 2018, the tax-free income for PIT has increased. The first tax rate was lowered in October 2018 and young workers (aged under 26 and with labour income below PLN 85,528) are exempted from the personal income tax since August 2019. Tax deductible costs for employees were increased in October 2019.
Redesign and increase the least distortive taxes, by establishing market-value-based property taxes and by taxing capital gains on investment properties.	No action taken.

Improving productivity, employment and well-being

To support the recovery and return to a sustainable growth path, Poland needs to boost innovation and productivity gains, notably in smaller firms. Progress towards more resilient and inclusive growth is held back by low skills, pervasive labour market inefficiencies, and difficulties of small and young dynamic firms to grow (Chapter 2). According to illustrative OECD simulations, structural reforms could increase GDP by 5.6% after 10 years (Box 1.3). The largest gains would come from reforming pension arrangements, developing childcare facilities and increasing the employability of low-skilled workers, through a reduction of their tax wedge and strengthened activation measures.

The Polish economy is shifting towards higher-skilled employment. Since transitioning from central planning, the service sector has expanded and manufacturing has become tightly integrated into global value chains, changing more and more the skill set that is needed in the labour market. The changing structure of the economy, as well as the increase in computerisation and automation, led to higher productivity. However, at the same time, the changing job profiles means that non-cognitive routine jobs are progressively disappearing. Employment is shifting from low- and medium-skilled jobs towards high-skilled jobs (Figure 1.25, Panel A). The growing demand for skilled workers is projected to continue (Cedefop, 2018) and providing workers with the right skills to adapt to a changing environment will sustain productivity growth (Panel B). Preparing the labour market for technological change is high on the political agenda and the government is preparing its skill strategy with the support of the OECD (2019d).

Enhancing labour market inclusiveness

Strengthening skills and their efficient use

Enhanced education and training will be essential to support the recovery and return to previous growth levels. Up-skilling and re-skilling will be crucial as the economic activity resumes. The number of jobseekers is expected to be higher than before and there may be permanent shifts in the demand for labour across sectors (OECD, 2020a). Training would help to swiftly reallocate displaced workers. Lifting up the skills of workers would also enable local firms to benefit from knowledge diffusion and technological adaptation to move production towards higher-value activities (OECD, 2017). In particular, the wider use of learning models at work could have a sizable effect on Poland's GDP (Box 1.3).

Figure 1.25. Upskilling and automation are challenging issues

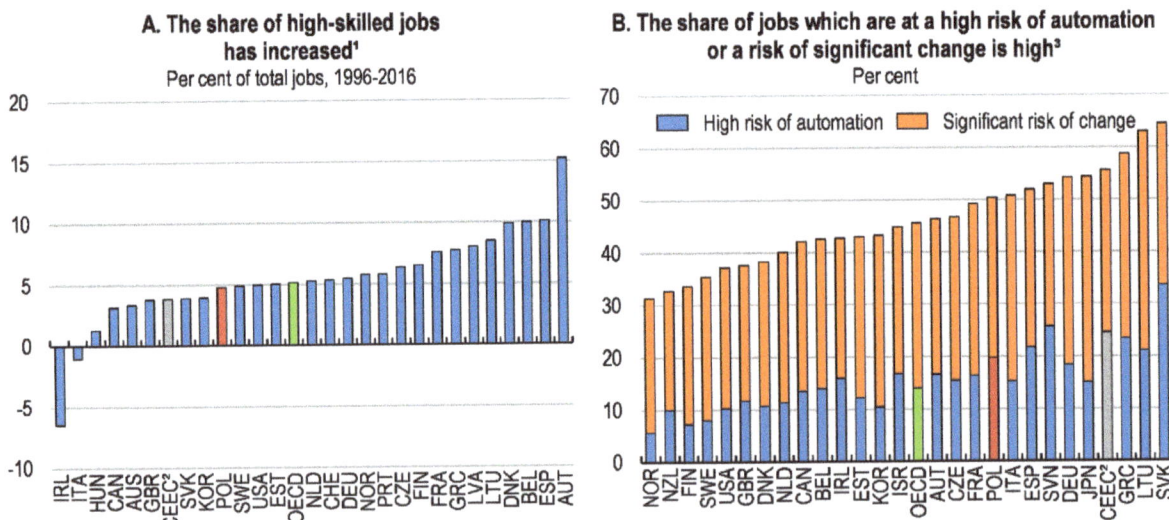

A. The share of high-skilled jobs has increased¹
Per cent of total jobs, 1996-2016

B. The share of jobs which are at a high risk of automation or a risk of significant change is high³
Per cent

High risk of automation   Significant risk of change

1. High-skill occupations are managers, professionals and technicians (ISCO88 codes: 1, 2 and 3). Middle skill occupations are clerks, machine operatives and crafts (codes: 4, 7 and 8). Low-skill occupations are sales and service occupations and elementary occupations (codes: 5 and 9). The time period covered is 2006-16, except for: Korea (2006 14); Australia (2006-15); Greece, Portugal and Latvia (2007-16); Italy (2007-15), Switzerland (2008-15); Canada, Ireland, and Luxembourg (2006-15).
2. CEEC is the average of Hungary and the Czech and Slovak Republics in Panel A, and of the Czech and Slovak Republics in Panel B.
3. Jobs are at high risk of automation if the likelihood of their job being automated is at least 70%. Jobs at risk of significant change are those with the likelihood of their job being automated estimated at between 50 and 70%. Data for Belgium correspond to Flanders and data for the United Kingdom to England and Northern Ireland.
Source: OECD (2019), OECD Employment Outlook 2019, OECD Publishing, Paris; and OECD calculations based on the Survey of Adult Skills (PIAAC) (2012); and Nedelkoska, L. and G. Quintini (2018), "Automation, skills use and training", OECD Social, Employment and Migration Working Papers, No. 202, OECD Publishing, Paris. https://doi.org/10.1787/2e2f4eea-en.

StatLink ᴍᴸᴤᴸ https://doi.org/10.1787/888934208412

Educational attainment is high in Poland, but many adults lack basic and digital skills. After considerable progress, Polish 15-year-olds are among the top performers in the OECD's Programme for International Student Assessment (PISA), finishing among the best of OECD countries in reading, science and mathematics in the 2018 PISA Survey (Figure 1.26, Panel A). Furthermore, the country has a high share of high performers and the lowest share of low performers in the OECD (Panel B) and low number of lagging students (OECD, 2019e). Yet, adult skills are below the PIAAC average, especially in numeracy (Panel C).

Participation in adult learning appears relatively low, according to international surveys. Low-skilled workers are particularly disengaged from learning (Figure 1.26, Panel D). This is also the case for those in rural areas and working in the numerous micro- and small-sized enterprises (Chapter 2). There is too little evaluation of the quality and effectiveness of training programmes (OECD, 2019d). The adoption of individual training accounts (Chapter 2) could promote lifelong learning, notably for those on temporary contracts (see below). This would make training rights "portable" from one job or employment status to another, therefore favouring labour reallocation. Yet, such system would require to secure adequate and predictable funding, to provide greater generosity for those most in need, to develop the availability of effective information, as well as advice and guidance would be critical to ensure its effectiveness (OECD, 2019f). Using digital channels to provide timely and relevant training and to disseminate information about training opportunities and career counselling can be quite effective if face-to-face interactions with Public Employment Services have to remain restricted (OECD, 2020d).

Figure 1.26. Educational outcomes have improved rapidly but there are significant skill gaps

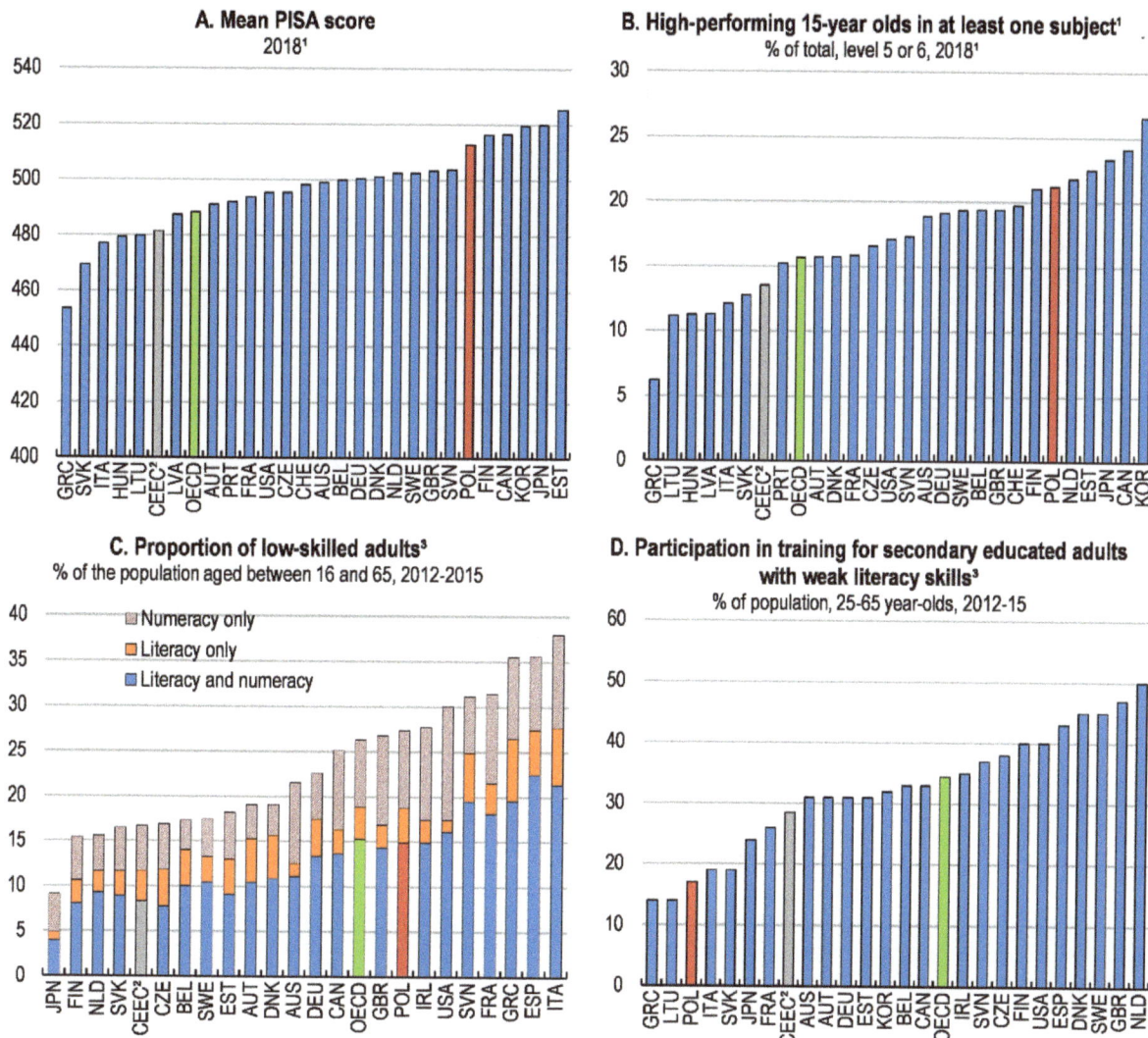

A. Mean PISA score
2018[1]

B. High-performing 15-year olds in at least one subject[1]
% of total, level 5 or 6, 2018[1]

C. Proportion of low-skilled adults[3]
% of the population aged between 16 and 65, 2012-2015

- Numeracy only
- Literacy only
- Literacy and numeracy

D. Participation in training for secondary educated adults with weak literacy skills[3]
% of population, 25-65 year-olds, 2012-15

1. The three PISA subjects are reading, mathematics and science; the average of score across these subjects is displayed in Panel A. PISA 2018 data for the Netherlands, Portugal and the United States did not meet the PISA technical standards but were accepted as largely comparable.

2. CEEC is the average of Hungary and the Czech and Slovak Republics, except in Panels C and D, where Hungary is missing.

3. Low-skilled adults are defined as those with a score of less than 2 on the scales of written comprehension and numeracy considered by the OECD's Survey of Adult Skills, in Panel C, and of written comprehension only in Panel D. The data are based solely on Flanders for Belgium and England for the United Kingdom.

Source: OECD (2019), PISA 2018 Results (Volume I): What Students Know and Can Do, OECD Publishing, Paris; OECD (2016), Skills Matter - Further Results from the Survey of Adult Skills, OECD skills surveys, OECD Publishing, Paris.

StatLink https://doi.org/10.1787/888934208431

Box 1.3. Potential impact of some OECD recommended reforms on growth

The impact of some key structural reforms proposed in this *Survey* are estimated using historical relationships between reforms and growth in OECD countries (Table 1.6). These estimates assume swift and full implementation of reforms.

Table 1.5. Potential impact of some reforms proposed in this Survey on GDP

Effect on the level of GDP

Policy	Measure	Effect in 2025	Effect in 2030
Increase in the effective retirement age[1,2]	Gradual increase in the statutory retirement age from 60 to 67 for women and 65 to 67 for men phased in over 2020 to 2040.	0.45%-1.02%	1.23%-3.17%
Additional spending on child-care and long-term care services[2]	Rebalancing of long-term care, childcare and child-benefit expenditures to wards spending for long-term care, childcare development and lower-income households.	0.57%	1.69%
Additional spending on business R&D[2]	Increase by 0.35% of GDP.	0.31%	0.59%
Improving product market regulations	Streamlining regulations for start-ups to the level of the OECD median.	0.09%	0.13%
Additional spending on training	Increasing training for the low-skilled and unemployed workers by 0.1% of GDP.	0.46%	0.58%
Lower tax wedge in particular for low-skilled workers	A reduction of the tax wedge for low-skilled workers equivalent to 0.4% of GDP.	0.22%	0.27%
Lower tax wedge in particular for low-skilled workers	Strengthening the progressivity of the personal income tax by increasing revenues by 0.6% of GDP (16% of the gap with the OECD average) and using these revenues to reduce general social security contributions, thereby reducing the labour tax wedge by around 0.1% of GDP	0.06%	0.07%
Total effects from structural reforms[3]		2.2%-2.7%	4.6%-6.5%

1. GDP gains for the increase in retirement age and spending on child-care and long-term care services are calculated based on the model of Cavalleri and Guillemette (2017).The range of estimates for the increase in retirement age corresponds to different estimates for the elasticity of elderly employment with respect to changes in the statutory retirement age, which are scaled based on the estimated changes in elderly employment in Poland in the last quarter of 2017 due to the lowering of the statutory retirement age. Estimates for the GDP effects of an increase in business R&D spending, additional spending on active labour market policies and change in the tax wedge are based on Égert and Gal (2017).
2. These recommendations are taken from the 2018 Survey. Such an increase is assumed to result from new public spending on higher education and research (Table 1.4).
3. The table does not fully take into account the impact of the tax reforms proposed in Table 1.4. Yet, the proposed tax reforms - VAT broadening and higher environmental and property taxes - are among the least harmful for growth according to recent OECD estimates (Akgun et al., 2017).
Source: OECD calculations based on Égert, B. and P. Gal (2017) "The quantification of structural reforms: A new framework", *OECD Economics Department Working Paper*, No. 1354 ; OECD (2018), OECD Economic Surveys: Poland 2018, OECD Publishing, Paris; Akgun, O., B. Cournède and J. Fournier (2017), "The effects of the tax mix on inequality and growth", *OECD Economics Department Working Papers*, No. 1447, OECD Publishing, Paris.

Reducing labour market frictions would improve the use of skills, by securing workers' labour market transitions and improving the geographical and social mobility of the most disadvantaged groups (Box 1.4; Lewandowski et al., 2020). Despite a booming labour market in the past years, regional disparities in employment rates have remained stable since 2007 (Statistics Poland, 2019b). Inter-regional mobility is the second lowest in the OECD (OECD, 2018a), and, within regions, disparities in unemployment rates are wide across municipalities. Past employment gains have been concentrated in urban regions (OECD, 2018g), and the lack of affordable housing prevents an efficient matching between workers and firms. All Polish regions rank among the bottom 20% of the OECD regions in number of rooms per person

(Figure 1.5) and, 43.9% of Poles aged 25-34 live with their parents in 2019. An estimated 40% of the population falls into the "rent gap" – remaining unable to purchase or rent a flat under commercial conditions, but with the earnings too high to qualify for social housing (Habitat for Humanity Poland, 2019). The 2017 "Apartment+" package support the construction of affordable housing for rent, with the possibility of eventually acquiring the flat. However, its take-up has been much weaker than anticipated: at the end of 2019, only about 3000 were finalised or under construction, as compared to the initial target of 100 000.

The high home-ownership rate and the poor quality of some local roads (Chapter 2) mean that mobility is not sufficient to avoid pockets with high unemployment. Some cities have large vacant land and buildings in their centres (EC, 2020a). Reducing registration fees and increasing periodic taxes on land and property by gradually aligning them with market prices would encourage owners to sell construction land. This would help develop a subsidised rental market and social housing (Box 1.4). Integrating spatial, economic and sectoral plans and developing the coverage of local spatial development plans would help to closely monitor urban developments and enhance the impacts of construction on productivity and well-being, notably by lowering the costs of developing and running public transport. Indeed, new construction have substantially sprawled in Poland (Figure 1.27), with negative consequences on daily commutes that are mainly by car. Boosting investment in public transport would help to support the recovery and promote worker reallocation, productivity growth and better air quality.

Figure 1.27. Urban sprawl could reinforce employment access issues

Change in average urban population density[1], inhabitants/km², 1990-2014

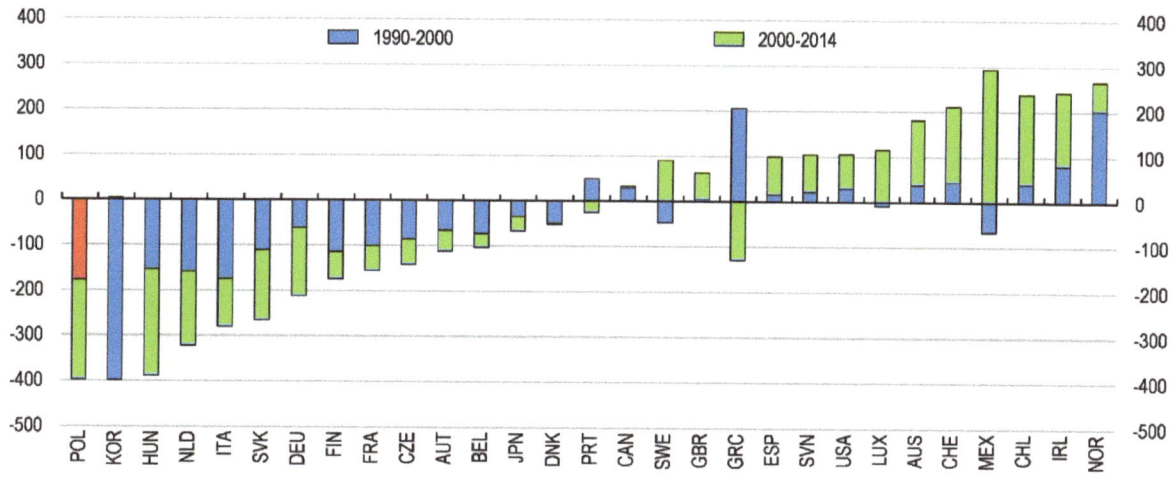

1. Urban population density refers only to population density in functional urban areas (FUAs): small cities not forming part of a functional urban area are not considered in the analysis. The full list of FUAs for France is available here: http://www.oecd.org/cfe/regional-policy/functional-urban-areas-all-france.pdf.
Source: OECD (2018), Rethinking Urban Sprawl: Moving Towards Sustainable Cities, OECD Publishing, Paris.

StatLink https://doi.org/10.1787/888934208450

Better information on job vacancies and candidates would contribute to promote the re-employment of displaced workers and have a positive impact on productivity (Algan et al., 2018 ; Skandalis, 2018). This could be done by providing greater assistance to long-term unemployed, low-skilled workers and SMEs, as well as adapting job search methods. For example, the French Public employment service has developed an application ("La Bonne Boîte") which allows jobseekers to target their unsolicited applications at enterprises that would be likely to employ them. Supporting SMEs in finding appropriate candidates (Chapter 2) and strengthening mobility vouchers would be useful complementary measures. The European Youth Guarantee provisions, an activation package introduced in 2014, includes job mobility vouchers, but other vouchers for unemployed people taking up employment outside their place of residence are low. They could be extended to interview and first time employment to boost search incentives and promote a more efficient use of skills.

> ### Box 1.4. Housing and labour market outcomes in Poland
>
> As in other OECD countries, the housing and labour markets are tightly linked in Poland, a country with a predominantly outright owned housing (84.2% of the population living in owned dwelling), a small rental market (4.2% renting a dwelling at market price), and large regional disparities in labour market situation. The quality of housing in Poland is rather low – overcrowding rate is high – although it has been steadily improving over last years.
>
> At the local level, regression analyses undergone for this Survey (Lewandowski et al., 2020) show that the spatial differences in construction activity and flat prices are weakly associated with differences in labour market situations. The housing stock in Poland has grown almost exclusively thanks to private construction and a substantial share of new flats has been built in the few largest cities where prices are the highest. Large differences in prices and liquidity between large cities, and towns and villages may constrain potential mobility of flat owners living in towns and villages.
>
> Relative wages do not appear to compensate the higher housing costs in the most dynamic local labour markets and cities. For tertiary educated workers, larger cities offer wage premia that may overweigh higher housing costs, but for workers without tertiary education, the wage gains appear relatively smaller than the relative housing costs, which may discourage internal migration towards localities with better labour market opportunities.
>
> Source: Lewandowski, P., Pigoń, A. and T. Świetlik (2020), *Housing and labour market outcomes in Poland*, Technical Background paper.

Improving job quality

The share of temporary contracts and self-employed remains high (Figure 1.6, Panel A). Despite a recent decline, temporary contracts still affect particularly young and low-skilled workers, who suffer from an associated wage penalty, and low career prospects and access to training (Figure 1.28; Gora et al., 2017). Non-standard workers were particularly vulnerable to the widespread shutdown due to COVID-19 containment measures (OECD, 2020a). The sectors most directly affected employ a large proportion of these non-standard workers. In addition, 2% (according to the recent labour Force Surveys) work on freelancing type of contracts based on general civil rather than labour law, and are not fully covered by social security contributions and workers' rights. The government implemented welcome measures to support self-employed and non-standard workers who were severely hit by lockdown measures (Box 1.1). Nevertheless, Temporary Work Agencies, for example, are not well covered by these measures.

The use of freelancing civil-law contracts is often illegal, but employers' probability of being inspected over their use of such contracts is below 1% (Gora et al., 2017). Few infractions are fined, and the average penalty is low (OECD, 2016). Hence, labour-law enforcement needs to be strengthened, as previous Surveys have argued. Around 3% of workers have no written contract at all according to Labour Force Statistics. Statistics Poland estimates employment in the informal or hidden economy at 5%. Informal workers remained beyond the scope of income support schemes promoted by the government after the COVID-19 outbreak. At the same time, the government should invest in communications to both workers and employers around minimum wage compliance and enforcement.

The ongoing rise in the minimum wage may adversely affect the economic recovery, employment and job quality. The 2020-21 hikes in the minimum wage (Box 1.2) will make the minimum-to-median wage ratio one of the highest in the OECD and significantly increase labour costs of low-wage workers (Figure 1.29, Panels A to C). The increases directly affect around 13% of workers (Statistics Poland, 2019b). The minimum wage has increased by 15.6% in 2020, while inflation is set to be close to 2.6%. The minimum wage will increase again by 7.7% in 2021 with inflation projected at 2.5%. Given the unprecedented fall in economic activity induced by the COVID-19 epidemic and the projected GDP contraction, there is a risk that the foreseen increases in labour costs deter employers from re-hiring displaced workers, especially low-wage, low-skill workers, or encourage them to increase more precarious forms of employment (Neumark, 2018). As the labour market impact of COVID-19 related confinement measures are likely to concentrate precisely on workers with lower wages and low skills, it becomes even more important not to discourage firms from employing the most vulnerable (EC, 2020b).

Figure 1.28. Temporary contracts tend not to be a stepping-stone for career development

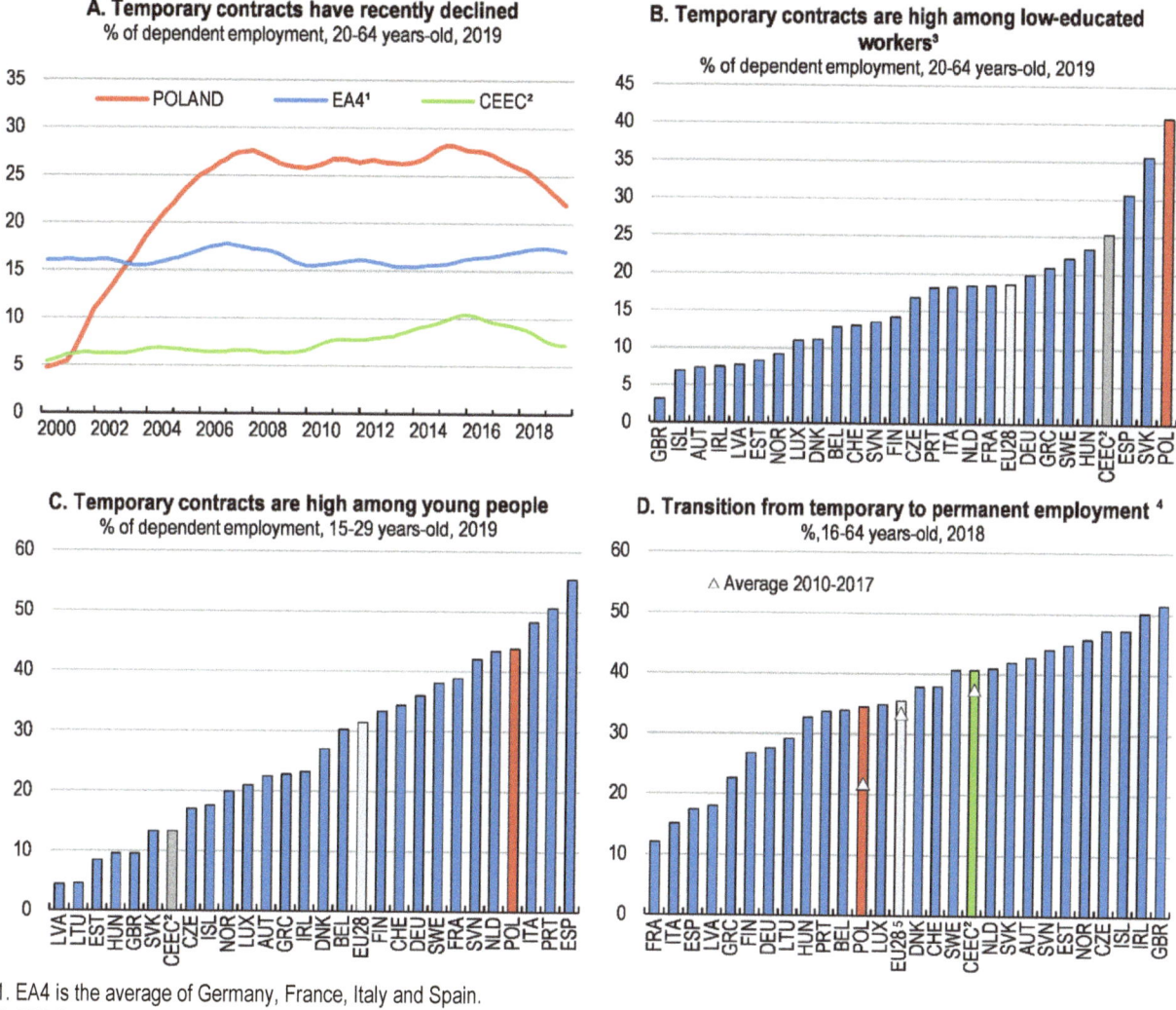

A. Temporary contracts have recently declined
% of dependent employment, 20-64 years-old, 2019

B. Temporary contracts are high among low-educated workers[3]
% of dependent employment, 20-64 years-old, 2019

C. Temporary contracts are high among young people
% of dependent employment, 15-29 years-old, 2019

D. Transition from temporary to permanent employment[4]
%, 16-64 years-old, 2018

1. EA4 is the average of Germany, France, Italy and Spain.
2. CEEC is the average of Hungary and the Czech and Slovak Republics.
3. Less than primary, primary and lower secondary educational attainment (ISCED levels 0-2).
4. Employees on temporary contract in year t-1 but declaring having been hired on a permanent contract in year t.
5. Unweighted average.
Source: Eurostat (2020), "Employment, Labour Force Statistics series" and "Labour transitions by type of contract", Eurostat Databases.

StatLink https://doi.org/10.1787/888934208469

Since 2017, in a welcome move, many atypical work arrangements have been covered by the minimum wage. In principle, the minimum wage also covers contracts for services between employer and self-employed. Yet, it does not apply to some forms of civil contracts, the so-called contracts for specific tasks (*umowa o dzieło*). Indeed, high minimum wage hikes have resulted in an increased use of such contracts in low-wage sectors in the United Kingdom for zero-hour contracts (Datta et al., 2019). In addition, even for workers that are covered by the statutory minimum-wage, non-compliance – that appears already high – could increase further (Goraus-Tanska and Lewandowski, 2019). However, the minimum wage increase could also have positive effects since it could provide incentives for firms to increase the skills of existing workers to improve their productivity. Some recent evidence points in that direction, as long as the downward wage rigidity does not prevent firms from partially passing on the cost of training to workers during the training period (D'Arcy, 2016). Another potential positive consequence would be to accelerate the shift of labour resources to larger and more efficient companies, provided there are no major obstacles to labour reallocation (Dustman et al., 2019).

Cutting labour taxes significantly on regular labour-law contracts with low wages as initiated in 2019 would create incentives for employers to re-hire displaced workers, reduce incentives to use civil-law and other irregular contracts and would make the tax system more progressive. This could be done by reducing or subsidising social contributions on lower wages, but other financing would be needed to maintain benefits for these groups. Introducing a targeted refundable earned income tax credit would even be more effective in reducing the tax burden on low-wage workers and increase their take-home pay (Boulhol, 2014). This would increase incentives for the unemployed to take a job at the minimum wage (Figure 1.29, Panel D), and incentives to work more hours at the minimum wage level that are set to remain weak (OECD, 2019g).

Figure 1.29. The minimum wage could increase substantially

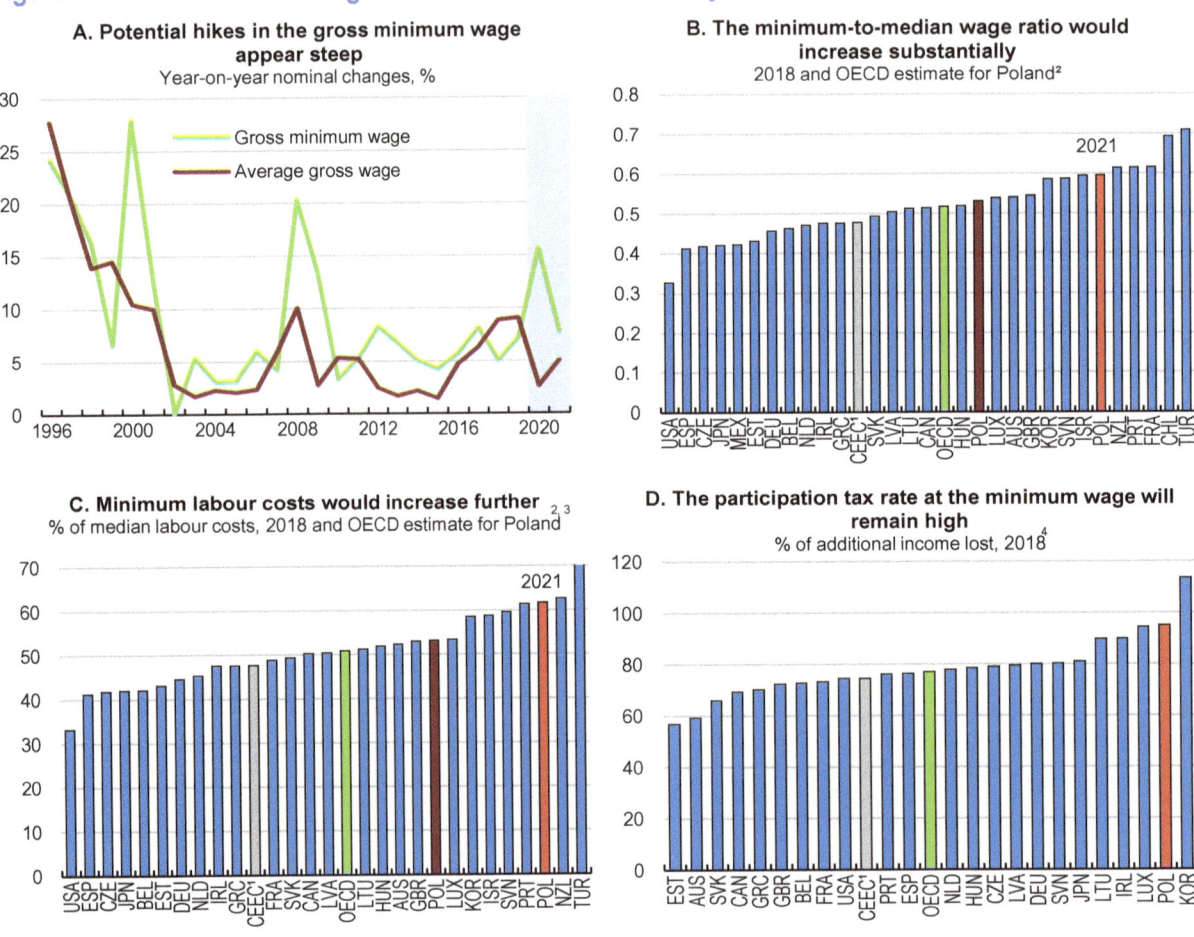

1. CEEC is the average of Hungary, the Czech and Slovak Republics.
2. The OECD estimate assumes that the median wage increase in line with the average gross wage projected over 2019-21 (OECD, 2019).
3. The OECD simulations are based on the Tax-Ben model and take into account the Polish tax and transfer system of 2018. Households are comprised of a single person aged 40 with no children who works in the private sector, generates all of his/her income from employment and possesses no other financial assets (OECD, 2019).
4. The participation tax rate when moving from unemployment to a full-time job at the minimum wage is due to higher taxes or lower benefits.
Source: OECD (2020), OECD Earnings Statistics (database); OECD (2019), OECD Economic Outlook: Statistics and Projections (database), November; OECD (2019), OECD Economic Surveys: France 2019, OECD Publishing, Paris.

StatLink ᵐᵖᵃ https://doi.org/10.1787/888934208488

Strengthening female employment

The female labour market situation has improved significantly, in many ways restoring the pre-transition situation of high female labour force participation and gender equality in education. The gender pay gap has been on a declining trend and the majority of employed women work full-time. The employment rate of 25-39 women is close to the European Union average. The share of women who reach management positions is also growing, with a fifth of the largest publicly listed companies' boards occupied by women. Yet, more effort is needed to encourage female participation, notably for the 60-64 old, who were affected by the lowering of the retirement age (see above), and the low-skilled, despite the recent increase of their employment rate. The extension of the 500+ family benefit in 2019 eliminated the potential negative effect of its initial means-testing (Magda et al., 2017). However, the employment rate of young women with children stagnated in 2018 and remains weak for the small number of low-educated mothers (Figure 1.30). Moreover, the COVID-19 economic crisis has been stark on women (OECD, 2020a). Women make up more than 95% of the long-term care workforce in Poland (OECD, 2020e). The closure of schools during the crisis likely amplified women's unpaid work burden and an on-line survey conducted by the CBOS Foundation reveals that women were disproportionally affected with income and job losses.

Figure 1.30. The employment rate of women with young children has stagnated

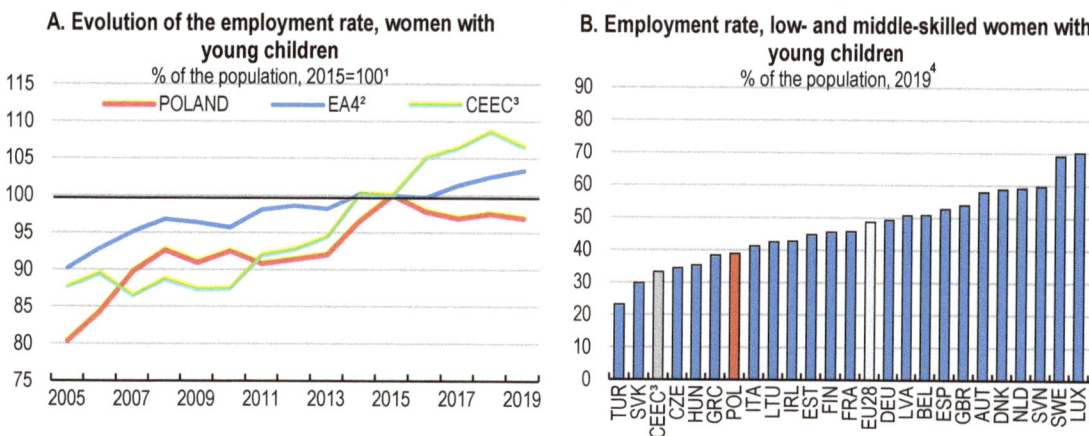

1. Data refer to women aged 20-49, with children less than 6 years old.
2. EA4 is the average of Germany, France, Italy and Spain.
3. CEEC is the average of Hungary and the Czech and Slovak Republics.
4. Low-skilled women refer to those with less than primary, primary and lower secondary educational attainment (ISCED levels 0-2), while middle-skilled women refers to those with upper secondary and post-secondary non-tertiary education (ISCED levels 3 and 4).
Source: Eurostat (2020), "Gender equality", Eurostat Database.

StatLink https://doi.org/10.1787/888934208507

Securing affordable childcare services is crucial to encourage female employment. More than 45% of inactive prime-age women cite care responsibilities as a reason for not participating in the labour market (OECD, 2018c). Poland witnessed one of the fastest increases in the enrolment of young children in education across OECD countries. The rate of 3-5 year-olds attending early childhood education has rapidly increased (Figure 1.31, Panel A), and 3-year-olds are legally entitled to a place in an early childhood education institution since 2017. However, access to early education for 0-2 years old remains largely insufficient despite a steady improvement according to EU-SILC data (Panel B).

The government estimates that the reformed *Maluch* (toddler) programme will help to create new places for toddlers and to increase their enrolment rate to 18% in 2020, although this would still be well below the OECD average. In particular, 58% communes in 2019 still did not have functioning pre-schools for 0-3 years old, posing a challenge especially in rural areas and for low-income households. As a result, little use is made of childcare by the lowest income households (OECD, 2020f), whose labour market participation is more sensitive to child care options (Goux and Maurin, 2010). In a welcome move, ongoing public programmes for childcare development target municipalities without any pre-schools, notably in rural areas. Continuing to improve access to childcare, and adapting it to the working hours of less skilled workers, would encourage less-qualified mothers to return to work while allowing for better social and economic mobility. Indeed, children of lower-educated parents would benefit strongly from high-quality early childhood education, as it yields considerable benefits for cognitive skills.

Other countries have recently implemented regulatory measures to legally enforce equal pay between genders. The gender-pay gap is relatively low Poland and Poland is supporting employers to monitor gender-pay gaps at the firm level. In France, for example, firms with at least 50 employees are obliged to publish indicators that measure pay gaps between women and men. Firms that fail to bring their score up to a minimum level within three years may incur financial penalties. In Iceland, the onus is no longer on the employee to prove that they are unpaid, but on the firm to prove they pay workers fairly. Employers must obtain a certification by an accredited auditor that their pay management system complies with a national equal pay standard. Poland could follow such examples to make further progress in closing the gender pay gap.

Figure 1.31. The use of formal childcare is improving

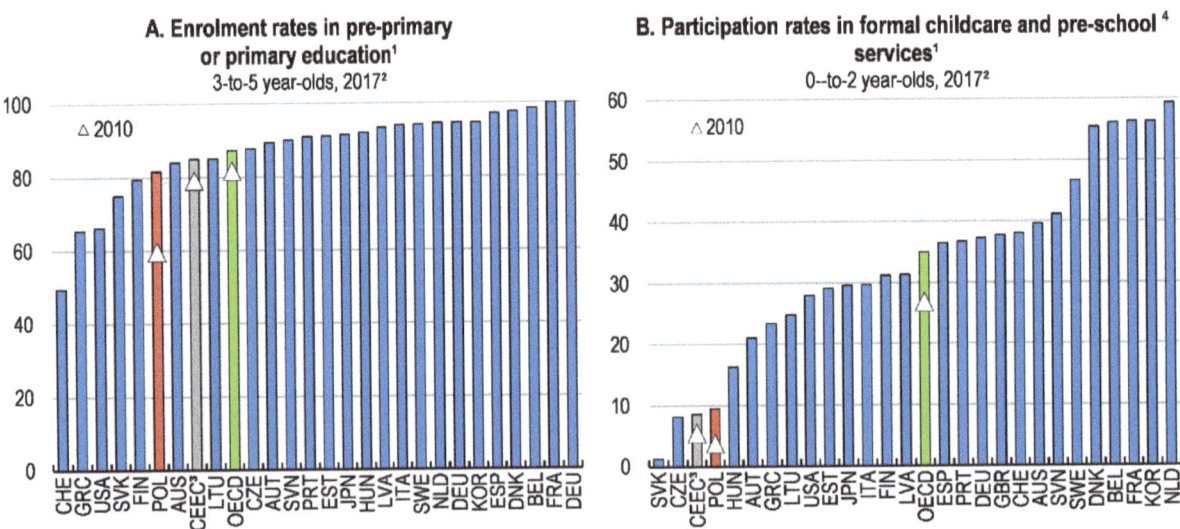

1. Potential mismatches between the enrolment data and the coverage of the population data (geographic coverage and/or the reference data used) may lead to overestimated or underestimated enrolment rates.
2. Or latest available year.
3. CEEC is the average of Hungary and the Czech and Slovak Republics.
4. Data refer to children using centre-based services (e.g. nurseries or daycare centres and pre-schools, both public and private), organised family daycare, and care services provided by paid professional childminders, excluding those using unpaid informal services provided by relatives, friends or neighbours.
Source: OECD (2020), OECD Family Statistics (database).

StatLink https://doi.org/10.1787/888934208526

Improving migration policies

To compensate for labour shortages in the context of an ageing society, policies can attract skilled labour into Poland. Poland became the largest temporary labour destination in the world (OECD, 2019h). By 2019, most migrants were from neighbouring countries, notably Ukraine from which temporary and seasonal migration has increased (Chmielewska et al., 2019). This has helped cushion the decline in the working-age population that started in 2011 (Strzelecki et al., 2020). Yet, the strong inflow of Ukrainians and from other neighbouring countries may not be sustainable, and opening up to workers from a wider set of countries is desirable. Moreover, the precarious situation of a majority of immigrant workers in Poland creates the risk that they move to another country when the opportunity arises (Chmielewska et al., 2019).

Migration policies should be improved to attract a broad range of skilled workers. Easy accessible information about educational degree verification, work opportunities and the availability of language courses could raise awareness among skilled workers to consider Poland as a destination. A clear migration strategy should help to monitor better the integration of foreigners in line with labour market needs together with the protection of their rights, notably access to education and training for them and their children (OECD, 2018c).

Easing the possibility of providing legal work to citizens from other countries through different work permits and faster resident permits would be helpful. The current administrative process for a standard resident permit for foreigners has not been able to cope with the strong inflow of foreigners. The length of the process of legalising their stay – through resident permits – has increased from 64 to 206 days over the last four years (NIK, 2019) and the duration of the procedures for work permits was close to 58 days in 2019, pushing many immigrants and their potential employers into precarious situations. There are common guidelines in all local offices regarding compulsory matters, but extending their period of validity could help reduce this congestion. Moreover, updating anti-discrimination policies and strengthening their implementation would help to confront ethnicity and nationality-based discriminations (UN, 2019; Antfolk et al., 2019). The government has successfully taken steps to help Polish farmers to recruit migrant labour force during the lockdown period. Some of the simplified procedures could remain in place even after the confinement measures are lifted and borders re-opened.

At the same time, the government should continue to strengthen its strategy to keep ties with the large expatriate community. Returning emigrants could bring skills, networks and financial capital (Brandt, 2016). Many OECD countries provide online hubs for their citizens abroad advertising jobs, training, and business and research opportunities in the home country (DFA, 2015). A job fair was recently organised in London and the authorities also created a website that offers some guidance to Polish workers abroad. Developing a diaspora skills database could help further to directly connect potential returning migrants with employers, as done in Portugal with the "Global Professional Mobility Platform". Tailored counselling and general assistance related to employment, housing, education and administrative procedures to start a small business, as the Irish "Back to Business" mentoring programme, have also proved quite effective (EC, 2014).

Table 1.6. Past OECD recommendations on labour market and migration policies

Main recent OECD recommendations	Actions taken since the 2018 Survey
Develop a national skills strategy with a strong basic skills component. Incentivise employers to develop workplace-based vocational education and adult training.	The general part of the Integrated Skills Strategy (ZSU) has been adopted in 2019. The detailed part is currently being developed with the support from the OECD which published the OECD Skills Strategy: Poland in December 2019.
Invest in childcare and long-term care facilities. Taper the phase out of the child benefit for the first child.	The Toddler+ programme helped to create an estimated 68 000 new places for toddlers from 2018 to 2020. The enrolment rate of children under 3 years old increased from 8.6%% in 2017 to 10.5% in 2018 (based on EU-SILC). Funding for new childcare institutions has increased in 2020. The previously means-tested child benefit was generalised in 2019.
Allow the public employment services to hire more skilled staff, and ensure that overall resources are better allocated to front-line placement tasks. Promote the adoption of best practices through performance management and benchmarking of providers.	No action taken
Consider introducing an earned-income tax for workers with a weaker attachment to the labour market.	No action taken
Develop a migration policy strategy to better monitor integration of foreigners in line with labour market needs, the protection of their rights and access to education and training for them and their children.	In 2018, the system of simplified registration procedure for employers was modified to ensure a higher level of control over the employment of foreigners. Moreover, a new type of work permit – the seasonal work permit entitling foreigners to work for 9 months over 12-month period – was introduced for employment in agriculture and seasonal branches.

Greening growth is essential for well-being

Bringing forward public investments that develop more sustainable alternatives could boost aggregate demand during the ongoing recovery and foster more sustainable growth (OECD, 2020g). Over the past couple of decades, energy and CO_2 emission intensities have been reduced considerably (Figure 1.32). Yet, the carbon intensity of the economy remains high and progress has stalled over the past few years. Coal still accounts for around 78% of electricity generation (Figure 1.33, Panel A) and 75% of coal capacity is over 25 years old. Consequently, many coal power plants have low level of efficiency and remain among Europe's largest contributors to CO_2 emissions and industrial air pollution (EC, 2019c).

Poland stimulus efforts should target to green further its energy mix. The authorities submitted their National Energy and Climate Plan to the European Commission at the end of 2019 and are preparing the Energy Policy of Poland until 2040. The updated 2020 draft Strategy notably aims at reducing the share of coal in electricity generation to 37-56% (depending on the carbon-price scenario) and boosting the share of renewables in gross final energy consumption to at least 23% by 2030. In addition, the 2020 update of the Nuclear Programme foresees that a first nuclear power plant will be commissioned by 2033 and 5 others by 2043. The government has yet to adopt its long-term strategy.

Despite significant progress (Figure 1.33, Panel B), Poland has room to strengthen its renewable electricity sector. Stricter EU emission standards and increasing CO_2 prices under the EU ETS make lignite-fired power plants increasingly expensive. Taking all costs into account, including environmental and closure costs when comparing the cost of different energy sources, would encourage new investment in renewable and less-polluting technologies (OECD, 2016; IEA, 2017). The draft Energy Policy envisages increasing the use of offshore wind and solar photovoltaic installations. Solar power generation increased twofold in 2019 and the 2019 auctions for renewables capacity will help develop solar power and onshore wind. Yet, the auctions for new renewable capacity are set to end in 2021 and building a more stable regulatory and incentive system would reduce uncertainty. Moreover, stringent regulations for onshore wind still prevent the use of larger and more-efficient turbines. The development of offshore wind will also require strengthening the transmission capacity in the northern part of the country.

Figure 1.32. Poland's energy and carbon intensities have declined but remain elevated

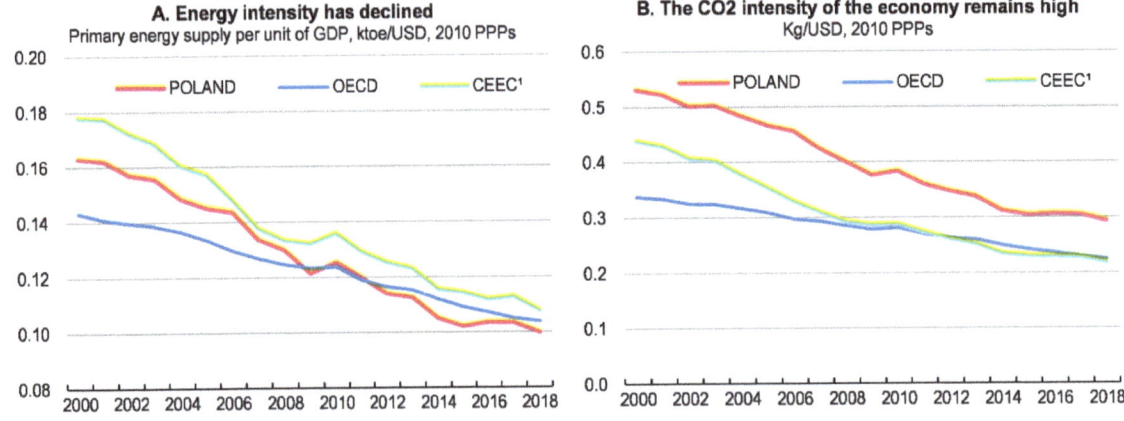

1. CEEC is the average of Hungary and the Czech and Slovak Republics.
Source: OECD (2020), OECD Green Growth Indicators (database).

StatLink ᐧᔆᒷ https://doi.org/10.1787/888934208545

Improvements in energy efficiency should continue, as they are the most cost-effective way of boosting competitiveness, increasing energy security and reducing the environmental footprint (IEA, 2018). The residential sector was responsible for 28% of final energy consumption in Poland in 2018. The energy intensity of space heating in Poland is one of the highest among EU countries. Due to the poor energy efficiency of buildings, energy affordability is an important issue, with as much as 10% of households in Poland suffered from energy poverty in 2017 (Sokołowski J. et al., 2019).

Deep retrofitting, through thermal insulations and replacement of inefficient equipment is key to improve energy performance. A large share of the existing building stock was built before 1990, with poor thermal standards. While progress has been made with regard to multi-apartment buildings, more than 70% of Polish single-family homes are either not or insufficiently insulated (Velux, 2018). The tightening of regulations on energy consumption in buildings, which is currently low, would help. The example of Nordic countries has shown that high insulation standards for buildings may result in energy intensity of heating among the lowest in the OECD countries despite cold climate (IEA, 2018). In addition, a combination of public support and imposing minimum requirements for reserve funds in multi-flat building renovation could help reinvigorate the numerous ageing multi-flat buildings, as in France.

Figure 1.33. Significant investments are needed in the electricity sector

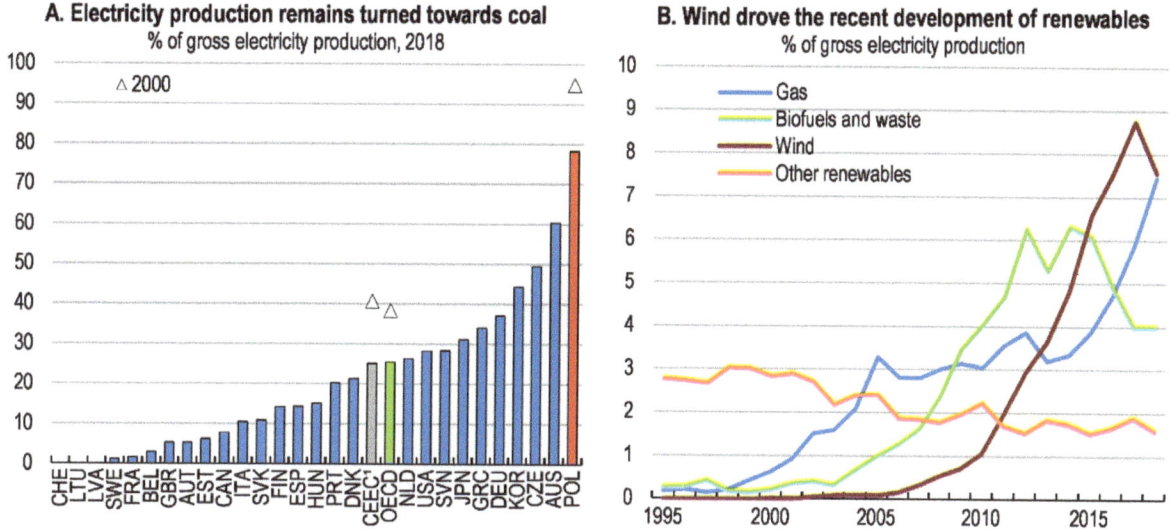

1. CEEC is the average of Hungary and the Czech and Slovak Republics.
Source: OECD (2020), OECD Electricity and Heat Generation Statistic (database).

StatLink https://doi.org/10.1787/888934208564

The emission of pollutants, in particular fine particles from heating installations of single-family houses, is the main cause of inappropriate air quality in large areas of Poland and is associated with too low energy efficiency in the heating sector. Air pollution is acute in many cities: among those evaluated in a report from the World Bank, 36 out of 50 most polluted European cities were in Poland (World Bank, 2018a and b). Air pollution has been found to lead to many premature deaths (Figure 1.34) and to have potential significant effects on productivity (Dechezleprêtre et al., 2019).

The government has taken welcome steps to address these challenges. In particular, the Clean Air programme, with a budget of PLN 103 billion, offers means-tested financial grants and loans for replacement of obsolete stoves and thermal retrofits to single-family houses until 2029. Another program, "Stop Smog", targets the poorest and most polluted municipalities. While the programs only started in 2018, their take-up has been so far much lower than anticipated (EC, 2020a). Complex administrative procedures and low income-thresholds for the highest grants constrained their implementation. Recent positive changes (administrative simplifications, premia for the installation of heat pumps and photovoltaic panels simultaneously, and the inclusion of banks in the provision of loans) could improve their take-up. In addition, regions (*voivodeships*) with areas exceeding the air-quality thresholds, introduced anti-smog regulations, aiming to limit the burning of fossil fuels in furnaces, notably in cities. Such legal requirements accompanied by fines for noncompliance, if properly implemented, should speed up the replacement of the heating systems.

Expanding and modernising the district heating network can help the clean energy transition. Poland has one of the largest district heating system in the European Union. However, most of the small district heating systems, which supply 40% of domestic heating, are old and inefficient (Forum Energii, 2019). They rely mostly on coal and incorporating more renewable energy sources would deliver cleaner energy to households. Poland should also expand its use of smart meters. Pilot smart meter projects in other countries have shown overall energy use reductions, with significant changes at peak times, like in the case of Ireland (BPIE, 2016).

Poland has also made efforts towards a circular economy. It adopted the EU Circular Economy Strategy in 2019. It identifies four priorities: sustainable production, sustainable consumption, bio-economy and new business models. Poland is also preparing its long-term "Strategy for Transformation to a Climate Neutral Economy". This document will define different scenarios for the development of the Polish economy to meet the objectives of the EU climate-energy policy and the target of the Paris Agreement in 2050. The Strategy will outline possible pathways to cut GHG emissions and their implications for the energy system and the economy by 2050.

The newly agreed "Next Generation EU" recovery plan will have dedicated funds to support the transition to climate neutrality, in line with the growth strategy outlined in the European Green Deal (Box 1.1). Poland should grasp the opportunity to enhance the resilience of its economy and society in the face of both the current recession and accelerating environmental challenges. In fact, several "green" sectors offer significant prospects for job creation, such as the renewable energy production sector (OECD, 2020h).

Figure 1.34. Air pollution levels are high and result in a high number of premature deaths

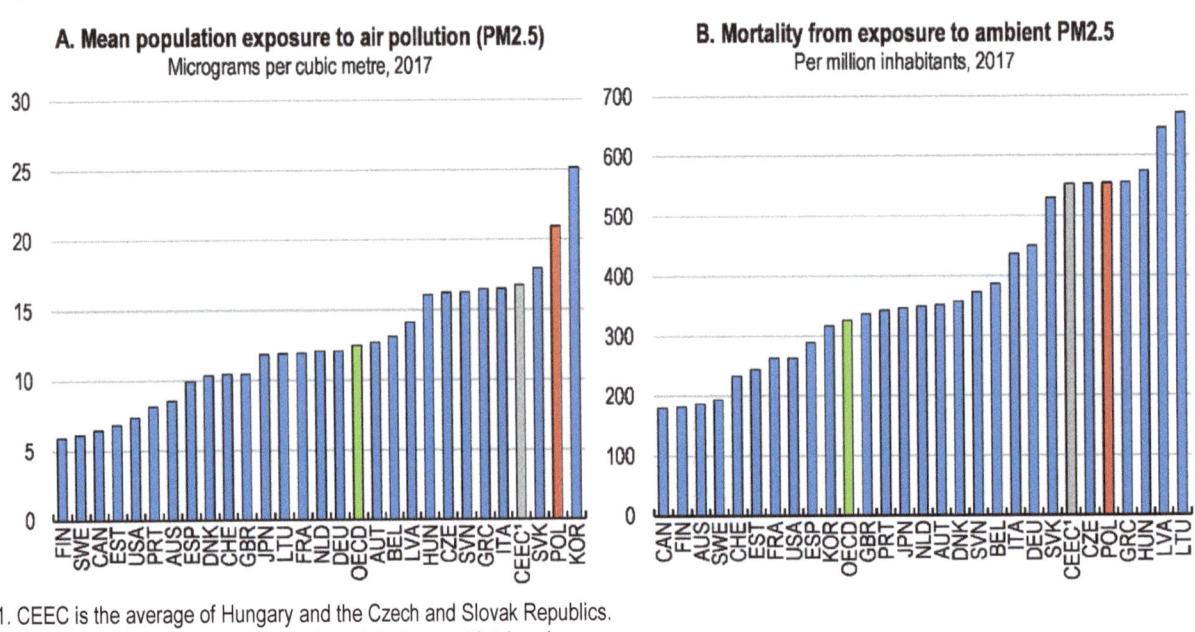

1. CEEC is the average of Hungary and the Czech and Slovak Republics.
Source: OECD (2020), OECD Green Growth Indicators (database).

StatLink https://doi.org/10.1787/888934208583

Mentoring firms could also have significant energy efficiency gains. There is no national programme to promote energy efficiency efforts of micro- and small firms, though EU funds and the EBRD provide dedicated support. As in other countries, SMEs face significant financial and informational barriers that are compounded by their weak management quality in Poland (Chapter 2; Bloom et al., 2010). Carefully evaluating and scaling up the effective measures of a 2018 EU-funded pilot programme for SMEs (Promotion of energy audits and energy efficiency investments in SMEs in Poland) would be positive. The project aims at improving knowledge about energy use and the effect of energy efficiency among SMEs and at raising awareness about energy management, including by encouraging the use of simplified energy audits.

Table 1.7. Past OECD recommendations on environmental policies

Main recent OECD recommendations	Actions taken since the 2018 Survey
Develop and implement clear and stable climate-change policies aligned with European and international objectives to reduce uncertainty for innovative green investments.	The National Energy and Climate Plan was submitted to the European Commission in December 2019. Work on the Energy Policy of Poland until 2040 is in progress. The update of the Polish Nuclear Power Programme has been approved by the Council of Ministers on 2 October 2020.
Ensure the stability and clarity of policies affecting investment decisions.	Mandatory consultations with stakeholders have often been short or avoided by laws proposed by the National Assembly members.

Preventing corruption and economic crimes

Poland's perceived corruption level appears relatively low compared to its peers, but remains above the OECD average (Figure 1.35, Panels A to C). Poland ranks just below the OECD average in most components of the Varieties of Democracy Index, with the judicial system assessed as the least corrupted (Panel D). Poland largely complies with the standards set by the Global Forum on Transparency and Exchange of Information for Tax Purposes which helps reducing money laundering risks.

Yet, GRECO (2019) and Transparency International (2019) have warned against the risks of increased political influence on the judiciary system. While the authorities argued that the judiciary system reform was designed to restore integrity of core State institutions, it risks concentrating the authority within a few central control bodies and decision makers and increase the role of the Minister of Justice in disciplinary proceedings (GRECO, 2019). Despite amendments in late 2019, the Council of Europe (2020) in an urgent opinion identified risks for the independence of judges recommended to increase the role of the judicial community for appointments, promotions and dismissals of judges.

Figure 1.35. There is room to further limit the risks of corruption

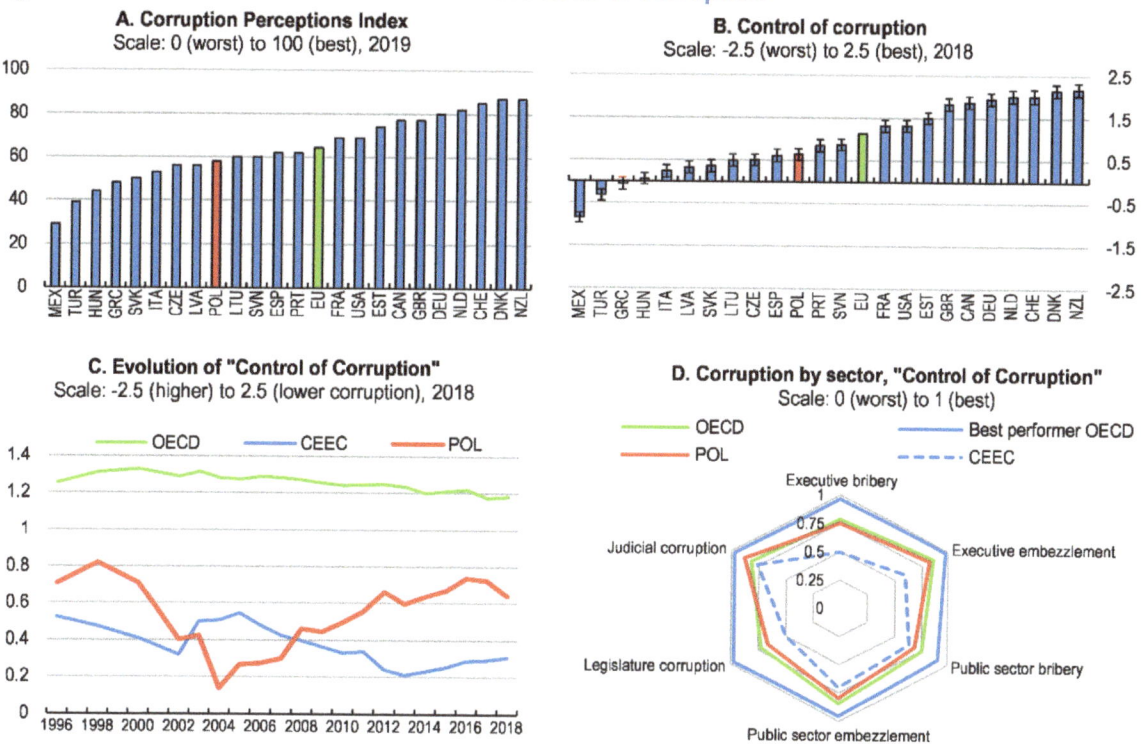

Note: Panel B shows the point estimate and the margin of error. Panel D shows sector-based subcomponents of the "Control of Corruption" indicator by the Varieties of Democracy Project. CEEC is the average of Hungary and the Czech and Slovak Republics.
Source: Panel A: Transparency International; Panels B & C: World Bank, Worldwide Governance Indicators; Panel D: Varieties of Democracy Institute; University of Gothenburg; and University of Notre Dame.

StatLink 🔗 https://doi.org/10.1787/888934208602

Transparency of the government's legislative process and the rules on access to information regarding lobbying activities emerge as key areas to improve corruption prevention (GRECO, 2019). More ambitious integrity policy aimed at parliamentarians is necessary for the rule of conduct and enforcement mechanism regarding gifts and benefits, conflicts of interest and accessory activities, as well as relations with lobbyists and other third parties. More transparent asset declarations and a revision of their immunities would also help limit risks of corruption.

The OECD Working Group on Bribery identified a number of challenges in fighting transnational corruption since 2013. In particular, companies cannot be held responsible for foreign bribery as long as the persons who perpetrated the offence are not convicted, and the fines for companies remain too low to be effective and dissuasive (OECD, 2018h). Whistle-blower protection is weak, with the "impunity" provision in the Penal Code inapplicable to the bribery of foreign public officials, and insufficient protective measures from retaliatory action for employees who report suspected acts of foreign bribery.

Other recommendations on macroeconomic and selected structural policies

(Memorandum item: key recommendations are presented in the Executive Summary)

FINDINGS	RECOMMENDATIONS
Macroeconomic policies and financial supervision	
The current financial supervision arrangements do not ensure a clear independence from the government.	Strengthen the process for nominating board members of the financial supervision authority.
The ex-ante scrutiny of the budget process and its macroeconomic assumptions rely on the Central Bank and the European Commission.	Task an independent institution to conduct ex-ante assessment of the government's fiscal plans and long-term fiscal sustainability analyses.
Inclusiveness, labour market and health issues	
Irregular work relationships are undermining productivity and well-being. They are also increasing risks of old-age poverty.	Strengthen labour law enforcement, and further align contributions on civil and labour law contracts
The rental market is weakly developed. Overcrowding is widespread and geographical mobility is relatively weak.	When the recovery is firmly underway, increase recurrent taxes on property, notably on vacant properties and land in urban areas.
	Strengthen geographical mobility support and activation measures.
High immigration from Eastern neighbours alleviated labour market pressures, but a lack of monitoring hampers the ability of policies to improve its impact on the labour market.	Develop a migration policy strategy to better monitor integration of foreigners in line with labour market needs, the protection of their rights and access to education and training for them.
Old-age work is low. Many households fail to see the benefits of postponing retirement.	Harmonise employment protection for all age groups.
	Ensure sufficient incentives and training to boost the effective retirement age.
	Strengthen further information about the benefits of working longer.
Special pension schemes have high fiscal costs and constrain workers mobility. Survivor pensions may have negative effect on labour supply.	Progressively align special pension schemes arrangements with the general rules.
	When the recovery is firmly underway, scale down survivors' pensions.
Social disparities in health conditions are high and linked to the prevalence of risky behaviours among lower-income households.	Strengthen information campaigns on behavioural risks, such as food and drinking habits.
	Review food and health standards.
Environment	
Regulatory requirements on housing heating system and housing efficiency are relatively weak.	Tighten regulations on energy consumption in buildings.
The take-up of energy efficiency measures and the rollout of demand-management system are low. Eligibility conditions to some support programmes are unduly restrictive for low-income households.	Ease eligibility conditions to energy efficiency programmes for low-income households
	Provide incentives for the use of smart meters.
Smaller firms make little use of potentially high energy efficiency gains.	Evaluate and scale up effective pilot information for SMEs on the benefits of energy efficiency savings and strengthen related energy-efficiency programmes.
Urban sprawl is substantial. The coverage of spatial plans is limited and their integration with other strategic document could improve.	Continue to strengthen integrated local spatial plans, by making their coverage mandatory in functional urban areas and increasing their coherence with other spatial plans.
Corruption	
Interactions between parliamentarians, lobbyists and other third parties are not fully transparent.	Provide the members of the Parliament with clear guidance on conflicts of interest.
	Develop a clearly defined mechanism to declare potential conflicts of interest of parliamentarians.
Whistle-blower protection is weak.	Improve protective measures for employees who report suspected acts of foreign bribery.
Business environment	
Private-sector R&D spending is very low, notably for SMEs, which hinders new technology adoption and innovation.	Incentivise SME employers to develop workplace -based vocational education and adult training.
General government contingent liabilities are high.	Ensure the full independence of the sectoral regulators.
	Pursue privatisation in competitive segments of the economy while ensuring sound governance of the remaining state-owned enterprises.

References

Albinowski, M. (2018), "Short-term and long-term employment effects of minimum wage. Evidence from Poland", Ministry of Finance Working Paper, No 29-2018, Warsaw.

Algan, Y. et al. (2018), "The Value of a Vacancy: Evidence from a Randomized Evaluation with Local Employment Agencies in France", Chaire sécurisation des parcours professionnels, No. 2018-05.

Antfolk, J, Szala, A and A. Öblom (2019), "Discrimination based on gender and ethnicity in English and Polish housing markets", Journal of Community and Applied Social Psychology; 29, pp. 222– 237.

Benzarti, Y., and D. Carloni (2019), "Who Really Benefits from Consumption Tax Cuts? Evidence from a Large VAT Reform in France." American Economic Journal: Economic Policy, 11 (1): 38-63.

Bledowski, P., A. Chlon-Dominczak, A. Fihel, A. Kielczewska, I. E. Kotowska, P. Lewandowski, I. Magda, M. Malec, M. Okolski and J. Tyrowicz, (2017), "Population ageing, labour market and public finance in Poland," Books and Reports published by IBS, Instytut Badan Strukturalnych, edited by P. Lewandowski and J. Rutkowski.

Bloom, N., C. Genakos, R. Martin and R. Sadun (2010), "Modern Management: Good for the Environment or Just Hot Air?," Economic Journal, vol. 120(544), pages 551-572, May.

Boone, J., J. Derboven, S. Kuypers, F. Figari and G. Verbist (2019), EWIGE 2 – Update and Extension of the EUROMOD Wealth Taxation Project, JRC Working Papers on Taxation and Structural Reforms, No. 07/2019, European Commission, Joint Research Centre (JRC), Seville.

Boulhol, H. (2014), "Making the Labour Market Work Better in Poland", OECD Economics Department Working Papers, No. 1124, OECD Publishing, Paris.

BPIE (2016), Smart buildings in a decarbonised energy system, Buildings Performance Institute Europe.

Brandt, N. (2016), "Making better use of skills and migration in Poland," OECD Economics Department Working Papers 1301, OECD Publishing, Paris.

Browne et al. (2019), Analysis of Policy reform in the EU – 2016-2018, OECD Publishing, Paris.

CASE/IAS (2019), Study and Reports on the VAT Gap in the EU-28 Member States: 2019 Final Report, Report TAXUD/2015/CC/131 for the Directorate General Taxation and Customs Union, Center for Social and Economic Research and Institute for Advanced Studies.

Cedefop (2018), Skills forecast trends and challenges to 2030, Cedefop.

Chmielewska et al., (2019) Informacja z badań ankietowych imigrantów w Bydgoszczy i we Wrocławiu w 2018 i 2019 roku, Narodowy Bank Polski.

Council of Europe (2020), Poland- Urgent Joint Opinion on the amendments to the Law on organisation on the Common Courts, the Law on the Supreme Court and other Laws, Opinion No. 977 / 2019, CDL-PI(2020)002-e.

Cribb, J., C. Emmerson and G. Tetlow (2016), "Signals matter? Large retirement responses to limited financial incentives", Labour Economics, Vol. 42, pp. 203-12.

Datta, N., G. Giupponi and S. Machin (2019), Zero Hours Contracts and Labour Market Policy, Economic Policy, eiz008, https://doi.org/10.1093/epolic/eiz008

Dechezleprêtre, A., N. Rivers and B. Stadler (2019), "The economic cost of air pollution: Evidence from Europe", OECD Economics Department Working Papers, No. 1584, OECD Publishing, Paris.

DFA (2015), Global Irish: Ireland's Diaspora Review, Department of Foreign Affairs.

Dube, A. (2019), Impacts of minimum wages: review of the international evidence, https://www.gov.uk/government/publications/impacts-of-minimum-wages-review-of-the-international-evidence.

Dustmann, C., Lindner, A., Schönberg, U., Umkehrer, M., and vom Berge, P., (2019) 'Reallocation Effects of the Minimum Wage: Evidence From Germany', Working Paper

EBA (2018), *2018 EU-wide stress test results*, European Bank Authority, 2 November 2018.

EBA (2019), EBA Dashboard - Q3 2019, European Bank Authority.

EC (2018a), The 2018 Ageing Report, European Commission.

EC (2018b), Strategic reports 2018 on the implementation of the European Structural and Investment Funds, European Commission.

EC (2018c), Pension adequacy report 2018, European Commission.

EC (2018d), "Revision of personal income tax in Poland: increase in the tax-free allowance for the lowest earners", *ESPN Flash Report*, No. 2017/13, European Commission.

EC (2019a), 2019 European Semester: Country Report – Poland, European Commission.

EC (2019b), Strategic reports 2019 on the implementation of the European Structural and Investment Funds, European Commission.

EC (2019c), Environmental Implementation Review 2019 – Poland, European Commission.

EC (2020a), 2020 European Semester: Country Report – Poland, European Commission.

EC (2020b), Science for Policy Briefs, The Impact of COVID confinement measures on EU labour market, The European Commission's science and knowledge service, Joint Research Centre.

ECJ (2019), In loan contracts concluded in Poland and indexed to a foreign currency, unfair terms relating to the difference in exchange rates cannot be replaced by general provisions of Polish civil law, Press Release, No 129/19, European Court of Justice, Luxembourg.

ERO (2020), Taryfy wszystkich czterech przedsiębiorców pełniących funkcję tzw. sprzedawców z urzędu zatwierdzone przez Prezesa URE, Energy Regulatory Office, Warsaw, https://www.ure.gov.pl/pl/urzad/informacje-ogolne/aktualnosci/8651,Taryfy-wszystkich-czterech-przedsiebiorcow-pelniacych-funkcje-tzw-sprzedawcow-z-.html

Eurostat (2020a), "Government finance statistics - Contingent liabilities and non-performing loans in the EU Member States in 2018", *Eurostat-News release*, No. 22/2020.

Eurostat (2020b), *Healthy life years (from 2004 onwards) (database)*, Eurostat.

Flues, F. and K. van Dender (2017), "The impact of energy taxes on the affordability of domestic energy", OECD Taxation Working Papers, No. 30, OECD Publishing, Paris.

Forum Energii (2019), Clean heat 2030: Strategy for heating.

Góra, M., P. Lewandowski and M. Lis (2017), "Temporary employment boom in Poland – a job quality vs. quantity trade-off?", Instytut Badan StrukturalnychWorking Paper No. 04/2017,Warsaw.

Goraus-Tanska K and P. Lewandowski, 2019. "Minimum wage violation in central and eastern Europe," International Labour Review, International Labour Organization, vol. 158(2), pages 297-336, June.

GRECO (2019), *Fourth Evaluation Round. Corruption Prevention in Respect of Members of Parliament, Judges and Prosecutors. Second Addendum to the Second Compliance Report Including Follow-Up to the Addendum to the Fourth Round Evaluation Report (Rule 34). Poland*, https://rm.coe.int/fourth-evaluation-round-corruption-prevention-in-respect-of-members-of/16809947b4

Growiec, J. et al. (2019), "The Contribution of Immigration from Ukraine to Economic Growth in Poland", NBP Working Paper No. 322, National Bank of Poland, Warsaw.

Statistics Poland (2019a), Sytuacja gospodarstw domowych w 2018 r. w świetle wyników badania budżetów gospodarstw domowych, Statistics Poland, Warsaw.

Statistics Poland (2019b), Wybrane zagadnienia rynku pracy (liczba osób z minimalnym wynagrodzeniem, „samozatrudnieni", umowy zlecenia, umowy o dzieło). Dane dla 2018 r, Statistics Poland, Warsaw.

Statistics Poland (2020), Wpływ epidemii COVID-19 na wybrane elementy rynku pracy w Polsce w pierwszym kwartale 2020 roku, Statistics Poland, Warsaw.

Habitat for Humanity Poland (2019), https://www.housingforall.eu/habitat-for-humanity-poland/

IEA (2017), Energy Policies of IEA Countries Poland 2016 Review, International Energy Agency.

IEA (2018), World Energy Outlook 2018, International Energy Agency.

IMF (2019), Republic of Poland : Financial System Stability Assessment, International Monetary Fund, Washington DC.

KNF (2019), Monthly data on the banking sector - October 2019, Komisja Nadzoru Finansowego, Warsaw.

Lewandowski, P., Pigoń, A. and T. Świetlik (2020), *Housing and labour market outcomes in Poland*, Technical Background paper.

MF (2019), Conditional liabilities of the general government sector, Ministry of Finance, https://www.gov.pl/web/finance/fiscal-data-for-eu-budgetary-surveillance

Ministry of Energy, 2018 Extract from the draft of EPP2040 - 23.11.2018.

NBP (2019), Financial Stability Report – December, National Bank of Poland, Warsaw.

NBP (2020a), Inflation Report - July, National Bank of Poland, Warsaw.

NBP (2020b), Financial Stability Report – June, National Bank of Poland, Warsaw.

NBP (2020c), Inflation Report - November, National Bank of Poland, Warsaw.

Neumark, D. (2018), Employment Effects of Minimum Wages, IZA World of Labour, Vol. 6.

NIK (2019), Państwo niegotowe na cudzoziemców, Najwyższa Izba Kontroli, Warsaw.

OECD (2015), Ageing and Employment Policies: Poland 2015, OECD Publishing, Paris.

OECD (2016), OECD Economic Surveys: Poland 2016, OECD Publishing, Paris.

OECD (2017), "How to make trade work for all" in OECD Economic outlook, OECD Publishing, Paris.

OECD (2018a), OECD Regions and Cities at a Glance 2018, OECD Publishing, Paris.

OECD (2018b), Good Jobs for All in a Changing World of Work: The OECD Jobs Strategy, OECD Publishing, Paris.

OECD (2018c), OECD Economic Surveys: Poland 2018, OECD Publishing, Paris.

OECD (2018d), OECD Pensions Outlook 2018, OECD Publishing, Paris.

OECD (2018e), Consumption Tax Trends 2018: VAT/GST and Excise Rates, Trends and Policy Issues, OECD Publishing, Paris.

OECD (2018f), Taxation of Household Savings, OECD Tax Policy Studies, No. 25, OECD Publishing, Paris.

OECD (2018g), OECD Rural Policy Reviews: Poland 2018, OECD Rural Policy Reviews, OECD Publishing, Paris.

OECD (2018h), Poland must make urgent legislative reforms to combat foreign bribery, OECD Publishing, Paris.

OECD (2019a), Main Findings from the 2018 OECD Risks that Matter Survey, OECD Publishing, Paris.

OECD (2019b), Pensions at a Glance 2019: OECD and G20 Indicators, OECD Publishing, Paris.

OECD (2019c), Taxing Energy Use 2019: Using Taxes for Climate Action, OECD Publishing, Paris.

OECD (2019d), OECD Skills Strategy Poland: Assessment and Recommendations, OECD Skills Studies, OECD Publishing, Paris.

OECD (2019e), PISA 2018 Results (Volume I): What Students Know and Can Do, OECD Publishing, Paris.

OECD (2019f), Individual Learning Accounts: Panacea or Pandora's Box?, OECD Publishing, Paris.

OECD (2019g), OECD Economic Surveys: France 2019, OECD Publishing, Paris.

OECD (2019h), International Migration Outlook 2019, OECD Publishing, Paris.

OECD (2020a), OECD Economic Outlook, Volume 2020, Issue 1, Issue Note 4: Distributional risks associated with non-standard work: Stylised facts and policy considerations, OECD Publishing, Paris.

OECD (2020b), Coronavirus (COVID-19): SME policy responses - OECD Policy Responses to Coronavirus (COVID-19), OECD Publishing, Paris.OECD (2020c), Housing prices (indicator), OECD Publishing, Paris.

OECD (2020d), OECD PMR Country-Fiche Poland, OECD Publishing, Paris.OECD (2020e), Women at the core of the fight against COVID-19 crisis - OECD Policy Responses to Coronavirus (COVID-19), OECD Publishing, Paris.

OECD (2020f), OECD Family Database, OECD Publishing, Paris.

OECD (2020g), OECD Policy Responses to Coronavirus (COVID-19) - COVID-19 and the low-carbon transition: Impacts and possible policy responses, OECD Publishing, Paris.

OECD (2020h), OECD Policy Responses to Coronavirus (COVID-19) – Making the green recovery work for jobs, income and growth, OECD Publishing, Paris.

OECD/EOHS (2019), Poland: Country Health Profile 2019, State of Health in the EU, OECD Publishing, Paris/European Observatory on Health Systems and Policies, Brussels

OECD/IEA (2016), Energy Policies of IEA Countries: Poland 2016 Review, OECD Publishing, Paris.

Republic of Poland (2019a), Convergence Programme – 2019 Update, Warsaw.

Republic of Poland (2019b), National Reform Programme – 2019, Warsaw.

Report of the Council of Ministers (2019), Sprawozdanie Rady Ministrów z realizacji ustawy z dnia 4 lutego 2011 r. o opiece nad dziećmi w wieku do lat 3 w 2018 r., Warsaw.

Skandalis, D. (2018), "Breaking News: Information About Firms' Hiring Needs Affects the Direction of Job Search", mimeo.

Sokołowski, J. et al. (2019), "Measuring energy poverty in Poland with the Multidimensional Energy Poverty Index", IBS Working Paper.

Sowada C et al. (2019), Poland: Health System Review, Health Systems in Transition, 21(1): 1–235.

Strzelecki, P. Jakub Growiec, Robert Wyszyński (2020), The contribution of immigration from Ukraine to economic growth in Poland, NBP Working Paper No. 322, Narodowy Bank Polski.

Tyrowicz, J. and N. Brandt (2017), "Simulating the effects of pension reforms in Poland in an overlapping generations model", Technical Background Paper, OECD, Paris.

UN (2019disc), "Concluding observations on the combined twenty-second to twenty-fourth periodic reports of Poland", Committee on the Elimination of Racial Discrimination, International Convention on the Elimination of All Forms of Racial Discrimination, CERD/C/POL/CO/22-24, United Nations.

Velux (2018), Barometr zdrowych domów 2018 (Healthy Homes Barometer)

Wojtyniak B. and Goryński P. (2018), Sytuacja zdrowotna ludności Polski i jej uwarunkowania, Narodowy Instytut Zdrowia Publicznego – Państwowy Zakład Higieny, Warsaw.

World Bank (2018a), Fighting Smog: Energy Efficiency and Anti-Smog in Single Family Buildings in Poland.

World Bank (2018b), Poland Energy Transition: The Path to Sustainability in the Electricity and Heating Sector.

Annex A. Progress on structural reforms

This Annex reviews action taken on recommendations from the March 2018 Survey that are not reported elsewhere in this Chapter.

Recommendations	Action taken since previous *Survey* (March 2018)
Product market competition and business environment	
Introduce fixed-term, non-renewable mandates for the President of the Competition Authority and all sectoral regulators, during which they cannot be dismissed without fault, and prevent revolving-door opportunities. Pursue privatisation in competitive sectors.	No action taken.
Reduce anti-competitive pressures resulting from the participation of Polish Airports State Enterprise (PPL) in many airport entities, and consider long-term concession agreements or privatisation for airport entities. Privatise the national air carrier (LOT).	No action taken.
Include a simplification component for SMEs to the government's tax compliance strategy.	The 2019 "package for SMEs" increased digitalisation of tax procedures and automatic filing of information already in the databases of public entities, partly reducing the tax compliance cost for the SMEs.
Strengthening higher education, research and innovation	
Enhance industry-science collaboration. Continue to increase funding for higher education and research over time, to merge small universities and independent research institutes to build strong research universities, and to allow underperforming institutions that do not improve over time to shut down.	The 2018 Act on Higher Education and Science strengthens the practical dimensions of education by supplementing practical-profile studies with a compulsory vocational practice, or a dual programme involving the employer. The Research Network: Lukasiewicz has been launched in 2019 to conduct scientific research, including industrial research.
Improve the quality of doctoral training by structuring it through coursework and tutoring and tightening entry criteria. Offer well-remunerated academic positions, and base career progression on an evaluation of research and teaching quality by faculty and external experts.	A wide-reaching reform of science and higher education was introduced in 2019 under the label "Constitution for Science". It included steps aimed at improving the quality of doctoral training and tightening entry criteria, thus making PhD training more selective.
If the take-up of the new R&D tax allowance is low among small innovative firms, adjust its provisions. Plan for national financing of business R&D and innovation programmes beyond the current EU budgetary cycle, if necessary.	The take-up of the R&D tax allowance has increased over 2018-2019. Yet, larger firms remain the main beneficiaries.

2 Boosting SMEs' internationalisation

The rapid internationalisation of the Polish economy has helped develop competitive export-led manufacturing and services sectors fostering robust growth and productivity performance. However, the benefits of this development have been unequal. Many small and medium-sized enterprises (SMEs), some regions and social groups have lagged behind. Poland's integration into world trade has largely focussed on downstream activities of value chains and relatively labour-intensive products that incorporate little domestic value added. The coronavirus (COVID-19) crisis has put additional pressures on SMEs. A broad range of well-coordinated policies is required to boost SMEs' internationalisation and their productivity, while easing labour reallocation during the ongoing recovery. Providing stronger support for training programmes in smaller firms and within small firms' networks would help them upgrade the skills of their workforce, notably for their managers, and ease new technology adoption and internationalisation. Streamlining regulations on start-ups and limiting regulatory and tax barriers to firm expansion would raise firm entry and growth. Strengthening post-insolvency second chance policies for honest entrepreneurs would ease resource reallocation and the adaptation of SMEs to an uncertain and rapidly changing international environment. Improving transport and digital infrastructure would lower trade costs and raise productivity. Ensuring that innovation policies adapt to smaller firms would boost their innovativeness and ease their integration in national and international value chains.

64 |

Poland's internationalisation has been remarkable but unequal

Poland's internationalisation has been a key driver of growth and income convergence since the transition process. Exports and imports in goods have outpaced GDP growth, notably through large exports and imports of intermediate goods (Eurostat, 2019). Services trade growth was also very strong, unlike in other Central and Eastern European (CEE) countries (Figure 2.1, Panels A and B). Exports of goods and services nearly quadrupled over the last two decades, and, export market share rose twofold. Competitive labour costs, proximity to European markets and the integration to global value chains (GVCs), as well as strong productivity gains explain the major part of the internationalisation and export performance (OECD, 2018a). Even during the 2011-16 global trade slowdown and until the coronavirus (COVID-19) crisis, Polish exports had continued to gather significant pace and raise their market share (Panel C). More than 40% of domestic employment nowadays depend on international markets (Panel D).

Figure 2.1. Poland's internationalisation and export performance have been impressive

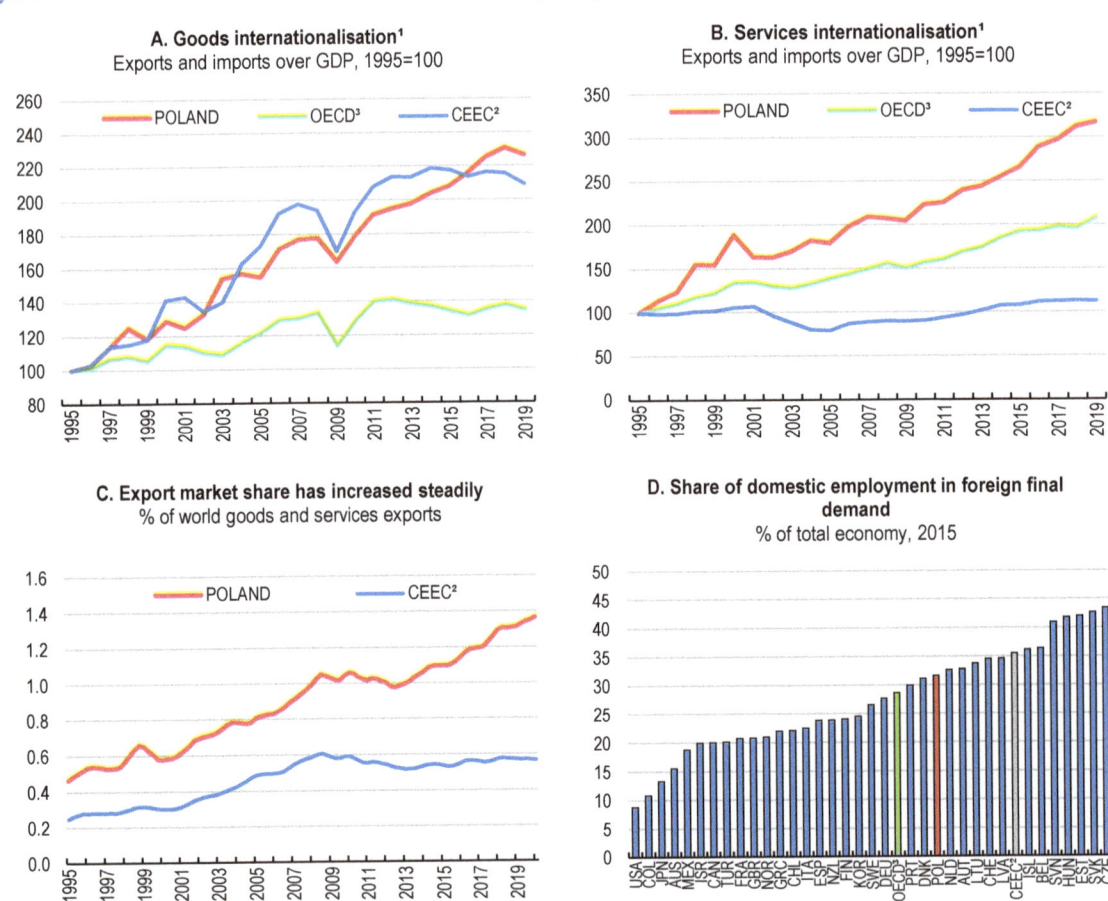

1. Internationalisation is proxied by the share of exports and imports divided by GDP.
2. CEEC is the average of Hungary and the Czech and Slovak Republics.
3. The OECD average is the unweighted average of OECD countries.
Source: OECD (2020), National account database; OECD (2020) Trade in Employment database.

StatLink https://doi.org/10.1787/888934208621

Poland's increasing trade openness and integration in GVCs, eased technology transfers and supported employment and productivity gains. During 1995-2011, Poland rapidly integrated into global value chains and received significant inward Foreign Direct Investment (FDI) in the manufacturing sector. Foreign affiliates played a key role in this development process and recent OECD estimates suggest that they are still responsible for 40% of GDP (Cadestin et al., 2019). As a result, the South-West of Poland, notably through the automotive sector, saw a rapid rise in GDP and incomes (Box 2.2). Indeed, the domestic sourcing of intermediates by foreign affiliates largely benefitted domestic firms, of which the majority are small and medium-sized enterprises (SMEs) (Hagemejer and Kolasa, 2011).

However, the development of SMEs' linkages with local, national and international networks could be reinforced and support further productivity and well-being gains. Poland's SMEs account for approximately 70% of persons employed in the business economy and around 51% of value added (Figure 2.2; OECD, 2019a). Yet, their internationalisation has been highly heterogeneous. Though a relatively large number of SMEs export directly (Figure 2.3, Panel A), SMEs still account for only a small share of direct exports (Panel B). They account for around 30% of direct exports, well below their share in employment or value-added. Moreover, most of these direct exports take place through medium-sized firms that, as large firms, saw a steep rise in their export intensity (Panel C).

Figure 2.2. SMEs play a key role in the Economy

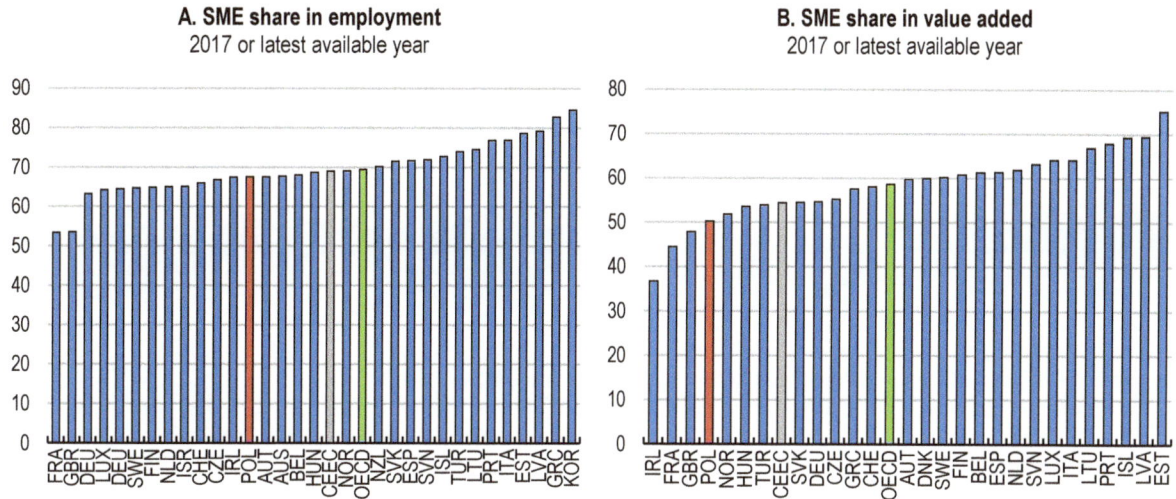

A. SME share in employment
2017 or latest available year

B. SME share in value added
2017 or latest available year

Note: All sectors of the business economy are included, except financial and insurance activities. CEEC is the average of Hungary and the Czech and Slovak Republics.
Source: OECD (2019), Structural Business Statistics.

StatLink ᵐˢᴾ https://doi.org/10.1787/888934208640

Poland's SMEs appear lagging in a number of forms of internationalisation. The share of SMEs in value-added exports is higher as SMEs export indirectly through upstream linkages with larger exporters, but the importance of SMEs for value-added export remains below the average level of Hungary and the Czech and Slovak Republics, or those of Italy, Portugal and Spain (Figure 2.3, Panel D). Indeed around 60% of SMEs' indirect exports reach foreign markets via large enterprises, the remaining 40% via other SMEs (OECD, 2018b). When they export directly, SMEs are more often occasional than persistent exporters and they export to closer markets (EC, 2018a; 2018b). SMEs engage less in imports of goods and services or may seek foreign suppliers, which could help them gain access to more sophisticated and competitively priced intermediates to enable productivity gains and upscale or upgrade production (López González and Sorescu, 2019). SMEs are also less likely to be the recipients of foreign direct investment (inward FDI) or to invest abroad (outward FDI).

This unequal internationalisation left behind some places that have high proportions of vulnerable people and low levels of economic activity. As in other OECD countries, exporting and foreign capital have been associated with faster productivity growth at the sector level, and internationalised firms, both through exporting and foreign direct investment, have performed better than non-internationalised firms (Szpunar and Hagemejer, 2018). This compounded the problems of lagging firms and regions, as long-term unemployment, poverty, and poor health and low social mobility often go hand in hand (OECD, 2019b).

Figure 2.3. SMEs internationalisation has been heterogeneous

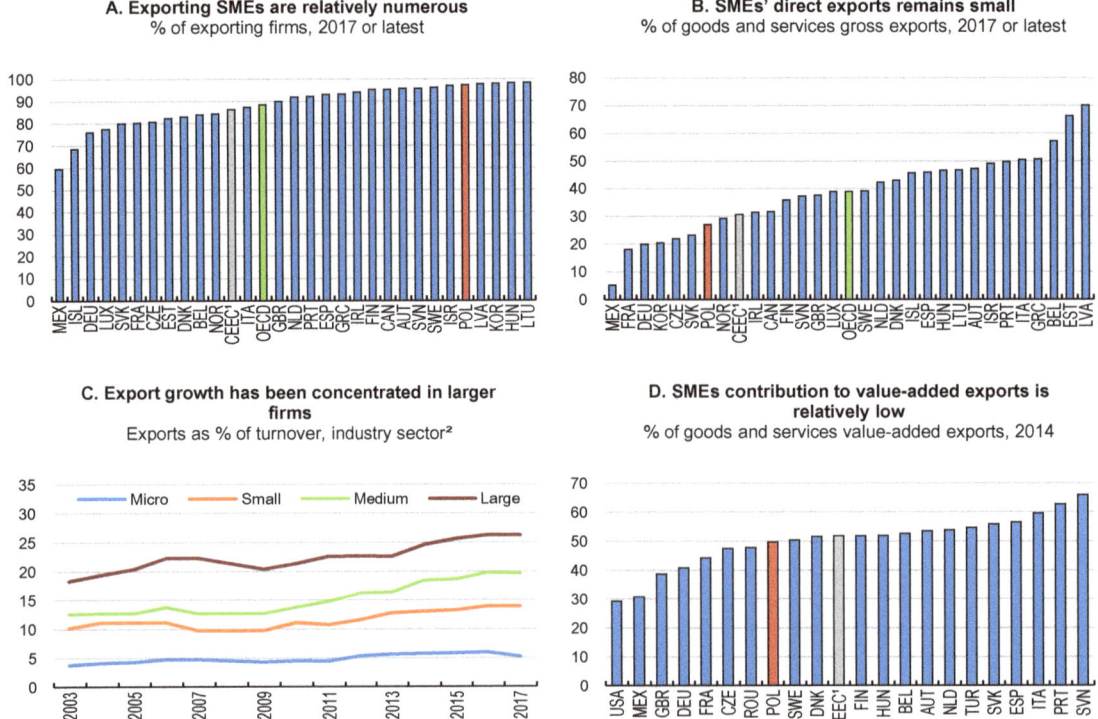

1. CEEC is the average of Hungary and the Czech and Slovak Republics.
2. For micro firms, exports over turnover is backcasted based on small firms over 2003-2009.
Source: OECD (2019), Structural Business Statistics, Trade by Enterprises Characteristics and National account databases; OECD (2018), "Accounting for firm heterogeneity in global value chains: The role of Small and Medium sized Enterprises", OECD Working Party on International Trade in Goods and Trade in Services Statistics, OECD publishing, Paris; OECD caclulations based on PARP (2019), *Raport o stanie sektora małych i średnich przedsiębiorstw w Polsce*, Polska Agencja Rozwoju Przedsiębiorczości, Warsaw and Ministry of Economic Development, Labour and Technology "Entrepreneurship in Poland" 2010 and 2011 reports.

StatLink 🔳🔳 https://doi.org/10.1787/888934208659

The global coronavirus pandemic had a large initial impact on Polish trade and vulnerable groups and regions were disproportionally affected (Box 2.1). At the same time, some well-internationalised sectors such as the automotive and transport industry have been hard hit. Stalling global investment has seen demand for capital goods plunge, in particular for cars. As during other crises, the internationalisation of firms appears to have played a role in the propagation of economic shocks, but they also seem to have helped firms to recover faster (OECD, 2020gvc). Following the initial coronavirus shock, Poland's trade bounced-back over the summer 2020. From 2019Q4 to 2020Q2, Poland's exports and imports of goods and services appear to have been more resilient than in many other European countries. Yet, in 2020Q2, exports and imports remained well below their 2019Q4 levels.

In response to long-standing issues that have been stressed in the 2017 Strategy for Responsible Development, the authorities have undertaken reforms to ease administrative business and trade procedures and increase R&D and innovation activities, as well as to reach a more even territorial development (Box 2.2 and Box 2.3). The authorities have also put in place extensive support measures that helped to cushion the initial coronavirus shock (Box 2.1). Yet, further efforts to ease resource reallocation while maintaining viable firms will also be required to deal with renewed challenges.

This chapter analyses how Poland's internationalisation and the digital transformation offer new opportunities for SMEs to integrate directly and indirectly into the global economy, raise their productivity and grow. It then looks at how policies can create the best policy environment to help SMEs – and the many people they employ – to take advantage of these opportunities.

Box 2.1. The global (COVID-19) pandemic and its effects on international trade and SMEs

SMEs have suffered heavily from the crisis

Government lockdowns and border closure have affected the supply of domestic and foreign goods and services, and trade plummeted between March and May 2020. Though Poland's exports and trade have been relatively resilient (OECD, 2020), early business surveys and employment data point that Polish SMEs and regions that had the weakest business dynamics are among the most affected by the crisis (Figure 2.4 and 1.6).

Figure 2.4. SMEs have been hard hit by the coronavirus crisis

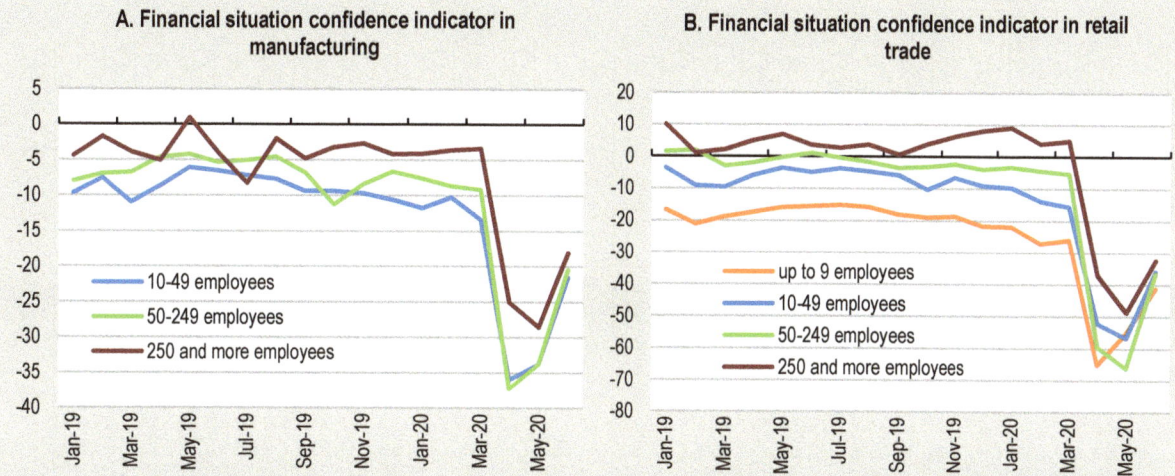

A. Financial situation confidence indicator in manufacturing

B. Financial situation confidence indicator in retail trade

Source: Statistics Poland (2020), Business tendency in manufacturing, construction, trade and services, 2000-2020, June 2020 update.

StatLink https://doi.org/10.1787/888934208678

The initial coronavirus shock also hit hard SMEs and regions that were well integrated in GVCs. Demand for cars has plunged over 2020 and is projected to recover only partially in 2021 (OECD, 2020d). Given the weight of the automotive industry in Polish exports, the crisis and the high uncertainty around future demand for cars, will put this industry and its suppliers under severe strain. The crisis, therefore, adds to the existing challenges facing the car manufacturing industry, such as changes in mobility patterns.

Policy responses

The Polish government took a series of early measures to limit the impact of the coronavirus crisis on SMEs. It increased their liquidity by announcing that micro enterprises (with less than 10 employees) experiencing a 50% drop in revenues would be exempted from social security contributions for three months, provided that their revenues in March would not exceed 300% of the average wage. Later, a 50% reduction was extended to small firms with less than 50 employees and revenues requirement dropped. It also eased their financing through an unprecedented loan scheme of PLN 100 billion launched in early April (Box 1.1) that was mainly targeted at SMEs, with ¾ of the funds dedicated to such firms and only ¼ available to large enterprises. Micro firms could receive up to PLN 324,000 and small and medium companies up to PLN 3.5 million each. The latest "anti-crisis package" established that micro loans of up to PLN 5,000, mostly concerning micro and small firms, would no longer need to be reimbursed as long as companies continued to operate for three months after the grant. It also suspended the statutory time limit to file for bankruptcy for firms affected by the coronavirus crisis and introduced new simplified restructuring procedures for all firms, which notably include a 4-month automatic stay on assets and out-of-court recovery proceedings, until 30 June 2021.

Source: OECD (2020), OECD Economic Outlook – June 2020, OECD publishing, Paris.

68

A bird's eye view of Poland's internationalisation and SMEs' landscape

Polish exports concentrate on medium and low-tech goods

Polish exports are well diversified in terms of composition. The agricultural sector, auto parts industry, and aviation and shipbuilding sectors have well-developed exports (Figure 2.4). A wide range of other exporting industries includes cosmetics, furniture, machinery, minerals, plastics and textiles, as well as services (Figure 2.5). This diversified structure has helped to cushion disruptive shocks. Until the coronavirus crisis, sharp contractions in final demand, which happened due to the concentrated exposure to cyclical industries in Slovakia and Hungary in 2009, had not been observed in Poland that tend to exports more consumer goods that are less sensitive to the global economic cycle than other CEE countries. During the 2018-19 global slowdown, Polish exports had continued to grow strongly, supported by renewed FDI inflows.

Figure 2.5. Polish exports have been robust, and well diversified

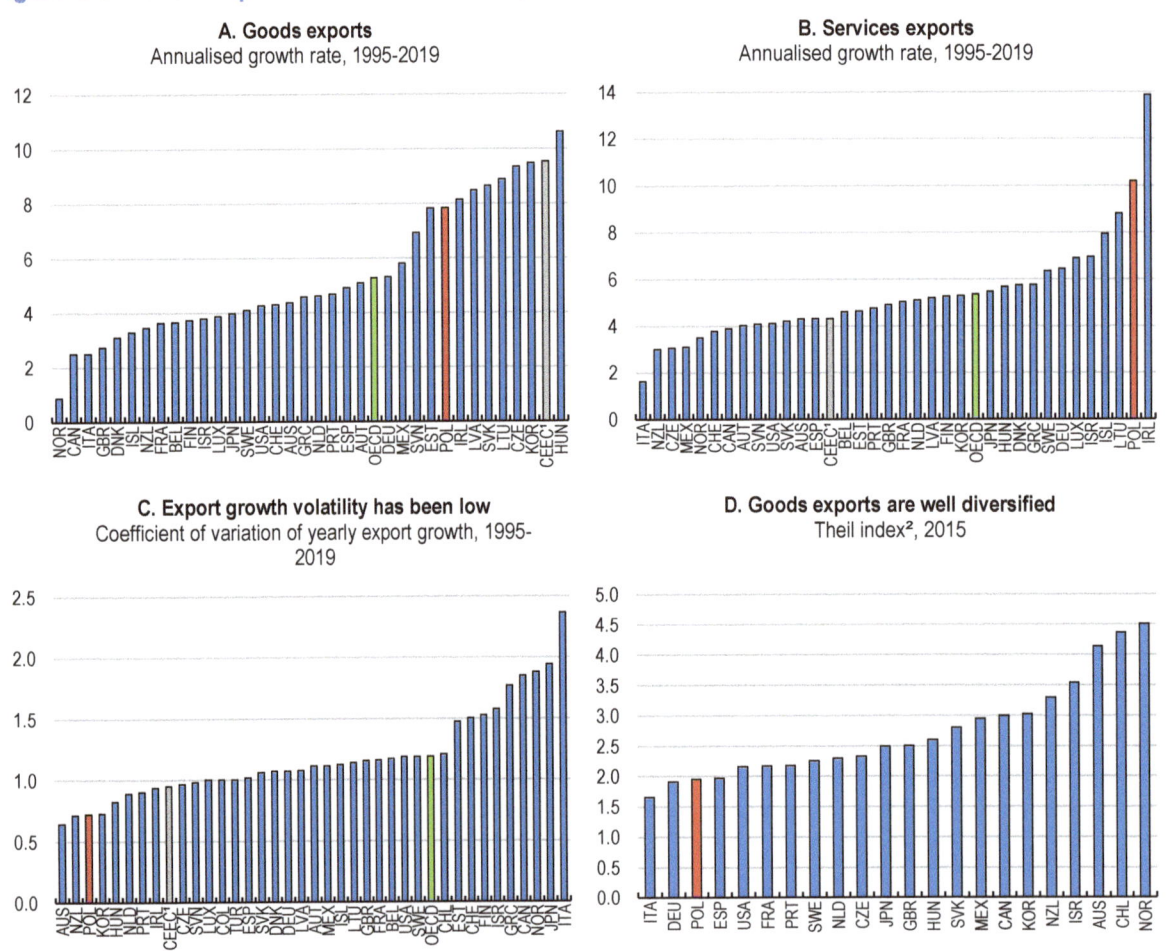

1. CEEC is the average of Hungary and the Czech and Slovak Republics.
2. Higher values of the index indicate higher concentration of export products. The Theil index is computed over export values in a 6-digit good classification (HS6 1992 classification) with 5,039 products per year.
Source: OECD (2020), National account database; OECD calculations based on CEPII (2019), BACI Database.

StatLink https://doi.org/10.1787/888934208697

As in other OECD countries, foreign multinationals play a key role in internationalisation (Cadestin et al., 2018). Poland's location next to Germany; the availability of a low-cost but skilled labour force; its European union membership since 2004; all combined with an historically cautious budgetary and financial policy, have preserved a stable economic and social environment and strong competitiveness. Inward FDI, as a share of GDP, have increased. Foreign investments have a well-diversified industry structure, though they are mostly concentrated in the capital region and the south-west of the country (Box 2.2). Thanks to these

OECD ECONOMIC SURVEYS: POLAND 2020 © OECD 2020

FDI inflows, mainly from the European Union (particularly from the Netherlands and Germany), Poland has become a significant exporter mainly through its integration into European GVC. For example, over 90% of automotive production in Poland is exported to Europe (mainly to Germany).

Multinationals supported the growth of services sectors. Jobs outsourced in business services (business processing, IT, and R&D) have nearly tripled over the past decade. Most of the growth has come from international companies' service centres that tend to be subsidiaries of the foreign companies using them (Box 2.2; McKinsey, 2015). In recent years, Poland also strengthened its position as a regional centre of logistics services, notably through importing consumer goods, such as clothing, footwear or electronics, from third countries into the EU, repackaging them in Polish warehouses and further distributing them to other European Union countries (Mroczek, 2019). The share of services in exports has increased rapidly from 16% in 1990 to more than 21% in 2018, but it remained below the OECD average of 30% in 2018.

Figure 2.6. The structure of Polish exports

Share of exports by sector and destination, 2019 or latest year available

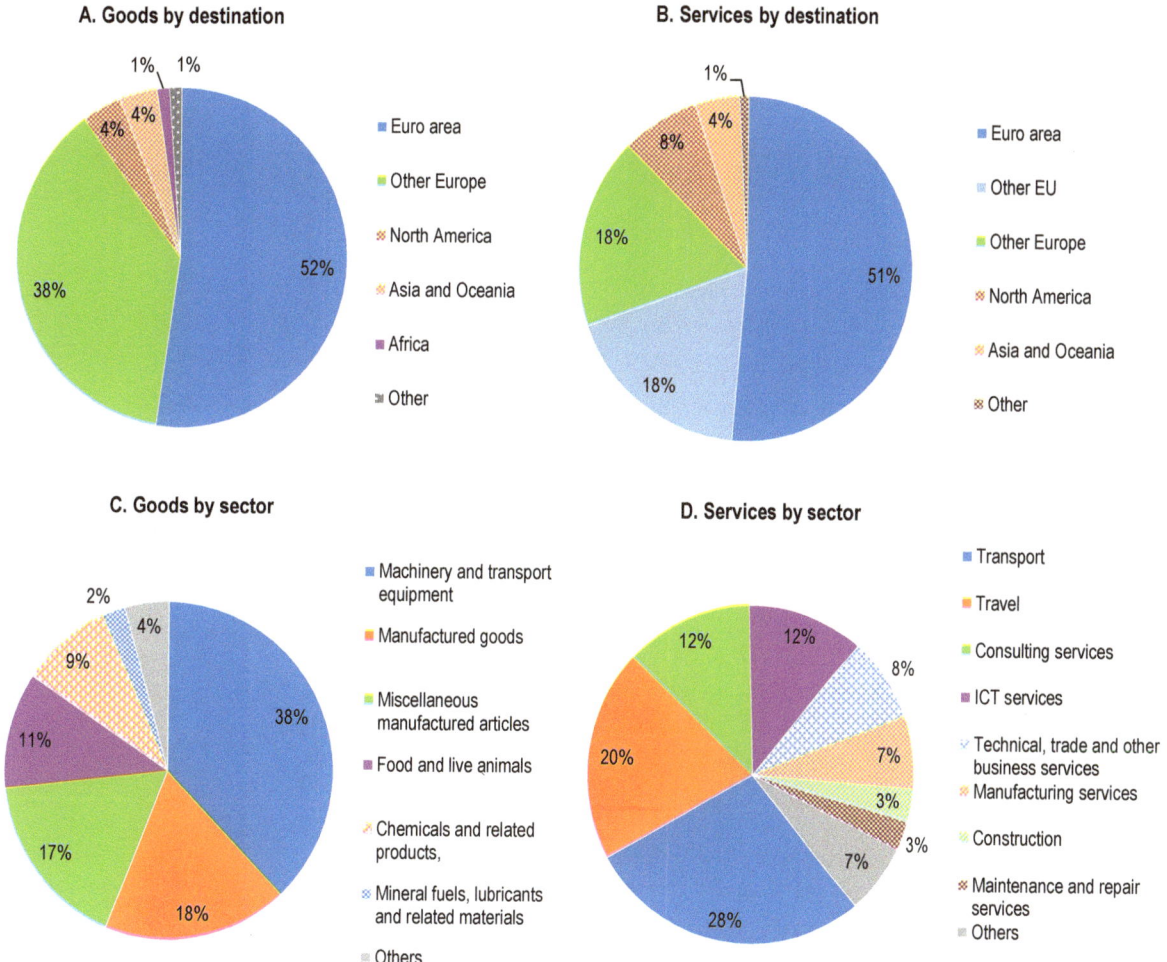

Note: Data on good exports refer to 2019, while data on services exports refer to 2018. In Panel C, Others include crude materials, beverages and tobacco, animal and vegetable oils, and commodities and transactions. In Panel D, Others include R&D services, financial services, insurance and pension, construction services, and cultural services.
Source: OECD (2020), International trade Statistics.

StatLink 🔗 https://doi.org/10.1787/888934208716

Box 2.2. The role of multinational enterprises in Polish exports and domestic value chains

Foreign firms play an important role in the Polish economy; they are responsible for around 30% of employment and around 44% of exports (Figure 2.7). The industries where foreign-owned firms produce more of the value added are often those that have a higher export orientation. On average, foreign-owned firms in Poland are twice as export intensive (share of exports in turnover) as domestically owned firms, and their export intensity is higher than the OECD median (OECD, 2017).The manufacturing sector highlights this point, with a high share of value added by foreign-owned firms and a high export orientation. In the manufacturing sector, foreign MNEs' exports reach 65%. In particular, in motor vehicles, foreign-owned firms account for 80% of employment and 90% of exports in value-added terms.

Figure 2.7. Foreign multinationals and exports are tightly linked

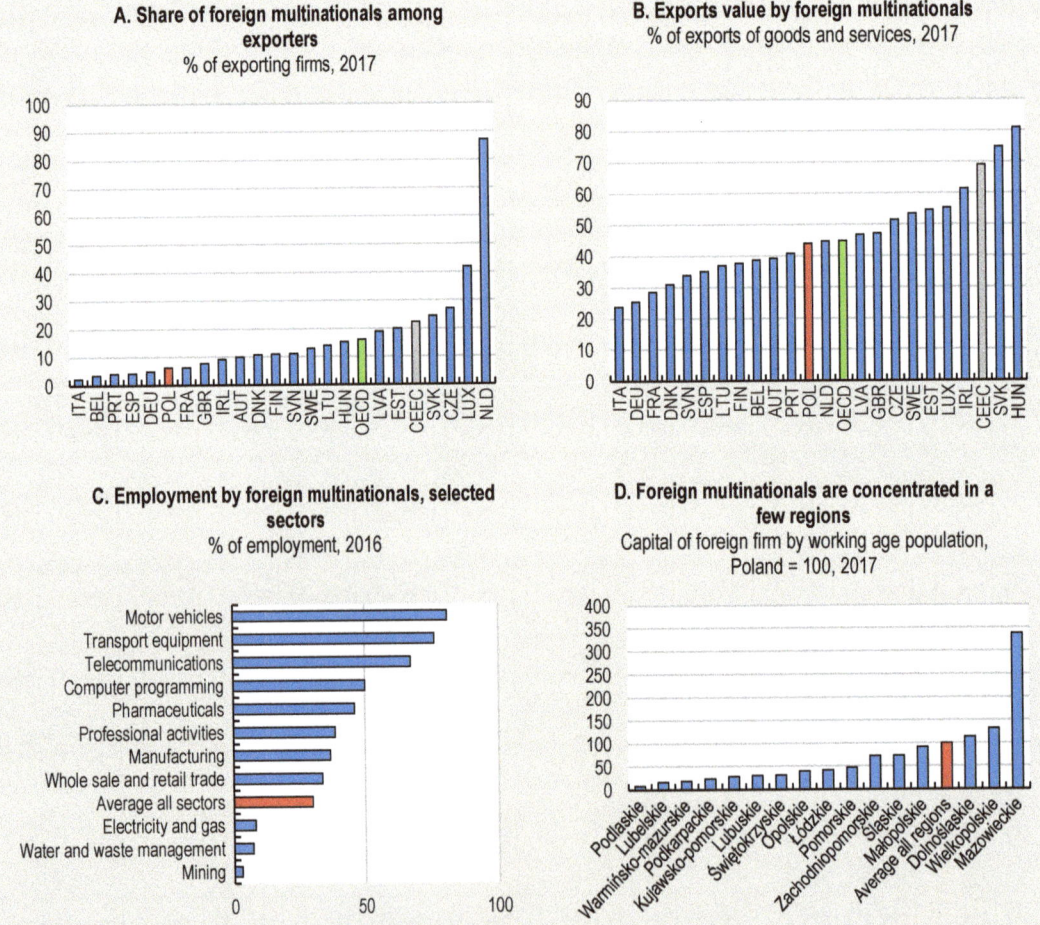

Note: CEEC is the average of Hungary and the Czech and Slovak Republics.
Source: OECD (2019), MNE database, Inward activity of multinationals and TEC database; Statistics Poland (2019), Entities with foreign capital participation.

StatLink https://doi.org/10.1787/888934208735

Foreign owned capital is concentrated in large firms, with a higher import content of exports and simultaneously relatively large upstream consequences, notably on smaller firms that act as supplier and indirect exporters. In Poland as in other OECD countries, domestic SMEs are the most important domestic suppliers to foreign affiliates (Cadestin et al., 2019).

Source: Cadestin, C., et al. (2019), "Multinational enterprises in domestic value chains", OECD Science, Technology and Industry Policy Papers, No. 63, OECD Publishing, Paris; OECD (2017), "Trade and investment in Poland", International trade, foreign direct investment and global value chains, OECD Publishing, Paris.

This increasing involvement in world trade has generated significant benefits. It has acted as a driving force for the economy, and this has been reflected in the strength of exports and the creation of value added from foreign demand since 1995. The sectors that are the most integrated into GVCs, and therefore the most export-focused, have developed comparative advantages, which have led to productivity gains that are stronger than in other sectors and other OECD countries (Miroudot and Cadestin, 2017; Berthou et al., 2015).

However, exports remained somehow specialised in relatively low-technology goods in 2017. The share of medium and high technology goods in Poland's export basket has doubled since 1995 (PARP, 2019a), but goods exports remain relatively less sophisticated than those of other CEE countries. Compared to Poland's level of development, its exports structure is tilted towards goods generally exported by lower-income countries (Figure 2.8, Panel A, Hausmann et al., 2007). Poland's exports' prices and quality, as proxied by trade unit values within narrowly defined type of goods, appears relatively low in the manufacturing sector (Panel B), which reflects a perceived specialisation in low-cost and low-quality goods (WEF, 2019). Original equipment manufacturers which operate globally still run largely labour-intensive and low value added production processes in Poland, and export few high-technology products. Poland's manufacturing exports are in the mature phase of their life cycle compared to many other OECD countries (Araujo et al., 2018), increasing the importance of innovation to sustain the future export performance of the economy.

Figure 2.8. Poland is specialised in low- and medium-tech exports

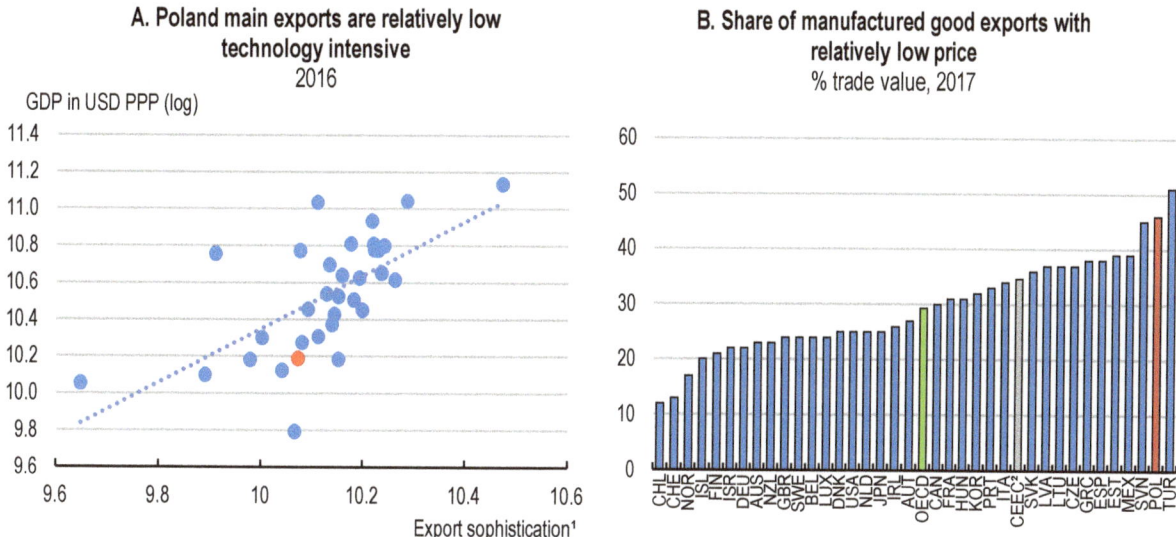

1. Export sophistication is defined as an average over exported goods as in Hausmann et al., (2007). For each good, a proxy for its sophistication is the average GDP per capita (in 2015 in PPP terms) of its destination markets. Computations use 180 destination countries and 6-digit good classification (1992 - HS6 classification).
2. CEEC is the average of Hungary and the Czech and Slovak Republics.
Source: OECD (2019), National Accounts Database. OECD calculations based on CEPII (2017), BACI Database and World Bank (2017), World Development Indicators; Comtrade Database; CEPII (2019), The Trade Unit Value Database.

StatLink 🔗 https://doi.org/10.1787/888934208754

Small size and low productivity hinder SME internationalisation

Internationalisation varies significantly by firm size and across sectors. The share of SMEs participating in direct exports is particularly low, notably for micro-firms. According to 2017 data, only about 12% of micro-firms participate in direct export activities in the manufacturing sector and less than 5% in key services sectors (Figure 2.9, Panels A and B). Moreover, their export intensity is relatively low and the average export value per exporting firm are smaller than in the average OECD country and other CEE countries (Panels C and F). The average exports of a Polish exporting firm are roughly 70% smaller in value terms than those of exporting firms in the average OECD country, though the gap varies from 80% for micro-firms to 60% for large firms. This suggests that beyond fixed costs and the participation in global trade, lower productivity and higher variable costs play a key role in explaining the export gap of Polish SMEs.

As in other OECD countries, only a few high-performing firms have become successful exporters. Exporters tend to be larger than non-exporting firms, more capital intensive and more productive (Albinowski et al., 2016; Szpunar and Hagemejer, 2018). The academic literature has traced this back to the existence of fixed costs of entering foreign markets, which only the most productive firms can recover once they become exporters (Melitz and Ottaviano, 2008). The geographical position of Poland is particularly favourable for potential exporters and firm internationalisation, as they benefit from rich neighbouring countries and enhanced access to markets through the European single market which reduces transaction costs. Yet, there remain barriers to cross-border activity hindering the European Single Market (Caldera Sánchez, 2018). And, as in other CEE countries, some fixed costs, such as the need to collect information about export markets, establishing commercial contacts, hiring multilingual staff or adapting products to be sold abroad, remain particularly binding for smaller firms (Morales et al., 2014).

Smaller firms face difficulties in becoming persistent exporters and scaling up their exports, which appears to be key drivers of productivity gains linked to internationalisation (Anderson and Lööf, 2009). The costs of adjusting products and company procedures to differences in culture, laws and technology of foreign buyers are relatively higher. Moreover, uncertainty in export relationships is generally high, notably in services sectors, because of the difficulty to enforce contracts across borders and the information asymmetry and geographical distance between the exchange partners. The complexity of firm's operations tend to increase with the number of product-destination couples exported (Guillou and Treibich, 2019). This also holds for exchange rate movements and their volatility that affect mostly smaller exporters in Poland (Albinowski et al., 2016).

Poland's SMEs are lagging other forms of internationalisation. When they engage in direct exports they tend to focus on the EU market or other trading partners, but rarely combine both export destinations contrary to larger firms and comparable firms in CEE countries (Figure 2.10). Selling goods and services through foreign affiliates is also less frequent in Poland. Moreover, Poland's SMEs appear less engaged in imports than SMEs in other OECD Countries. Micro-firms have an importing intensity, as measured as the ratio of imports over turnover, twice below the OECD average, both in manufacturing and services sectors, and much smaller than that of larger firms. Poland's SMEs, in addition to facing barriers to export, have difficulties in overcoming some of the costs associated with importing – and integrating in GVCs – such as finding reliable suppliers and ensuring that the imported products have the right specifications.

The lagging internationalisation of SMEs reflects their weak productivity and small size. Polish SMEs have relatively low productivity, notably the numerous micro-enterprises, according to 2017 data. Their relative productivity is among the lowest in the OECD (Figure 2.11). Indeed, micro-enterprises account for a high share of employment in Poland compared to the OECD average and other CEE countries, in the services and manufacturing sectors (Figure 2.12). Before the coronavirus crisis, a plethora of start-ups experienced significant difficulties to survive and grow, despite a dynamic economy and the crisis legacy will compound these difficulties. The firm size distribution implies that a large share of firms face relatively higher costs and challenges than larger exporters due to their lower human resources and capital. These firms are disproportionally affected by barriers such as tariffs, quotas and stringent rules of origin, as applied in the whole European Union, due to fixed compliance costs that do not vary with the amount traded and the inability of SMEs to spread these costs over large export values (Rouzet et al., 2017).

Figure 2.9. Smaller firms have low export intensity in manufacturing and services sectors
2017

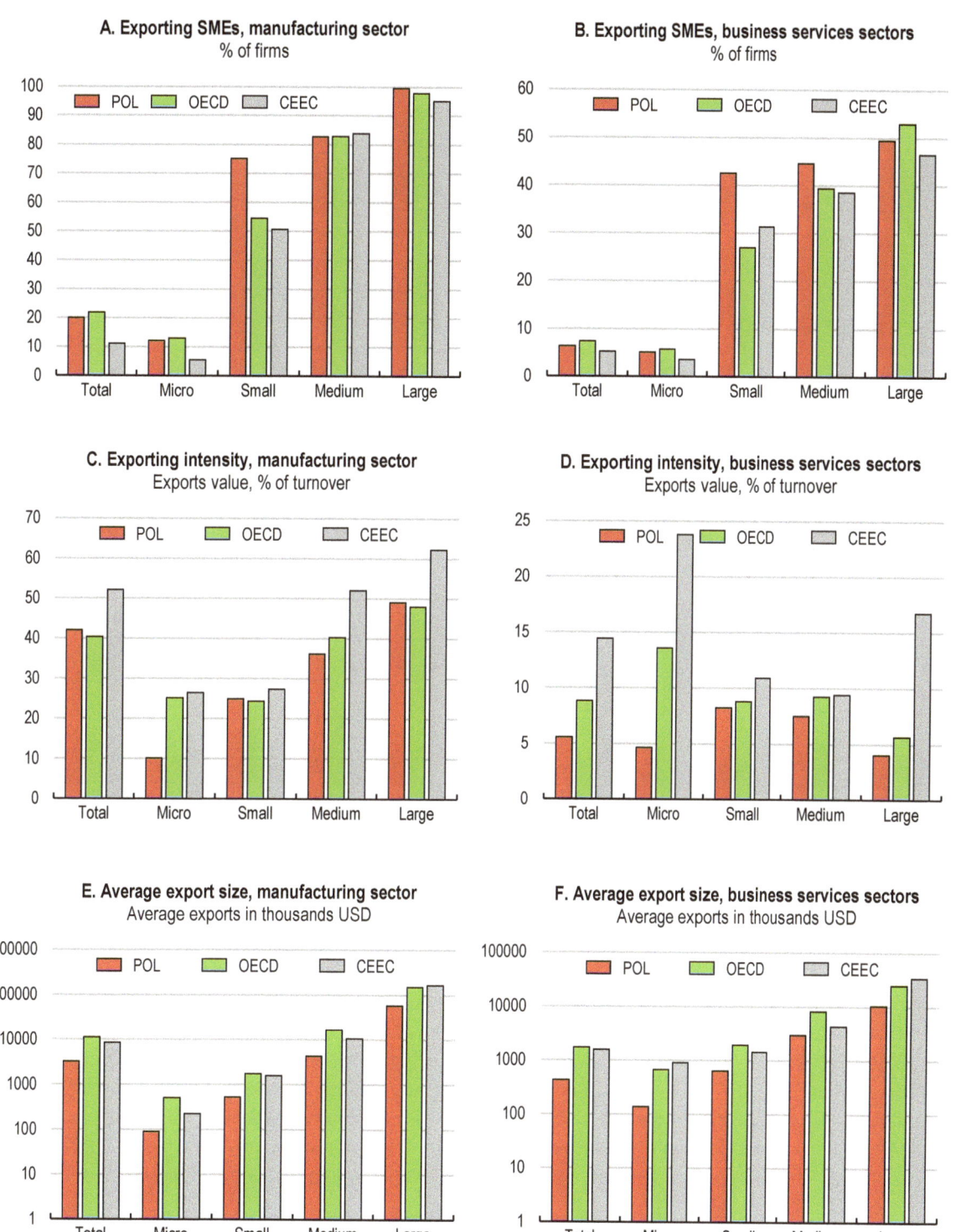

Note: CEEC is the average of Hungary and the Czech and Slovak Republics. Business services sectors include wholesale and retail trade, transportation and storage, information and communication, professional, scientific and technical activities and administrative and support service activities.
Source: OECD calculations based on OECD (2019), Structural Business Statistics, Trade by Enterprises Characteristics and National account databases.

StatLink https://doi.org/10.1787/888934208773

74

Figure 2.10. Micro-firms lag multiple forms of internationalisation

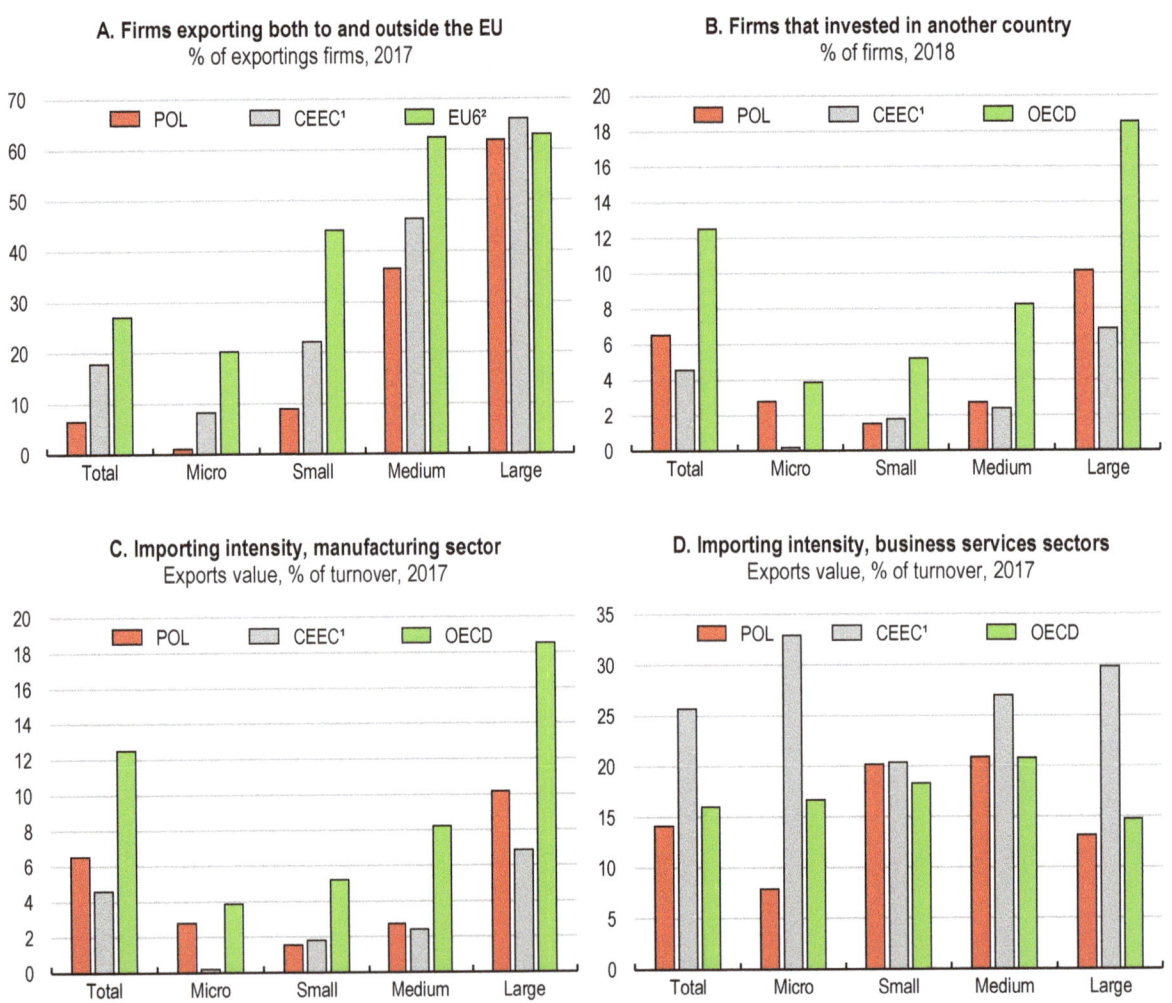

1. CEEC is the average of Hungary and the Czech and Slovak Republics.
2. EU6 is the average of Denmark, Germany, Italy, Netherlands, Portugal and Spain.
Source: OECD calculations based on OECD (2019), Structural Business Statistics, Trade by Enterprises Characteristics and National account databases; EIB (2019), EIB Investment Survey.

StatLink https://doi.org/10.1787/888934208792

The internationalisation and productivity gaps of smaller firms have large social and territorial implications. For example, micro firms pay on average salary that are only 50% the one of large firms (Statistics Poland, 2019). SMEs' employees have also lower employment opportunities, lower quality job and low training opportunities (see below). This also contributes to strong regional divides. Widely internationalised large and foreign-owned firms concentrate more than two thirds of their employment in 5 of the 16 Polish regions, while SMEs are more equally spread (Figure 2.13, Panel A). In particular, the share of micro and small firms in employment is strongly negatively associated with GDP per capita at the regional level (Panel B).

Figure 2.11. SMEs productivity is weak and young firms lack opportunities to grow

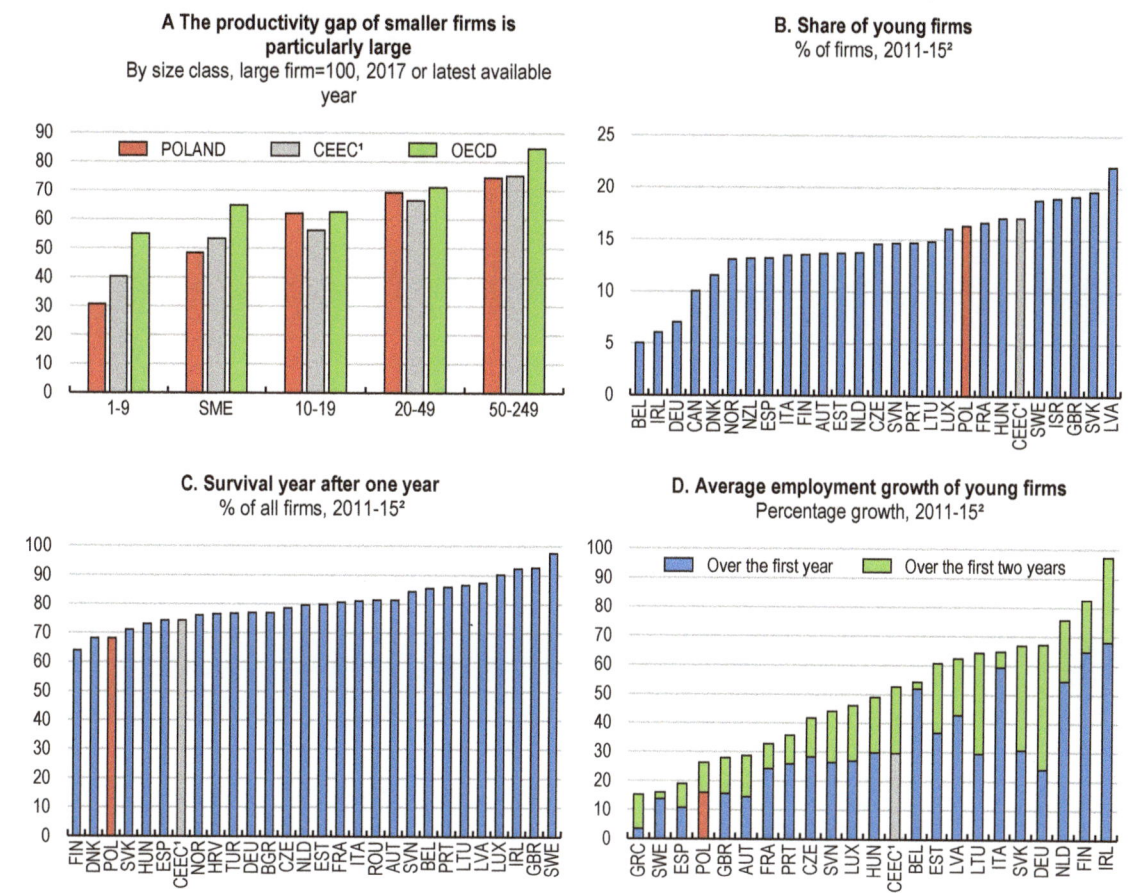

1. CEEC is the average of Hungary and the Czech and Slovak Republics.
2. Average of available years. Young firms are those less than two years old.
Source: OECD calculations based on OECD (2019), Structural Business Statistics, Trade by Enterprises Characteristics and National account databases; Eurostat (2019), "Structural Business Statistics", Eurostat Database.

StatLink ⟡ https://doi.org/10.1787/888934208811

Figure 2.12. Micro-firms account for a high share of employment
By size class, 2017

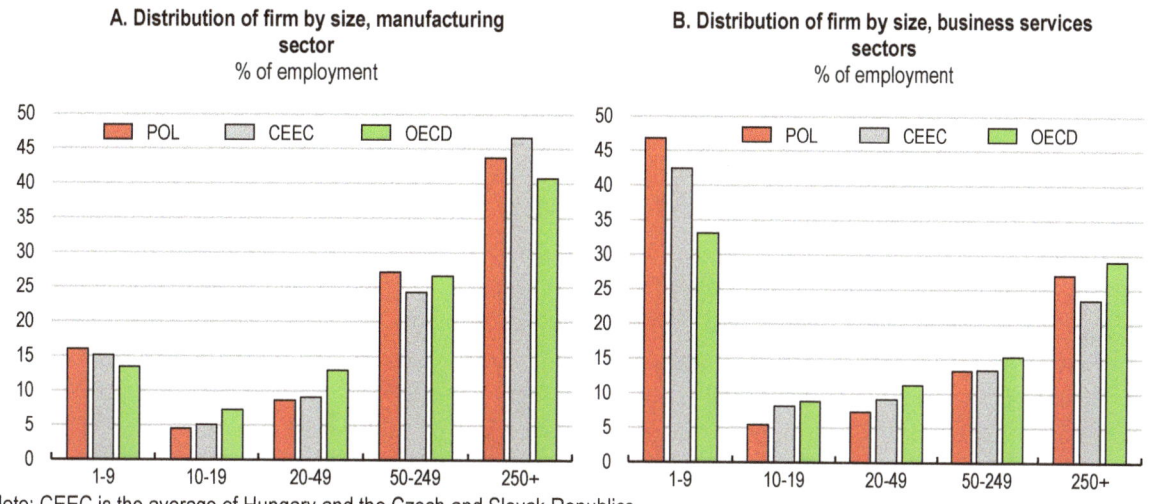

Note: CEEC is the average of Hungary and the Czech and Slovak Republics.
Source: OECD calculations based on OECD (2019), Structural Business Statistics.

StatLink ⟡ https://doi.org/10.1787/888934208830

Figure 2.13. SMEs' gaps have significant economic and social consequences

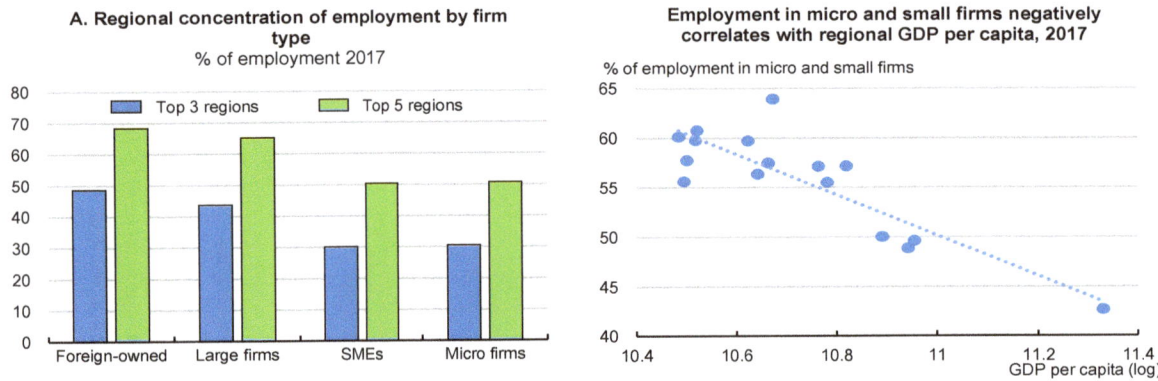

Note: Regions correspond to Poland's 16 regions (voivodeships).
Source: OECD calculations based on Statistics Poland (2019), regional accounts and non-financial entities database.

StatLink 🔗 https://doi.org/10.1787/888934208849

Boosting SMEs' internationalisation through a better business environment

Policies that promote activities in which firms and workers are particularly competitive and that foster business dynamism and ease linkages between large exporters and smaller firms would help reap additional gains from trade (OECD, 2017a). Lowering the administrative burden that weighs especially on smaller and younger firms would reduce entry and fixed costs of participating in global trade. A broader firm internationalisation would result in greater diffusion of knowledge, technology and know-how, with positive effects on employment and labour market inclusiveness (Gal and Theising, 2015; Causa et al. 2016).

Easing further administrative costs for potential exporters

Improvement in product market regulation has been significant over the last decades, but several aspects of the business environment continue to harm SMEs performance, productivity and internationalisation (Figure 2.14). The authorities have recently implemented measures to ease business creation and growth, notably, lower administrative requirements for new and smaller firms and the possibility of a simplified joint stock company with low capital requirements to facilitate start-ups (Box 2.3 and Box 2.4). The measures also foresee more legal certainty for firms when it comes to paying taxes and audits, and a reduction of paperwork.

Despite these reforms, some administrative and regulatory procedures remain burdensome. In particular administrative requirements necessary to set up new firms, whether limited liability companies or personally owned enterprises, remained relatively burdensome in 2018-19. A large number of procedures have to be fulfilled (OECD, 2019c; World bank, 2019) and some related regulations could be streamlined. For example, in the Podkarpackie and Lubelskie regions (voivodeships), in 2017-18, more than five food inspection services had responsibilities to enforce food requirements, with little standardisation and coordination, which was significantly increasing compliance costs (Drozd et al., 2018).

Streamlining court proceedings could facilitate contract and payment enforcements, particularly important for SMEs and services, and raise productivity growth by shortening bankruptcy procedures. This would help to face the expected wave of insolvent firms when the government starts to withdraw if the recovery remains weak. Before the crisis, it took about three months more than the OECD average for a typical case, with substantial variations across cities leading to high uncertainty (World Bank, 2019). Courts and judges were often overburdened by small, non-litigious cases and the take-up of e-technologies had been low, despite high judicial spending and the 2015 reform easing ICT use for civil proceedings (CEPEJ, 2016; World Bank, 2013 and 2016). Moreover, bankruptcy procedures remained lengthy (OECD, 2018a).

Ensuring that sound firms are given a fair chance to survive the coronavirus crisis and that there is not a proliferation of 'zombie' firms and misallocation of resources is key to the recovery. This should be addressed in three phases (OECD, 2020a): *i)* preventing sound firms from entering insolvency proceedings, *ii)* ensuring insolvency regimes and other policies can deal with the wave of insolvencies, and *iii)* policies to address the debt overhang problem to enable a "fresh start" for individuals and firms. Poland took early action to avoid premature liquidations, create a breathing space for firms facing difficulties and ease procedures (Box 2.1). Yet, to prepare for the recovery, developing special insolvency procedures for SMEs, such as simplified or pre-packaged in-court proceedings or the possibility to have instalments in the payment of administrative expenses related to the insolvency proceedings, is also warranted, as SMEs are frequently unable to cover the costs of formal insolvency proceedings (Adalet McGowan et al., 2017). Moreover, limiting in the short and longer term, the burden of non-litigious cases on judges could free up some resources, as in commercial-court cases. Such measures would have positive side effects on payment delays, as frequent arrears are particularly harmful for SMEs and recent measures to limit their abuse rely on efficient court procedures (Lewiatan, 2019; MR, 2019a).

Figure 2.14. Selected features of the OECD product market regulation indicators

Index scale 0 to 6 from most to least competition-friendly regulation, 2018

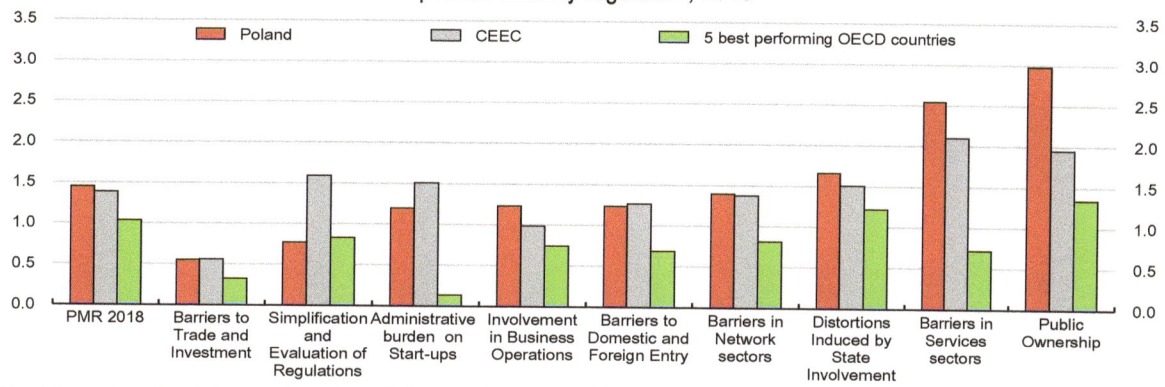

Note: Information refers to laws and regulation in force on 1 January 2018. The USA and Estonia are not yet included in the PMR database.
Source: OECD (2019), OECD 2018 PMR database.

StatLink https://doi.org/10.1787/888934208868

Services regulations have also significant room for improvement, since services inputs are often sourced domestically and key to access foreign markets. Services account for 35% of gross exports, but 55% of value-added exports, indicating that Poland's exports of goods rely intensively on services inputs. However, some services professions still face relative high barriers to entry and, in the case of lawyers and notaries restrictions to their conducts (Figure 2.15 and Figure 2.16, Panel A). Occupational licensing and the lack of a temporary licensing system for foreign practitioners obstruct market entry and competition by professionals from outside the European Economic Area (OECD, 2019d).

The OECD Services Trade Restrictiveness Indicator (STRI) also highlights horizontal barriers to international trade in services. Labour market tests and quotas for natural persons seeking to provide services in the country on a temporary basis as intra-corporate transferees, contractual services suppliers and independent services suppliers tend to lower international mobility. Procedures to obtain business visas and register a company are all significantly more numerous, costly or longer than best practice (OECD, 2019d). Relatively weak regulatory transparency and complex administrative procedures tend to add to firm operational expenses (Figure 2.16, Panel B). This setting weigh particularly on SMEs and potential exporters, as larger firms are better equipped to succeed in complex regulatory environments because of their broader resources, in-house legal expertise, existing networks of business partners, and the benefits of scale to absorb overhead costs (Rouzet et al., 2017).

78 |

Figure 2.15. Some administrative procedures remain burdensome

Burden on new firms[1], scale 0-6 from least to most restrictive, 2018

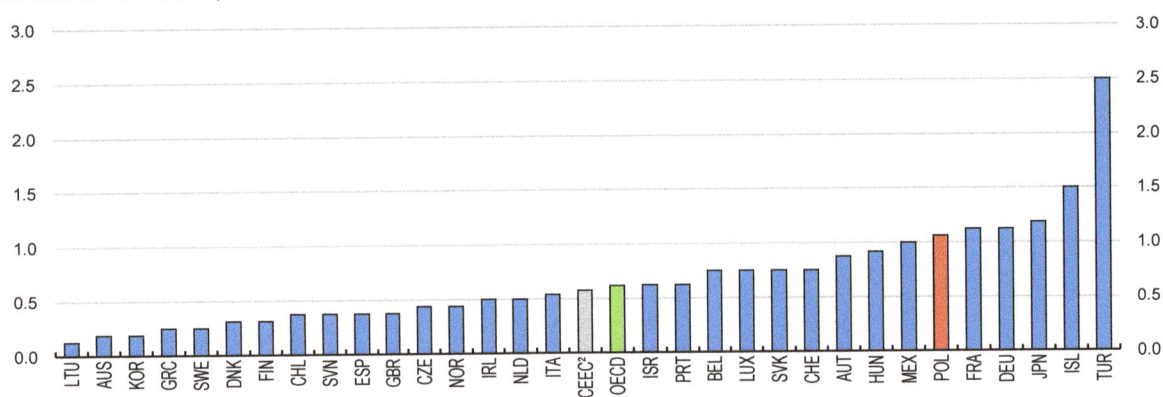

1. Administrative requirements to set up limited liability companies and personally-owned enterprises.
2. CEEC is the average of Hungary and the Czech and Slovak Republics.
Source: OECD (2019), OECD 2018 PMR database.

StatLink https://doi.org/10.1787/888934208887

Figure 2.16. Some services trade barriers remain important

Services Trade Restrictiveness Index by sector, 2019

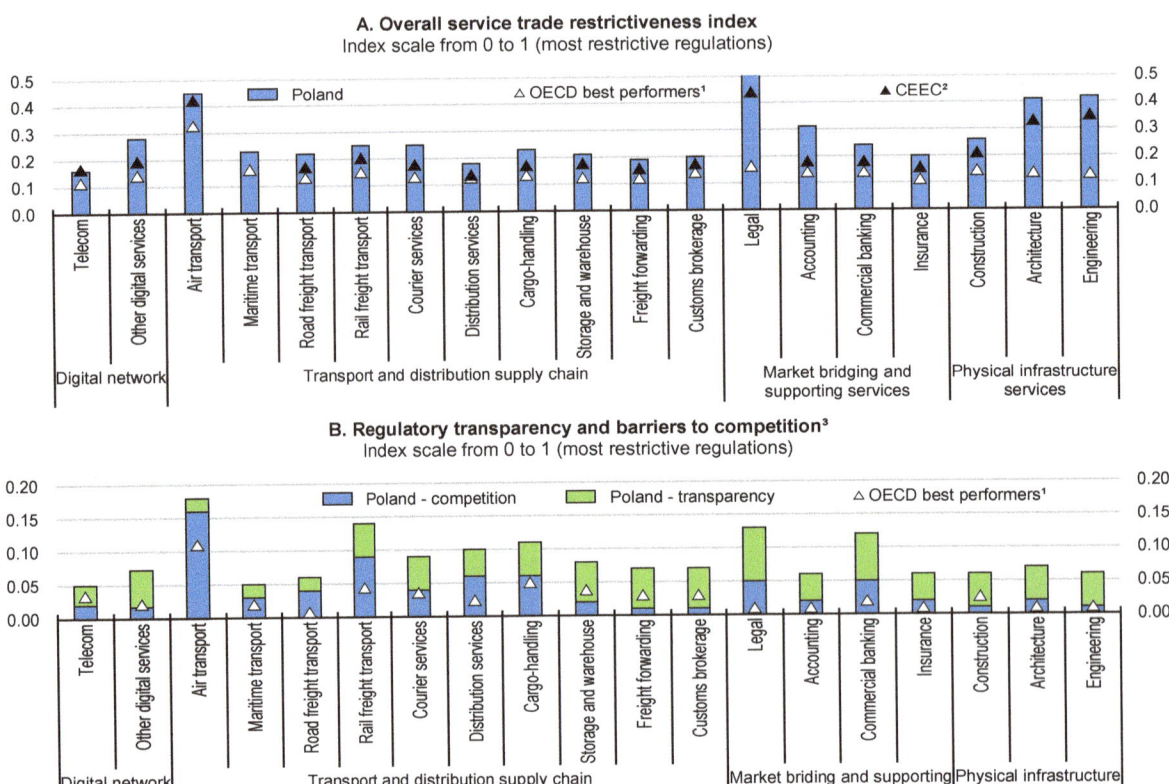

1. The OECD best performers is the average of the five countries with regulations the most conducive to trade.
2. CEEC is the average of Hungary, Czech and Slovak Republics.
3. Most of the measures recorded as barriers to competition and issues related to regulatory transparency apply equally to domestic and foreign firms.
Source: OECD (2020), Services Trade Restrictiveness Index (database).

StatLink https://doi.org/10.1787/888934208906

Strong regulatory governance is key to achieve further simplification. Poland has substantially improved its regulatory system (OECD, 2019c). Since 2015, public consultations are a general principle of the regulation making process, except for laws initiated by the Parliament. Existing consultations are often too quick or insufficiently taken into account (EC, 2019a; 2019b; and 2020). According to a recent exercise by the Supreme Audit Chamber, only a third of the impact assessments examined had been performed correctly (NIK, 2018a). Strengthening the role of consultations in the legislative process, allowing for sufficient time to gather relevant stakeholders' views and building on some ministries' best practices, would help lower the administrative burden resulting from frequent law changes (NIK, 2018a).

Easing tax compliance and ensuring sound public support for SMEs

Reducing further tax compliance costs for SMEs

Tax administration remains particularly cumbersome for smaller firms and potential exporters. While there are various methods for measuring tax compliance costs (Box 2.3), the widely used World Bank Doing Business Indicators suggest that paying taxes takes many more hours in Poland than other OECD countries, despite the increased digitalisation of tax procedures and pre-filling of information on tax returns if available (Figure 2.17). In particular, the system of reduced VAT rates – despite its ongoing simplification – remains overarching (KPI). The payment of social security contributions also appears time consuming (World Bank, 2019).

The development of e-procedures could help to ease tax compliance. Although the process of reporting, paying and auditing taxes is now done electronically, time spent by a typical Polish company on meeting tax obligations has increased (EC, 2019a). Electronic Invoicing Systems could be streamlined to increase compliance and allow businesses to issue and receive invoices that are immediately available to the tax authorities. Such system could also provide, free of charge, a simplified and complete accounting framework to users. For example, in collaboration with software developers, Danish tax authorities embedded tax-related guidance and other functionalities in accounting software solutions targeted to small businesses.

Figure 2.17. Tax compliance costs remain elevated

Time needed to pay taxes[1], hours per year, 2019

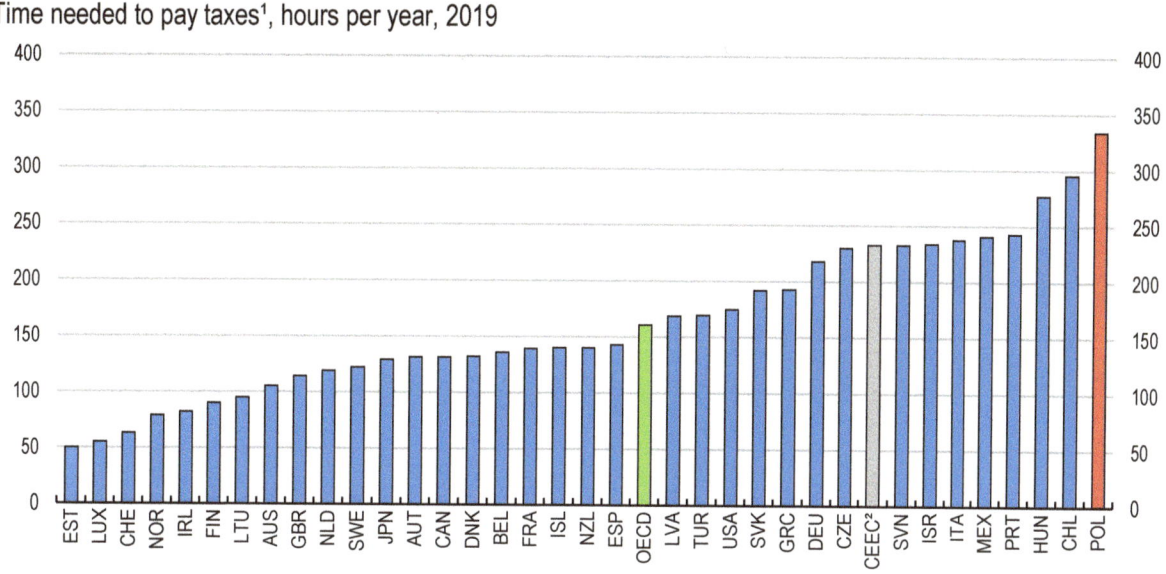

1. The time to comply with tax laws measures the time taken to prepare, file and pay three major types of taxes and contributions: the corporate income tax, value added or sales tax and labour taxes, including payroll taxes and social contributions.
2. CEEC is the average of Hungary and the Czech and Slovak Republics.
Source: World Bank (2019), Doing Business 2020.

StatLink https://doi.org/10.1787/888934208925

Ensuring appropriate fiscal support for smaller firms

Tax reliefs for smaller firms have been reformed recently. A reduced Corporate Income Tax rate and reformed Special Economic Zones aim to improve support for smaller firms both through a lower tax rate and through increase access for SMEs (Box 2.3). Special tax regimes for small and initially unprofitable firms, especially in a country with relatively high informality, can ease tax compliance and related fixed costs, particularly burdensome for SMEs (OECD, 2015). However, as shown by the experience of other OECD countries, reduced rates may also lead to misreporting of taxable income or size (Bergner et al., 2017), reducing incentives for dynamic firms to scale up and carry out exporting and innovative activities, like in France or Spain (Garicano et al., 2016; Almunia and Lopez-Rodriguez, 2013). The significant tax-rate gap of 10 percentage points between SMEs and larger firms in Poland could increase these risks. In addition, international evidence tends to show that small firms' investment decisions are less sensitive to corporate taxes changes (OECD, 2010; OECD, 2015).

The costs and benefits of having such system should be reviewed – as planned - and, if needed, transitional measures should be introduced to smooth cliff edge effects when businesses transition from the preferential status. For example, employment-based or other thresholds could apply if reached for five consecutive years, as recently done in France. Yet, frequent tax and regulatory changes should be avoided as they induce significant adjustment costs for SMEs. Regional disparities create further difficulties, as the tax administration interpretations are only locally binding (OECD, 2018a).

Ex post evaluation efforts of fiscal measures for SMEs should also be strengthened, notably to include the full economic impact and incorporate more systematically rigorous research designs. *Ex post* evaluations can be required at the request of the Council of Ministers or subsidiary bodies (OECD, 2018x). They are also mandatory in several instances, notably for the heavily relied on EU-funded programmes (Figure 2.18). Yet, such efforts have been partly lacking (OECD, 2016a). For example, the agency in charge of business innovation subsidies has no obligation to monitor their effectiveness, though it granted support worth 0.3% of GDP in 2015 (NIK, 2016). Moreover, evidence about the effectiveness of the 2017 R&D tax break is also lacking though its take-up has increased rapidly. Defining *ex ante* the timing of the evaluation would have allowed a more efficient adjustment of the scheme and avoided incentives for firms to delay investments. More generally, systematically evaluating business support schemes would help to ensure that they are constantly improved based on experience and that the most effective programmes are strengthened in the longer term.

Figure 2.18. Business and SMEs' support are heavily reliant on EU funds

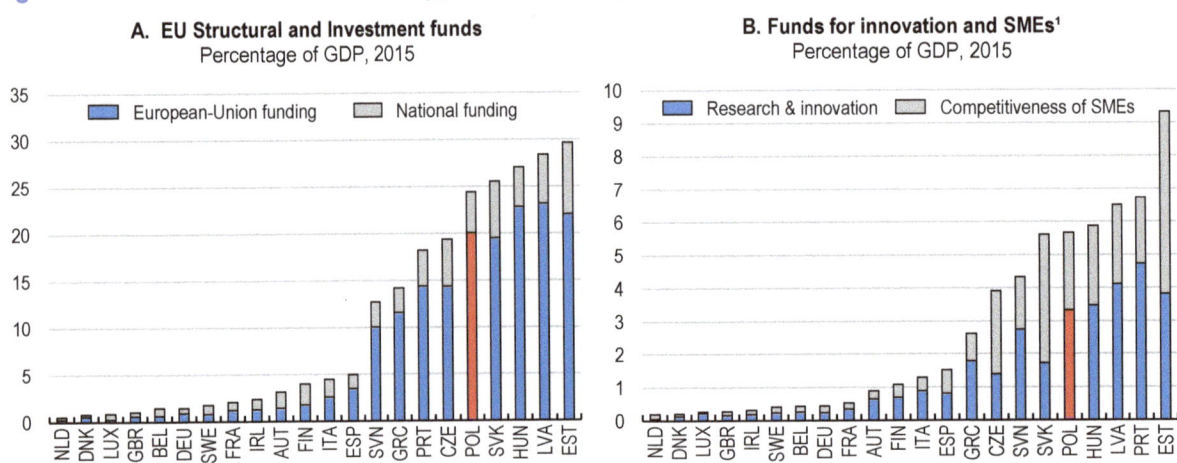

A. EU Structural and Investment funds
Percentage of GDP, 2015

B. Funds for innovation and SMEs[1]
Percentage of GDP, 2015

1. EU and domestic funding. The data refers to European Structural and Investment Funds with thematic objectives "Research & Innovation" and "Competitiveness of SMEs". For comparison across countries, the figure excludes some measures for technical assistance that represent 3.4% of expenditures under the Smart Growth operational programme in Poland.
Source: European Commission (2016), ESIF Finance dataset.

StatLink ᴍᴴᴴᴸ https://doi.org/10.1787/888934208944

Box 2.3. Recent policy initiatives and ongoing discussions to support SMEs

The 2018 Business constitution and "100 Changes for Enterprises"

The measures aims at reducing the administrative burden, as well as simplifying bureaucratic procedures, notably for small and medium-sized enterprises and foreign investors. Key changes include:

- Simplified registration procedures and an exemption for the smallest businesses (whose turnover does not exceed half the minimum wage). The threshold for full accounting obligations was also lifted from EUR 1.2 million turnover annually to EUR 2 million. In addition, new firms benefit from a "right to error" for a one-year period.
- Social security exemptions for the first six months of setting up a business. Entrepreneurs may benefit from reduced contributions, through the so-called "small ZUS" scheme over the next two years.
- Measures aimed at improving the administrative trust for businesses. Notably: presumption good faith and creation of the Ombudsman for small and medium-sized enterprises; ministries are required to publish simple explanations of administrative rules and tax laws; companies need to keep financial statements only for five years now rather than indefinitely.
- A new law also allows to prevent cessation of legal personality of an enterprise – notably family-owned and smaller firms – in the case of death of the entrepreneur, by setting rules for temporary management of business activity after death of an entrepreneur.

The 2018 reform of special economic zones (SEZ)

The previous network of special economic zones (used mainly by larger industrial companies) was transformed into a countrywide investment tax credit with the view of boosting SMEs' take-up. The level of support depends notably on firm size, the local unemployment rate and other qualitative criteria, such as the assessed potential of sector, as well as the expected social and environmental effects. As a result, refundable tax credits for CIT and PIT (for non-legal entities) depend on the initial investment, the region and firm size. They amount to: i) 10% to 50% of the initial investment for large enterprises; ii) 20% to 60% for medium-sized enterprises, iii) 30% to 70% for micro and small enterprises.

The 2019 reduction in corporate income tax rate for SMEs

The authorities reduced the corporate income tax rate for SMEs to 9% (instead of 15% since 2016 and the standard rate of 19%). It applies to firms having annual turnover equal or less than EUR 1.2 million. In order to prevent tax optimisation, this reduced rate does not apply to taxpayers starting their activity, if their activity was created as result of transformation of one company into another company or of a company division.

The 2019 simplified joint stock company

The new simplified joint stock company (P.S.A.) will facilitate starting up a business in March 2021. It has low capital requirements, possibly only 1 PLN, simplified registration online within 24 hours and light procedures to dissolve the company.

The 2019 changes to the programme supporting investments of major importance over 2011-30

The reform aimed to ease access to SMEs by amending project requirements and introducing qualitative assessments. The minimum eligible costs and the job creation thresholds for R&D investments were lowered. Cash grant supplements can now be awarded in less developed regions and to cover training costs. In addition, the assessment of investment projects now includes qualitative objectives such as sustainable development, social responsibility and scientific development.

The 2020 regulation on late payments

The new regulation introduced legally binding deadlines for payments, which is set to help address arrears and support enterprises' financial liquidity.

The "Estonian CIT"

The authorities are considering the introduction of a new voluntary Corporate Income Tax (CIT) scheme for SMEs. Under the new measure, SMEs with revenues below PLN 50 million (approximately EUR 11 million), whose passive revenues do not exceed those from operating activities and whose shareholders are individuals, would not pay income tax as long as revenues are reinvested. CIT collection would only occur when these SMEs pay out dividends to shareholders. The scheme is expected to reduce obstacles for SMEs development, boost investment and employment.

Increasing SMEs innovation, its diffusion and productivity

Poland's business sector spends relatively little in the generation of knowledge-based capital. Both business research and development (as a percentage of GDP) and the number of patents (per capita) are in the OECD's lowest quadrant (OECD, 2018a). This partly reflects the dominance of SMEs in the economy. While many SMEs may be unlikely to develop radical innovations, empirical evidence suggests that performing research activity is important for their ability to demystify new technologies being developed abroad and adapt them to suit their production processes (Griffith, Redding and Reenen, 2004).

Stimulating private-sector research and innovation, which has been stable as a share of GDP could help raise SMEs internationalisation (Figure 2.19). Indeed, the low level of business R&D spending largely reflects little investment by local firms, especially SMEs, hindering the diffusion of innovation and GVC integration, which requires state-of-the-art producing processes. More than 70% of SMEs reported not to have state-of-the art machinery and equipment in 2018 (EIB, 2019).

Figure 2.19. SMEs lag R&D investment and innovation

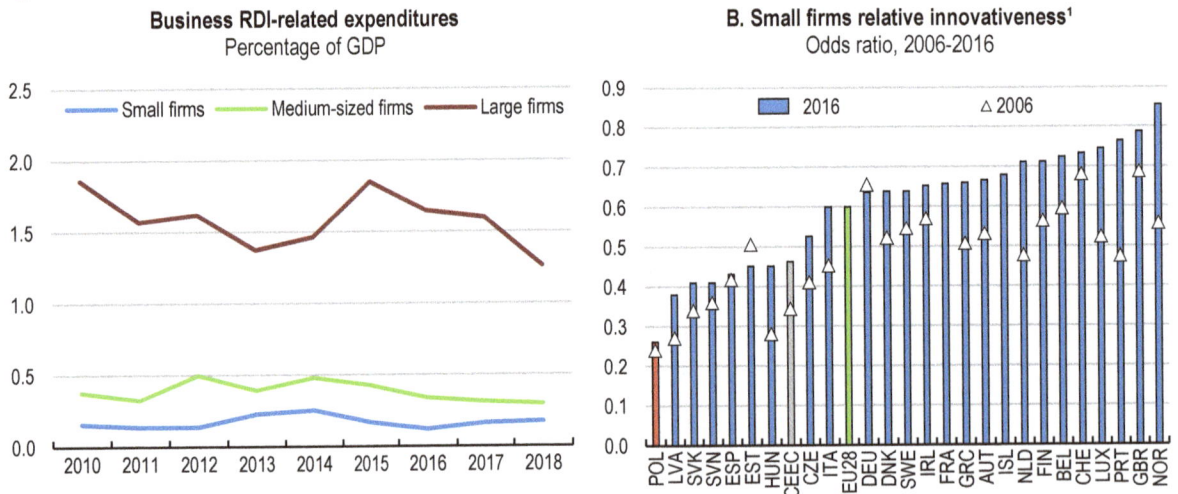

1. Share of innovative firms among 10-49 employee firms divided by the share of innovative firms among firms with over 250 employees.
Source: OECD calculations based on Statistics Poland (2017; 2019 and 2020), Expenditures on Innovation Activities, Statistics Poland, Warsaw and OECD (2020), National account database; Eurostat (2019), "Community Innovation Surveys (CIS) 2006-16", Eurostat Database.
StatLink https://doi.org/10.1787/888934208963

To stimulate research, development and innovation, public support for SMEs, start-ups and businesses has increased sharply. In particular, tax incentives have steadily increased through several reforms of the 2016 R&D tax allowance. For example, the tax-deductible proportion of R&D expenditure on labour increased from 30% to 100% over 2016-18. In 2017, the authorities also expanded the list of tax-deductible R&D spending, made the subsidy refundable for start-ups in the first year of business activity (two years for SMEs) and extended the credit carry-forward option from three to six years. As a result, the number of taxpayers using the relief increased significantly from 638 in 2016 to 1186 in 2017 (PIE, 2019).

However, the total amount spent in R&D support is still low, at 0.11% of GDP in 2017 (OECD, 2019e). Moreover, the average amount in claimed expenditures for tax credit remains high, suggesting small firms are taking less advantage. If take-up of the R&D tax relief by innovative SMEs remains low, making the tax credit refundable for SMEs operating more than two years and beyond the first year of a start-up could help boost SMEs' R&D spending. Developing standardised definitions for R&D expenditures, compiling a common list of qualified costs and offering services to assist firms in tax-claiming procedures (e.g. online information and simplified claims forms) would also help (OECD, 2018a).

The authorities could also give greater priority to direct support schemes. Grants are easier to monitor than general tax deductions, which require more checks. A well-designed and targeted strategy, based on closer co-operation between public research entities and businesses, could also help strengthen the country's research capacities. In fact, science-industry linkages remain generally weak (OECD, 2018a). Austria, for instance, is pursuing interesting initiatives thanks to the COMET (Competence Centres for Excellent Technology) programme and the Christian Doppler Laboratories (Comet, 2018; Cdg, 2018), which have been successful in promoting cooperation between companies and application-oriented research over the past two decades, especially in the automotive industry (Harms, 2018).

Trade facilitation has improved

Trade policies have successfully increased SMEs' ability to handle fixed costs associated with exporting and importing. According to the OECD Trade Facilitation Indicator, Poland exceeds or is close to the best performers in all areas (OECD, 2019f). Poland's performance has improved between 2015 and 2017 in terms of information availability and streamlining of procedures. Similarly, the cost of importing and exporting is low in international comparison (World Bank, 2019). Yet, the efficiency of custom clearance processes could still be improved (World Bank, 2017, OECD, 2019f). Expanding the use of pre-arrival processing and of Authorised Operators could help reduce variable costs, increase the value of imports and exports, as well as support timely delivery to consumers.

In a welcome move, the authorities recently reformed the exports promotion and investment framework to provide Polish companies with more help to expand into foreign market (Box 2.4). In 2017, the Polish Investment and Trade Agency (PAIH) replaced the Polish Information and Foreign Investment Agency (PAIiIZ) as the main institution responsible for promotion and facilitation of foreign investment. The government has also extended the mandate of its investment promotion agency to export promotion and increased its resources significantly. Since 2017, Polish sectoral brands promotion programs have been launched in Asia, Africa and Latin America, helping particularly SMEs. To offer on-site direct assistance, PAIH also runs a network of Foreign Trade Offices that are notably focused on distant markets with rapid growth potential for Polish exporters and investors (Box 2.4). The Polish Investment and Trade Agency (PAIH) does not offer financial instruments (except Polish Tech Bridges), but help to get support for international expansion from other financial institutions belonging to the Polish Development Fund (PFR). Apart from the support from PAIH, the Ministry of Economic Development encourages SMEs' internationalisation. For example, since 2016, Polish sectoral brands promotion programs (BPPs) have been carried out, to promote selected industries (based on their estimated export potential). SMEs may also obtain support to cover part of the costs related to participation in fairs, trainings and economic missions as well as other specific information and promotion undertakings. In addition, the Ministry plans to launch a new online portal to facilitate and promote SMEs' exports. This strategy is welcome, as coherent export support services have been lacking so far, and evidence suggests that high-quality investment promotion services tend to translate into stronger FDI inflows (Harding and Javorcik, 2013) with potential benefits for innovation and productivity.

The regular organisation of business meetings and SME associations with Foreign Trade Offices of the Polish Investment and Trade Agency (PAIH) could be a useful mechanism for helping Polish SMEs to reduce search costs and overcome trust barriers, to adopt superior management practices, and to raise productivity. International evidence as shown that such business networks may have a causal impact on firm performance (Cai and Szeidl, 2018). The example of Germany's structured network of public and private organisations could help to strengthen the Polish framework in this direction. The German Chambers of Commerce Abroad act as a link between the local and regional levels and the federal Germany Trade and Invest network in Embassies and consulates through the domestic regional Chambers of Industry and Commerce. The public-private cofinancing of the German Chambers of Commerce Abroad also helps to ensure the relevance of their actions (EESC, 2018). Austria's internationalisation initiative "go-international", also targets SMEs and builds on public-private financing to establish export relationships for the first time, or to open up new markets abroad. The initiative provides various support measures through a collaboration between the Ministry for Digital and Economic Affairs and the Federal Economic Chamber.

Developing local clusters and SMEs' consortia could boost internationalisation

Export consortia appear to be rare (MR, 2019b) and collaboration between companies is perceived as weak (Figure 2.20). To promote knowledge exchange, notably of export markets, and agglomeration economies, Poland has tried to develop local clusters and sectoral consortia. For example, the Torun region provided seed funding to several companies to establish a cluster and compete as a unique group offering complete solutions to potential contractors in other countries (Filippaios, 2018). Scaling up such experience could create successful exporters and innovation hubs by promoting the cooperation of interconnected firms, suppliers and research institutions (Marchese et al., 2019), capitalising on the already strong spatial concentration of exporting and innovation activities in Poland (Albinowski et al., 2016).

SMEs could combine their human and financial resources by creating networks of small businesses or collaborating with larger firms for exporting activity or training (see below). Participating in an export consortium reduces the risks and costs involved in penetrating foreign markets for SMEs (Unido, 2005). This could be done by creating a new legal form to accommodate export consortia and incentivising the participation of small businesses with grants or tax benefits (OECD, 2017b). For example, the Italian Institute for Foreign Trade gives grants to export consortia to incentivise their development. In order to qualify, export consortia must comprise a minimum number of SMEs.

Figure 2.20. Strengthening firms' cooperative linkages and clusters could support SMEs

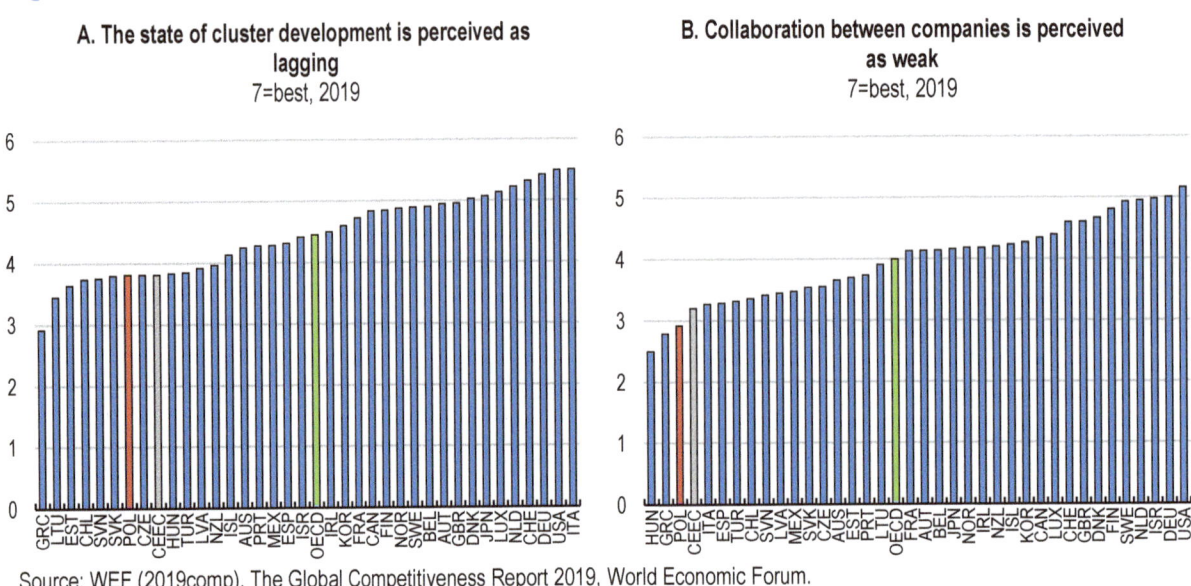

Source: WEF (2019comp), The Global Competitiveness Report 2019, World Economic Forum.

StatLink ⓘⓢⓛ https://doi.org/10.1787/888934208982

Polish cluster initiatives are relatively recent, and few have proven effective so far. There are around 130 clusters in Poland (PARP, 2020). In particular, the 15 National Key Clusters (NKC) have to define a business strategy and provide business services for their members. Yet, in many cases, the clusters' innovative activity and orientation towards foreign markets is low and their financial viability without subsidies is questionable (OECD, 2018a). Many lack a common business strategy for their members and make insufficient use of mentoring, coaching and business development services. The management of these structures often lack information about innovative activity and economic results of the participating firms, precluding effective evaluation (NBP, 2016; NIK, 2016). PARP currently provides information on clusters activities every second year, investigating and benchmarking the activities of National Key Clusters and a sample of other clusters. A prerequisite could be to develop, as planned, a database of potential suppliers for exporters and large MNEs. This would ease the integration of SMEs into domestic and global value chains, as done in Czech Republic through the "CzechInvest" project, which connects foreign investors with potential suppliers.

Going forward, the government is focusing its support on a small group of 15 National Key Clusters selected competitively as the most promising initiatives in terms of size, management quality, innovative activity and presence in foreign markets. Public support is meant to help them expand further abroad. Given that little is known about effective policies to support clusters, it seems sensible to concentrate on framework conditions, such as internationalisation, investment in infrastructure and training. This should include efforts to improve cluster management in line with the requirement to have an explicit strategy, as well as links to research institutions. Publicly supported clusters, technology parks and similar initiatives should be required to set up a plan on how to increase own earnings. Those failing to gradually reach viability should eventually lose their subsidies. Beyond benchmarking exercises and the regulator monitoring of clusters, a robust evaluation framework is needed to better understand what works. National and local initiatives should be regularly evaluated, as international evidence on spillovers and productivity effects of place-based incentives has been mixed so far (Slattery and Zidar, 2020), despite studies showing positive agglomeration effects on innovation (Carlino and Kerr, 2015).

There is still scope to improve technical assistance and mentoring to small businesses at the local level. SMEs are often located in lagging regions (Figure 2.13). Building on the existing local business centres and contact points for EU funds, at the municipal or regional level, local support institutions could be strengthened. Such practices have been experienced for the development of business services centres in some medium-sized cities (Radom, Tarnów, Elbląg and Chełm) to help promote their attractiveness (MR, 2019c). To avoid making such centres excessively dependent on local budgets, some national financing from an earmarked subsidy of the state budget could facilitate cooperation between firms and local institutions.

Box 2.4. Main institutions supporting SMEs and their internationalisation

The Polish Agency for Enterprise Development (PARP)

The Polish Agency for Enterprise Development (PARP) manages a wide range of instruments and programmes designed to support business development, innovation and SMEs:

- During the 2014-20 financial perspective for European Funds, PARP has been providing financial instruments to help SMEs in the promotion of product brands, support SMEs' internationalisation in Eastern Poland and promote the internationalisation of "National Key Clusters" (KKK). In 2020-22, new industry promotion programs have also been introduced.
- In 2018, it launched the SMEs' Development Centre. This web portal offer information and consulting services to SMEs.
- In 2019, to help small and young companies in gathering capital for their development, PARP introduced a new development loan for micro and small companies. The loan can be used for purchase and delivery of new fixed assets, purchase of software, integration of purchased software with an existing machine park or IT system.
- PARP also finances investment in management skills through a human resources programme co-funding training with firms, as well as the innovation manager academy, and a range of programme designed at boosting SME's innovativeness (Box 2.5).

The Polish Investment and Trade Agency (PAIH)

The Polish Investment and Trade Agency (PAIH) supports both the foreign expansion of Polish business and the inflow of FDI into Poland. Actions targeted towards SMEs include:

- A network of Foreign Trade Offices that are responsible for providing free-of-charge support for exporters and investors abroad.
- The 2018 Tech Bridges project, funded by the European Regional Development Fund, which supports foreign expansion of start-ups and SMEs with high potential.
- Networking events: in 2018, PAIH organised the first Support Forum for Polish Business Abroad - PAIH Expo - for SMEs which planned to or had already been pursuing foreign expansion. The event presented public services supporting participation in foreign markets.

The state-owned development bank (BGK)

The national promotional and development bank (BGK) promotes entrepreneurship and the development of micro companies and SMEs by offering guarantees, surety instruments, as well as loan and equity instruments:

- To ease access to bank loans, BGK grants de minimis guarantees in cooperation with commercial banks. In co-operation with the EIB group, BGK supports SMEs by providing portfolio guarantees to commercial banks counter-guaranteed by the guarantee of the European Investment Fund.
- BGK provides trade finance instruments and direct loans for larger transactions for SMEs and larger firms. The PAE programme launched in 2017 also offers guarantee against the risk of non-payment under letter of credits from commercial banks.
- For the implementation of the 2014-20 European Structural Investment funds, BGK operates funds of funds for 15 regional and 2 national programmes. These programmes provide preferential loans, guarantees and equity instruments for SMEs through financial intermediaries to address investment and innovation needs and financing gaps, as well as the impact of the coronavirus crisis.

BGK is also in charge of the "Loan for technological innovations" for SMEs financed through European Regional Development Fund (ERDF). BGK provides non-repayable support for loans granted by commercial banks that may reach up to 70% of total eligible costs of investment.

The Export Credit Insurance Corporation (KUKE)

The company provides export credit insurance with State Treasury backing, notably for markets exposed to higher political risk. Its operations focus on insuring trade receivables arising from the sales of goods and services with deferred payment, as well as providing bonds.

Increasing skills to foster integration in global value chains

Raising skills through better life-long training

With its relatively low wage costs, Poland has increased its exports and turned itself into an attractive market for foreign investors. The workforce is increasingly educated, suggesting significant opportunities for further internationalisation. Poland foreign language skills, in particular English, are generally well ranked in international comparison and have increased rapidly (EF, 2019). Yet, the internationalisation of Polish firms tends to rely on relatively low skills and few knowledge-intensive services compared to other OECD countries. In addition, the share of adults having a high-skill level is lower than neighbouring countries and the OECD average (Figure 2.21).

A vital condition for improving SMEs internationalisation is the existence of a sufficiently large pool of workers with a high level of education and skills. Before the coronavirus crisis, the unemployment rate was at a 20-year low and business surveys indicated labour shortages as a key factor limiting production, across firm size (Figure 2.22, Panels A and B). In the short term, the education and training system will face strong needs to facilitate the reallocation of displaced workers towards sectors and firms that have high potential. In the longer term, it will be important to strengthen the skills needed for the adoption of technological innovations (OECD, 2019g; Lang and Mendez Tavares, 2018). Indeed, automation is set to affect a significant share of jobs, while population ageing is set to lower labour supply (Panels C and D).

The high rate at which skills become obsolete makes it harder for seniors to find work, whereas demographic ageing requires better employability and working conditions of older workers. According to forecasts produced by the national statistics institute, if nothing changes, the active population growth rate will be only just over half that of the total population between 2017 and 2070. Seniors will therefore have to work until later in life, which means they need to fight against stereotypes and discriminations.

Digitalisation may accelerate skill depreciation for many workers, increasing inequality. Almost 50% of jobs in Poland could become redundant or risk changing substantially due to new technologies (Figure 2.22, Panel C). Automation and digitalisation are set to further reduce demand for manual and repetitive tasks, and increase demand for interpersonal and problem-solving skills to ensure machines' and workers' complementarity (OECD, 2018c).

Figure 2.21. The share of high-skilled adults and their contribution to GVCs is low

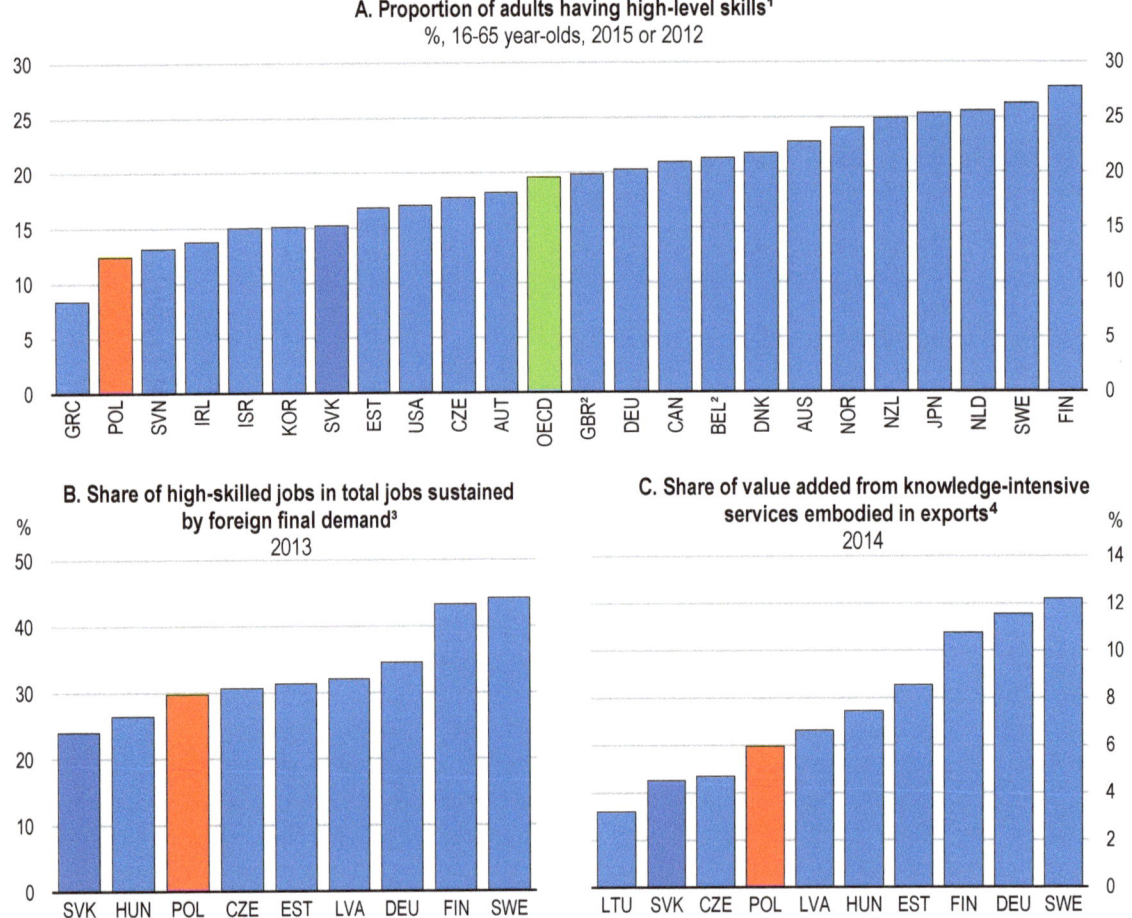

A. Proportion of adults having high-level skills[1]
%, 16-65 year-olds, 2015 or 2012

B. Share of high-skilled jobs in total jobs sustained by foreign final demand[3]
2013

C. Share of value added from knowledge-intensive services embodied in exports[4]
2014

1. Average of percentage of adults scoring at PIAAC literacy or numeracy proficiency level 4 or 5, or scoring at problem solving in technology-rich environments level 2 or 3.
2. Data for Belgium refer only to Flanders, and data for the United Kingdom refer only to England.
3. OECD calculation of the decomposition of total employment sustained by exports into three groups of skills intensity defined according to major groups of the International Standard Classification of Occupations 2008: High-skilled occupations (ISCO-08 major Groups 1 to 3), medium-skilled (4 to 7) and low-skilled (8 and 9).
4. OECD estimates based on the OECD Inter-Country Input-Output (ICIO) table and the OECD Bilateral Trade Database by Industry and End-Use (BTDIxE).
Source: OECD (2017), Education at a Glance 2017: OECD Indicators ; OECD (2017), Skills Outlook 2017: Skills and Global Value Chains; OECD/WTO (2016), Statistics on Trade in Value Added (database).

StatLink ⟶ https://doi.org/10.1787/888934209001

Enhanced lifelong learning will be essential. The percentage of adults with little education attainment has increased and participation in continuous training is relatively low, despite the estimated high returns to job related training (Fialho et al., 2019). As in many OECD countries, low-skilled, unemployed and inactive workers struggle to access training, notably formal training courses (OECD, 2017c). Despite recent improvements, namely through the European Social Fund operational programme "Knowledge Education Development", which aims at promoting lifelong learning and is regularly assessed, there is still little evaluation of the quality and effectiveness of training programmes (OECD, 2019h).

Figure 2.22. Shortages of skilled staff, demographic ageing and automation remain major issues

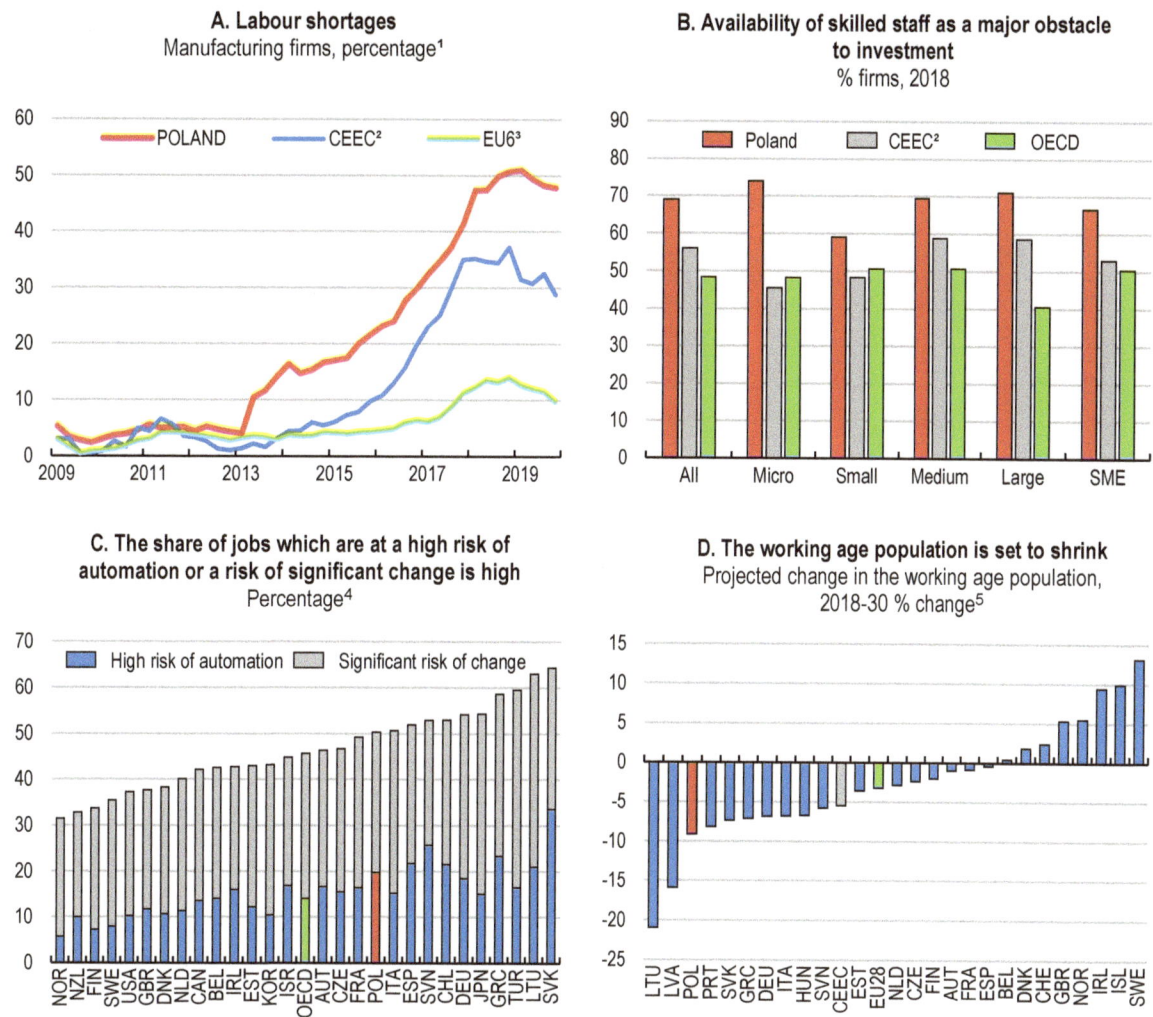

A. Labour shortages
Manufacturing firms, percentage[1]

B. Availability of skilled staff as a major obstacle to investment
% firms, 2018

C. The share of jobs which are at a high risk of automation or a risk of significant change is high
Percentage[4]

D. The working age population is set to shrink
Projected change in the working age population, 2018-30 % change[5]

1. Percentage of manufacturing firms pointing to labour shortages as a factor limiting production.
2. CEEC is the average of Hungary and the Czech and Slovak Republics. Jobs are at high risk of automation if the likelihood of their job being automated is at least 70%.
3. EU6 is the average of France, Germany, Italy, Spain, Denmark, and the Netherlands.
4. Jobs at risk of significant change are those with the likelihood of their job being automated estimated at between 50 and 70%. Data for Belgium correspond to Flanders and data for the United Kingdom to England and Northern Ireland.
5. Eurostat baseline projections including migrations, the working-age population refer to those between 15 and 64 years old.
Source: European Commission (2019), Business and consumer survey database; EIB (2019); OECD calculations based on the Survey of Adult Skills (PIAAC) (2012); and Nedelkoska, L. and G. Quintini (2018), "Automation, skills use and training", OECD Social, Employment and Migration Working Papers, No. 202, , https://doi.org/10.1787/2e2f4eea-en; Eurostat (2019), Population projections.

StatLink ᐧ https://doi.org/10.1787/888934209020

Workplace training for SMEs is particularly costly (Figure 2.24, Panel A). There is fewer staff and resources, the retention rates are low and the risk of poaching by other firms is high (OECD, 2019i). Providing additional financial support and technical assistance to SMEs would help to increase work-based learning opportunities. Financial support for the development of programmes and cost reimbursement have proved to be the most effective initiatives in improving SMEs work-based learning (Strzebońska, 2017).

Figure 2.23. Training is low and insufficiently targeted, 2016

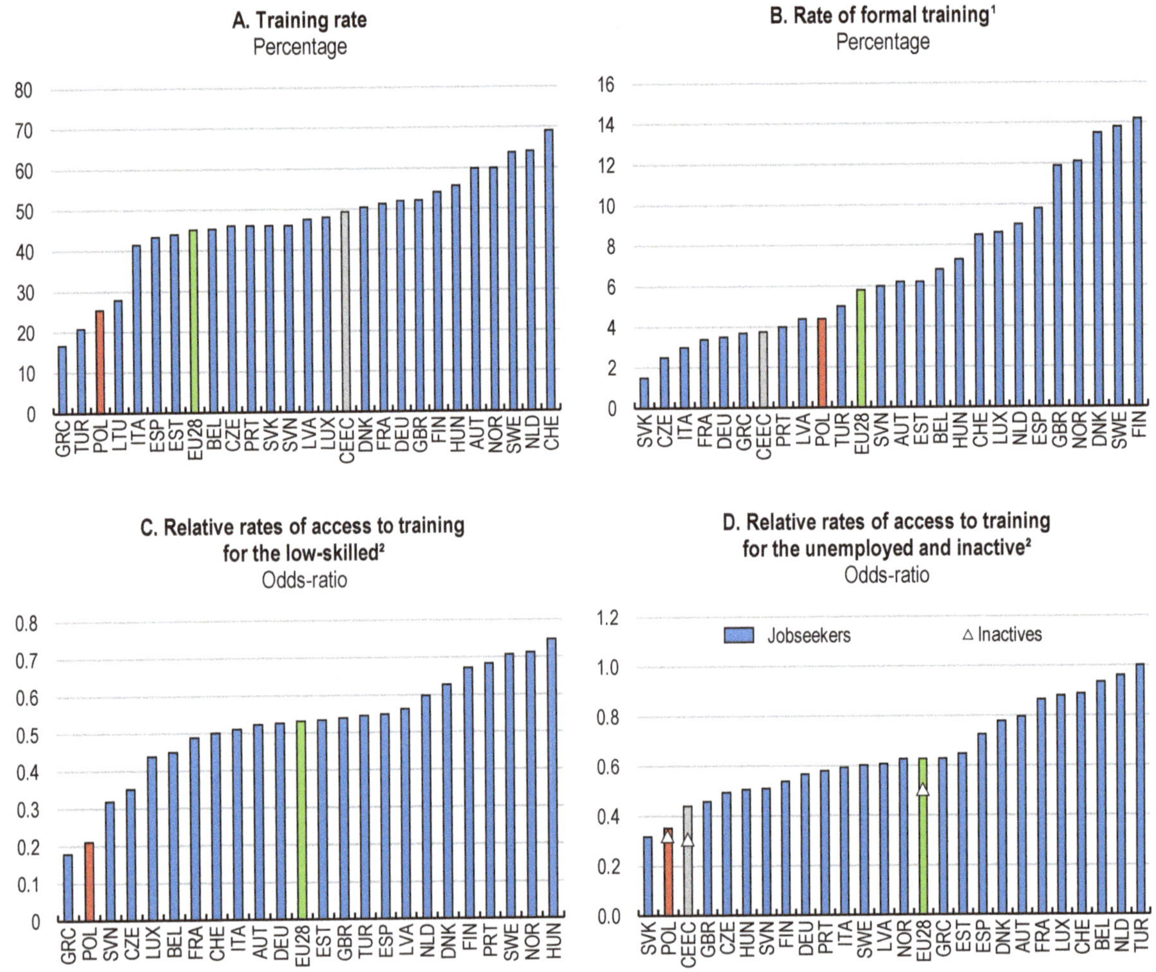

A. Training rate
Percentage

B. Rate of formal training[1]
Percentage

C. Relative rates of access to training for the low-skilled[2]
Odds-ratio

D. Relative rates of access to training for the unemployed and inactive[2]
Odds-ratio

Jobseekers   △ Inactives

1. Adults aged between 25 and 64 enrolled in education or training during the last twelve months.
2. Participation rate of adults with education up to the first cycle of secondary education (unemployed or inactive in Panel D) compared to the participation rate of all adults.
Source: Eurostat (2019), "Adult training: Participation rate in education and training", Eurostat database.

StatLink ᴍᴸ℠ https://doi.org/10.1787/888934209039

Public financing of training could offer more support for SMEs (Figure 2.24, Panel B). Co-financing of employees' training is mainly provided through the National Training Fund (NTF) and European funds. Any enterprise can apply to the KFS for an 80% refund of training costs, while micro-sized enterprises can apply for 100%, up to a maximum of 300% of Poland's average monthly salary per employee. In 2017, over 18 000 enterprises received KFS funds, half of which were micro-sized enterprises. However, uptake of the KFS has been limited and many applications are unsuccessful. In 2017, 32% of KFS applications were unsuccessful, because the funds were exhausted (OECD, 2019i).

Another important factor is the lack of awareness of current arrangements for work-based learning (OECD, 2019h). In addition, the available information often uses too technical and complicated language (Strzebońska, 2017). Workshops' and focus groups' participants confirmed that financial and informational barriers prevent SMEs from engaging in work-based learning. Poland could benefit from the experiences of other OECD countries in improving SMEs' participation in work-based learning (Box 2.5). For example, the Polish Agency for Enterprise Development (PARP) should continue to improve the Database of Development Services (BUR), which is widely used by SMEs, to make the portal more user-friendly and comprehensive in terms of the programmes included, user satisfaction data, career and development counselling, recognition of prior learning and available public funding (OECD, 2019h and Box 2.6).

Conditions to access training should be adapted to support the unemployed and non-standard workers. Though Public employment services (PES) focus on supporting unemployed people in adapting their skills to new labour market needs, they have limited funding and staffing (OECD, 2018a). The rapid turnover of workers on temporary contracts does not incentivise training participation. Adopting individual training accounts, as in France, would make the training rights "portable" from one job or employment status to another, and potentially improve access to lifelong learning for low-skilled workers. Yet, this would also require improved access to effective information and guidance to be fully effective (OECD, 2019j).

Box 2.5. Boosting SMEs participation in adult learning, international examples

Training associations in Switzerland

In Switzerland, the government established vocational training associations (Lehrbetriebsverbünde) in 2004. These associations of two or more training firms share apprentices, whose training is organised across several firms on a rotating basis. The aim is to enable the engagement of firms that lack the capacity and resources to provide the full training of an apprentice, and to lower the financial and administrative burden on individual firms. The Confederation subsidises the associations with initial funding during the first three years for marketing, administrative and other costs necessary to set up the joint training programme. After this initial support, the training associations are supposed to be financially independent. An evaluation found that the majority of firms participating in training associations would not have engaged in training otherwise.

Support for SMEs' training in Flanders (Belgium)

The SME Wallet (KMO-portefeuille) is targeted exclusively at SMEs and is designed to help them grow and become more competitive through training and advisory services. The SME Wallet covers 20-30% of training costs, depending on the size of the enterprise, with a maximum budget of EUR 7,500 per year. SMEs can apply for subsidies online to receive a direct transfer. Employers determine their own training needs and there is no targeting element (OECD, 2017[6]). A recent impact assessment determined that participating firms achieved higher growth than a control group.

Source: OECD (2019), OECD Skills Strategy Poland: Assessment and Recommendations, OECD Skills Studies, OECD Publishing, Paris, https://doi.org/10.1787/b377fbcc-en; OECD (2019), OECD Skills Strategy Flanders: Assessment and Recommendations, OECD Skills Studies, OECD Publishing, Paris, https://doi.org/10.1787/9789264309791-en. Kuczera M., V. Kis and G. Wurzburg (2009), OECD Reviews of Vocational Education and Training: A Learning for Jobs Review of Korea 2009, https://doi.org/10.1787/9789264113879-en.

Figure 2.24. Public funding for training is low and small firms provide low access to training

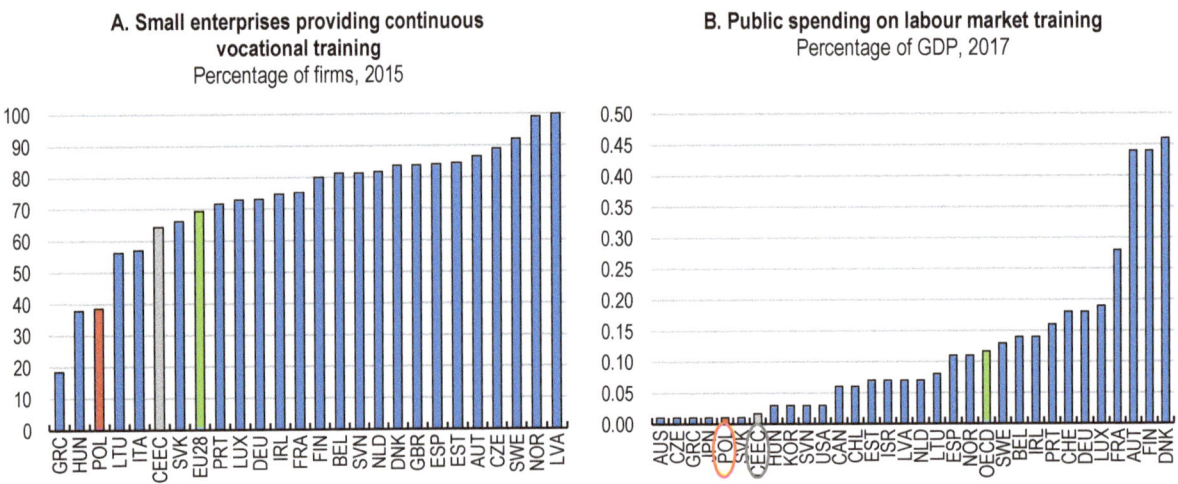

Note: Continuing vocational training (CVT) are training measures or activities which have as their primary objectives the acquisition of new competences or the development and improvement of existing ones and which must be financed at least partly by the enterprises for their persons employed who either have a working contract or who benefit directly from their work for the enterprise such as unpaid family workers and casual workers.
Source: OECD (2019) Employment and Labour Market Statistics: Labour market programmes: expenditure and participants ; Eurostat (2019), Continuing vocational training in enterprises database.

StatLink https://doi.org/10.1787/888934209058

Supporting better management skills for SMEs

Many SMEs do not have strong human resource infrastructures to implement training policies and, more generally, internationalisation and growth strategies. A number of studies shows that management skills can be improved, with positive effects on internationalisation (Figure 2.25; Bloom et al., 2018). As in other CEE countries, SMEs with a structure that is favourable to innovation and its diffusion are underrepresented (Lorenz and Potter, 2019). The limited number of highly skilled managers is considered one of the main barriers to growth, and the lack of support from management is a barrier to innovation (Zadura-Lichota, 2015) including the adoption of digital tools (see below) or efficient energy management process (Chapter 1). For example, high-performance workplace practices are less frequent in medium than large companies (PARP, 2019b; OECD, 2017a).

New initiatives have contributed to develop managerial skills in SMEs at different stages of business expansion, notably to access foreign markets (Box 2.6). Yet, the government could play a stronger role in disseminating high-performing organisational and management practices. Another step would be to adopt such practices in public administrations and the numerous government-owned enterprises (Figure 2.14), with potential spillovers to the private sector (OECD, 2019i).

Several OECD countries, including Australia, the Netherlands, New Zealand and Sweden have implemented programmes to improve the managerial and organisational performance of firms. For example, the Finnish Workplace Development Programme (TYKE from 1996 to 2003, TYKES from 2004 to 2010, thereafter Liideri) aimed to disseminate new work and management practices, and to develop a "learning organisation" culture to counter sluggish productivity growth in many traditional industries. Networks played an increasing role and there was a strong emphasis on disseminating good practices and mutual learning. Qualitative evaluations suggest that the programmes did promote workplace innovation and productivity. Coaching, promoting best practices and disseminating these through the creation of networks of firms are also common features of other countries' programmes (OECD, 2019j).

Building on these international practices and the assessment of its own initiatives, the Polish authorities could consider establishing a co-operation network to identify and disseminate best practices for stimulating a learning culture in the workplace. Employers, unions and sectoral training providers, with support from the government, could establish this network. The chambers of commerce and group-based interventions can be particularly important, especially SMEs, to share good management practices (Lacovone et al., 2019).

Figure 2.25. Management skills appear lagging, notably for domestic firms

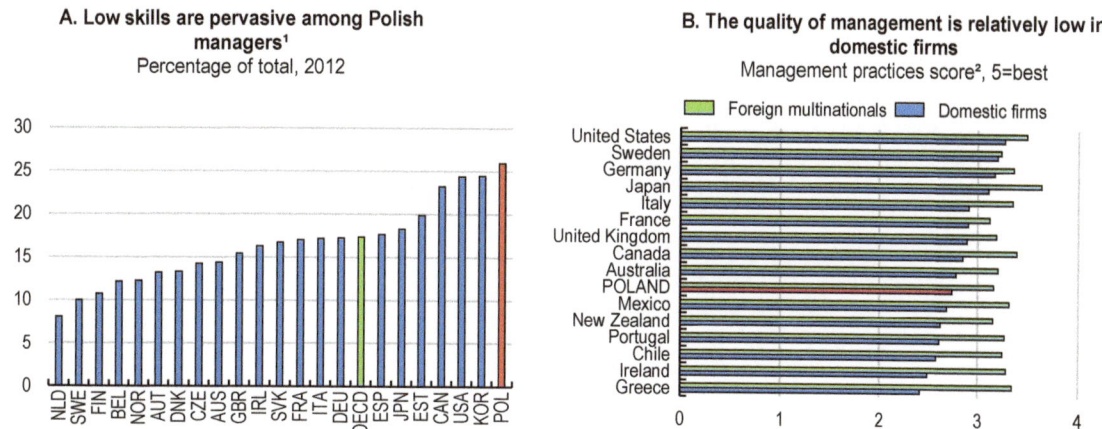

A. Low skills are pervasive among Polish managers[1]
Percentage of total, 2012

B. The quality of management is relatively low in domestic firms
Management practices score[2], 5=best

1. Share of managers with at least upper secondary education scoring below level 2 in at least one of the PIAAC proficiency scales, i.e. literacy, numeracy and problem-solving in technology-rich environments.
2. Scores are a measure of management practices across 5 key areas of management: operations management, performance monitoring, target setting, leadership management and talent management. Scores are scaled from 1 (worst practice) to 5 (best practice), 2012-2015.
Source: OECD (2013), OECD Skills Outlook 2013 (database); N. Bloom, C. Genakos, R. Sadun and J. Van Reenen (2012), "Management practices across firms and countries", NBER Working Paper, No. 17850.

StatLink 🔗 https://doi.org/10.1787/888934209077

Facilitating the immigration of skilled workers

Facilitating the immigration of skilled workers could play an important role in overcoming local skills shortages and improving SMEs' internationalisation. Immigrants' country and language knowledge may reduce uncertainty and improve the governance of foreign operations (Ottaviano et al., 2018). Over recent years, immigrants from Ukraine and other neighbouring countries have contributed to a surge in labour supply. They reached an estimated 5% of the Polish labour force in 2016, and their inflow helped cushion the decline in the working-age population that started in 2011.Immigration had an estimated contribution of about 11% of Poland's economic growth over 2013-18 (Growiec et al., 2019). Yet, most Ukrainian migration is still short term and such strong migration inflows are unlikely to become permanent, leaving SMEs and other firms with potential large skill shortages in the medium term.

To improve Poland's attractiveness as a workplace for third-country nationals, a clear migration strategy should be finalised. Such strategy should help to better monitor the labour market integration of foreigners and protect their rights, namely access to education and training for them and their children (OECD, 2018a). It is also necessary to increase the provision of legal stay and work to citizens from other countries: the current administrative procedures are not adapted to cope with the rapidly growing number of foreigners coming to Poland. The timing to process applications for resident permits has increased more than threefold: from 64 to 206 days over the last four years (NIK, 2019). There are common guidelines for applicants, but extending permits' period of validity could also help reduce the congestion. Updating and enforcing anti-discrimination policies, taking into account labour and housing markets barriers for immigrants, would help to confront ethnicity and nationality-based discriminations (UN, 2019).

At the same time, the government should continue to strengthen ties with the large expatriate community. In particular, as the United Kingdom prepares to exit the European Union, further efforts to attract Polish workers who have migrated to the United Kingdom could be envisaged. Returning emigrants could bring skills, networks and financial capital (Brandt, 2016). Many OECD countries provide online hubs for their citizens abroad advertising jobs, training, and business and research opportunities at home (OECD, 2013; DFA, 2015). A job fair was recently organised in London and the authorities also created a website that offers some guidance to Polish workers abroad. In addition, the authorities could consider the development of a diaspora skills database to directly connect potential returning migrants with employers, as done in Portugal with the "Global Professional Mobility Platform". Tailored counselling and general assistance related to employment, housing, education and administrative procedures to start a small business, as the Irish "Back to Business" mentoring programme, have also proved quite effective (EC, 2014).

Harnessing the benefits of digitalisation to support SMEs' exports

Poland's transition to a digital economy is lagging compared to similar economies (Figure 2.26). The diffusion of advanced digital technologies is limited, particularly for SMEs (Figure 2.27). Yet, there is evidence that firms using online tools are more likely to export to more countries and obtain larger shares of turnovers from exports (OECD, 2019k). Developing the use of high-performing digital tools would stimulate productivity and employment, particularly for start-ups (DeStefano et al., 2019). There is also evidence that access to high-speed internet would increase the ability of firms to find the right business partners abroad and import goods that meet their needs (Malgouyres et al., 2019).

Figure 2.26. Poland's digital transition has been relatively lagging

A. Digital economy and society indicator (DESI¹) and GDP per capita

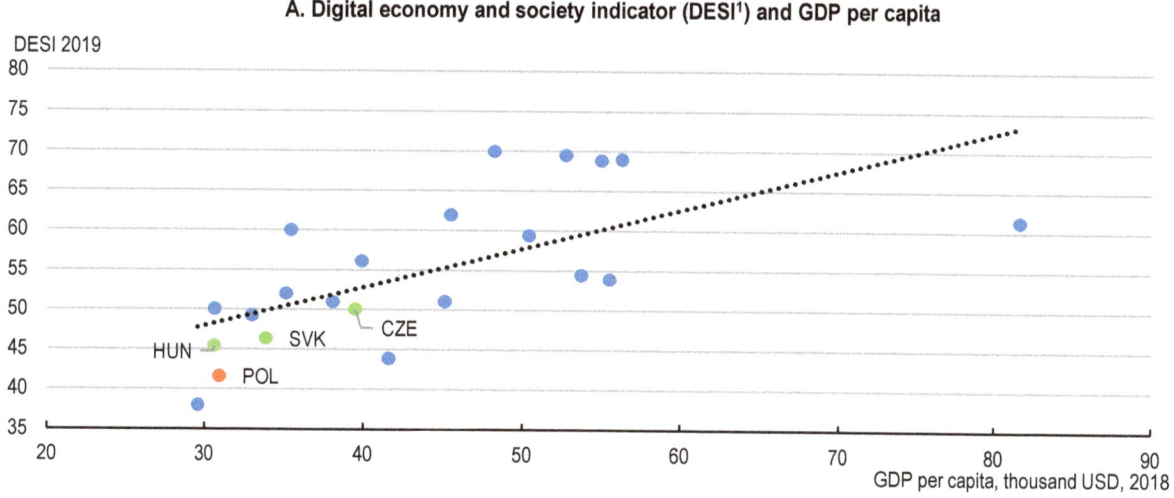

B. Value added by information industries², 2016
As a percentage of total value added

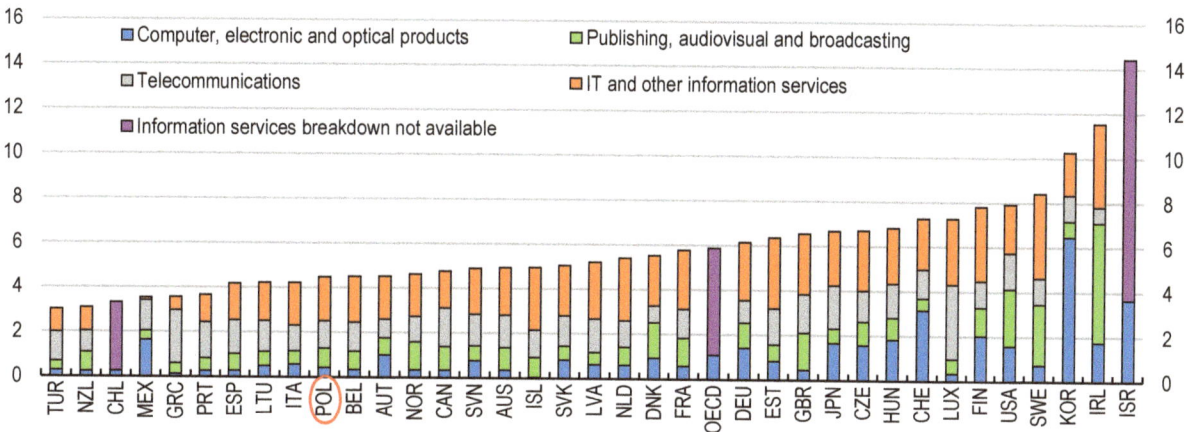

1. The Digital Economy and Society Index (DESI) is a composite index by the European Commission based on i) the deployment of broadband infrastructure and its quality; ii) endowment with ICT skills; iii) the variety of activities performed by citizens online; iv) the digitalisation of businesses and in particular SMEs; and v) the digitalisation of public services.
2. Information industries cover the following ISIC Rev.4 Divisions: Computer, electronic and optical products (26); Publishing, audiovisual and broadcasting (58 to 60); Telecommunications (61) and IT and other information services (62, 63). For Latvia, New Zealand, Poland, Portugal, Spain, Sweden and Turkey, the value added shares refer to 2015.
Source: European Commission, Digital Economy and Society Index (DESI) 2019; OECD (2019), National Accounts Statistics (database); and OECD (2019), Measuring Digital Transformation.

StatLink https://doi.org/10.1787/888934209096

Poland is stepping up efforts to promote the use of digital public services, which can help stimulate digitalisation. Poland also performs well in terms of its open data policy relative to many EU countries (EC, 2019c). Yet, key challenges to digitalisation remain. The authorities need to facilitate the rollout of high-quality digital infrastructure, encourage the uptake of digital tools by SMEs and boost ICT skills.

Developing high-quality digital infrastructure

High-quality digital infrastructure is a necessary condition to reap the full benefits of digitalisation and speed up firms' internationalisation. Poland's National Broadband Plan (*Naradowy Plan Szerokopasmowy*) aims at a full coverage of high-speed broadband internet (of at least 30 Mb/s) by the end of 2020 and its 2020 update define targets of higher speeds (of at least 100 Mb/s) as well as 5G connectivity in large cities by 2025. The "Digital Poland" programme, which is predominantly financed from EU structural funds, supports access to fast broadband in rural areas (EUR 2.5 bn or 0.5% of 2018 GDP). In addition, the authorities have set up a new national Broadband Fund in 2020 to accelerate the deployment of high-speed broadband in rural areas (PLN 140 million per year or 0.01% of 2018 GDP).

Figure 2.27. SMEs lag in the adoption of more sophisticated digital technologies

Enterprises using cloud computing services, by firm size, as a percentage of enterprises in each employment size class, 2018 or latest year available

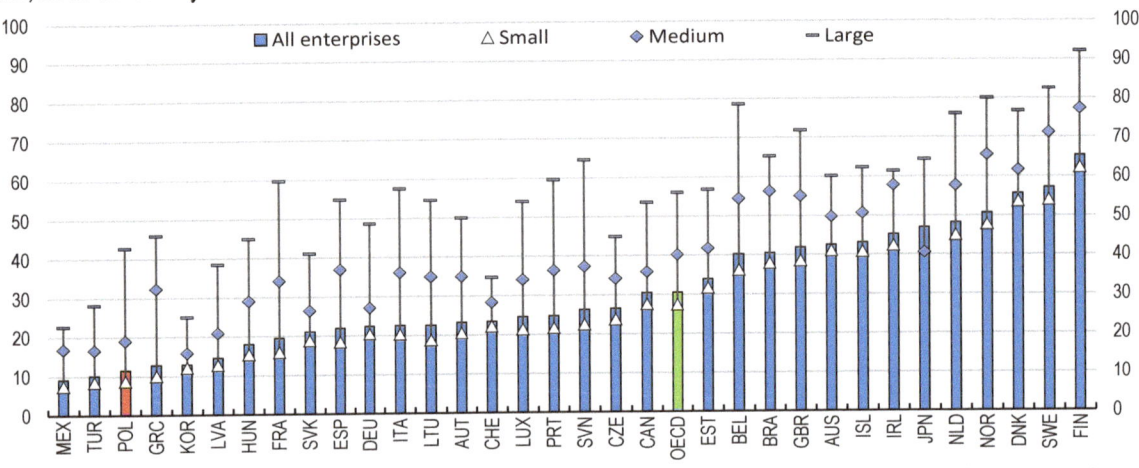

Note: Cloud computing refers to ICT services used over the Internet as a set of computing resources to access software, computing power, storage capacity and so on. Data refer to manufacturing and non-financial market services enterprises with ten or more persons employed, unless otherwise stated. Size classes are defined as: small (10-49 persons employed), medium (50-249) and large (250 and more).
Source: OECD (2019), ICT Access and Usage by Businesses (database).

StatLink ᵐˢᴸ https://doi.org/10.1787/888934209115

Poland's access to fast broadband has improved rapidly and the 2020 update of the National Broadband Plan is aligned with the European Commission's Digital Agenda for Europe. Yet, the deployment, access and use of very-fast broadband networks remain hampered by remaining regulatory barriers that are not conducive to private investment in higher-speed networks. In particular, Poland is still far from having achieved the foreseen connectivity of at least 30Mb/s for its whole population in 2020 (EC, 2020desi).

Restrictive regulations and the high cost of providing services in some geographical areas have hindered the rollout of high-quality digital infrastructure. Until January 2020 and the "Mega-Act" on broadband roll-out, some local governments could demand hefty rental fees for the use of roads to set up digital infrastructure. Fees levied by local authorities have then be capped, a new Broadband Fund was created (see above), the monitoring of the existing infrastructure has improved and rules for building access have been amended. New welcome regulations have also aimed at making the usage limits of electromagnetic fields more flexible in 2019. Indeed, the strict electromagnetic field levels in Poland and the challenging spectrum coordination with neighbouring non-EU countries have also created barriers to digital investment (EC, 2017; 2020desi). Moreover, as other European countries, Poland had to postpone the assignment of the 5G spectrum auctions due to the coronavirus pandemic. To remove remaining obstacles to private investment, more could be done to ease regulation and reduce uncertainty in spectrum auctions by developing robust auction rules (Figure 2.28; EC, 2019c).

OECD ECONOMIC SURVEYS: POLAND 2020 © OECD 2020

Adequate regulation can help promote private investment in digital infrastructure and expand coverage. Poland's telecommunications regulator, UKE, regularly intervenes to settle disputes over access to land and buildings, while preventing the need to duplicate infrastructure by different operators (UKE, 2019). To more systematically address these concerns, the German authorities introduced regulation to make it mandatory to lay fibre optic cables in the construction of new roads and it is already mandatory in Poland for the construction of new buildings. Poland could expand this requirement to speed up the deployment of fibre. Promoting further infrastructure sharing and the co-ordination of civil works between communication and utility operators can reduce costs for network and services providers, while promoting the development of new and innovative services for end users (OECD, 2019l). Co-investment arrangements are in place in countries such as the Netherlands, Spain and Switzerland to overcome large capital expenditures and share risks (OECD, 2019m).

Figure 2.28. Barriers to the deployment of digital infrastructure are elevated

Digital Services Trade Restrictiveness Index, 2018

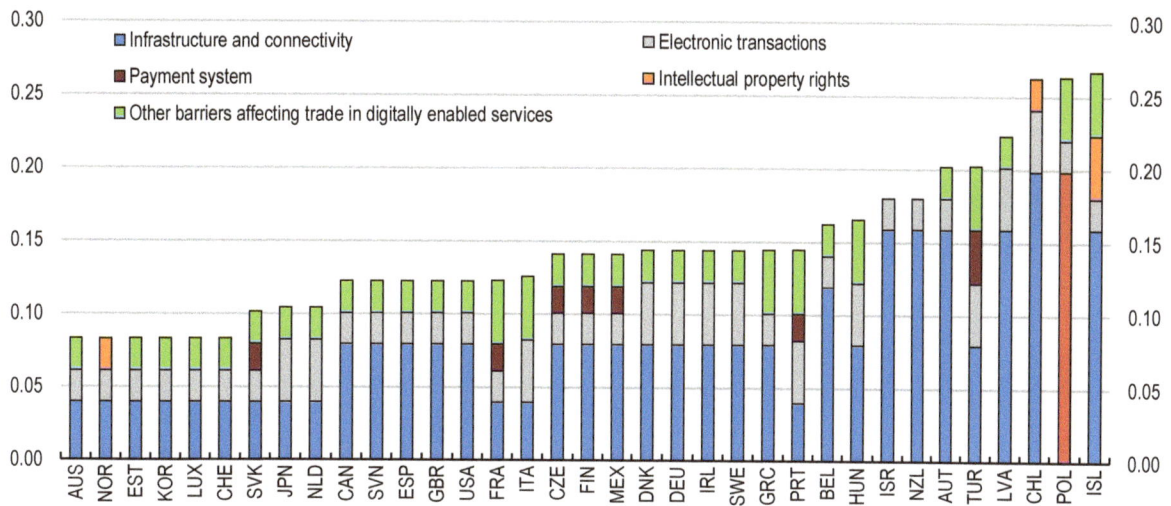

Source: OECD (2019), *Digital Services Trade Restrictiveness Index* (database).

StatLink 🔢 https://doi.org/10.1787/888934209134

Improving end-users information regarding broadband performance would strengthen incentives for private operators to upgrade the quality of their network. Broadband speed in Poland is broadly in line with the OECD average, but coverage of rural areas is weaker than in the average EU country (Figure 2.29). Beyond efforts to improve broadband networks and speed-up the deployment of high-speed mobile broadband, effective monitoring of broadband performance is key, since download speeds advertised by telecommunication operators may differ markedly from actual download speeds experienced by end-users. UKE provides information about broadband performance of the different operators, such as coverage and speed. It also certified an end-user mechanism that is available through applications to measure the speed of data transmission for fixed-line transmission in 2018. Yet, it could do more to provide timely information on broadband performance. The National Information Society Agency in Korea is a good example of an agency providing high quality information on broadband performance to end-users, reflecting official testing by regulators, self-evaluation by operators and quality evaluation by users (OECD, 2019l). Monitoring alternative metrics to evaluate broadband reliability such as latency – that is, the round-trip time for information between two devices of the network – will be necessary, since the latest digital applications require ultra-reliable broadband (OECD, 2019n).

Figure 2.29. The quality of Poland's digital network needs to improve further

A. Average experienced download speed of fixed broadband connections, 2018
Ookla and M-lab measurements

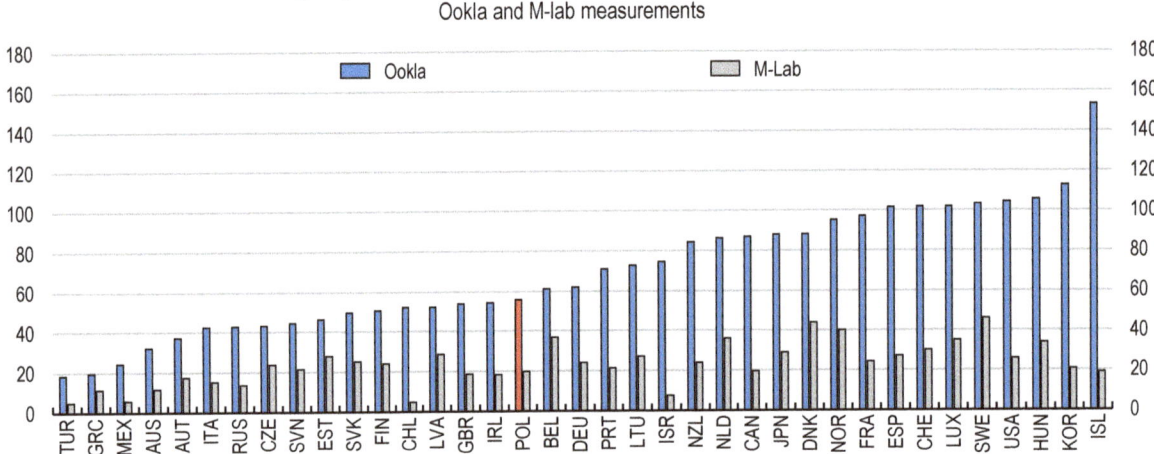

B. Households in areas where fixed broadband with a contracted speed of 30 Mbps or more is available, 2017
As a percentage of households in each category

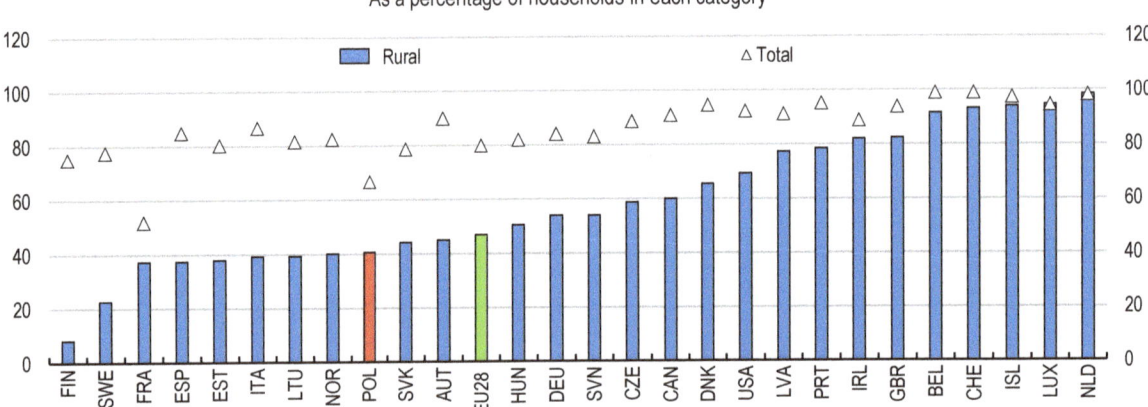

Source: OECD (2019), Measuring the Digital Transformation 2019, based on Ookla, October 2018 and M-Lab (Worldwide broadband speed league) as measured between June 2017 and May 2018; and OECD (2019), Measuring the Digital Transformation 2019, based on CRTC, Communications Monitoring Report, 2017 (Canada); EC, Study on Broadband Coverage in Europe 2017 (European Union) and FCC, 2018 Broadband Deployment Report (United States).

StatLink 🔗 https://doi.org/10.1787/888934209153

Using and sharing big data between private and public sectors could help boosting the internationalisation and productivity of SMEs, as well as the development of new products, processes and organisational methods, notably through artificial intelligence and the Internet of Things. Access to data is crucial for competition and innovation in the digital economy (OECD, 2019o). Poland has made significant progress and ranks above the OECD average in terms of Open Government Data according to the OECD Open Useful Re-Usable data (OURdata) Index (OECD, 2019p). Yet, Polish SMEs still lag behind larger firms and SMEs in other European countries (Eurostat, 2020). Fixed costs and sometimes excessively restrictive access to data could partly explain this low take-up. Supporting the development of public data hubs and e-health could be encouraged further, while limiting the associated risks (Box 2.7). This would require bolstering SMEs' capacity in terms of data and cyber security (see below).

> ## Box 2.7. Good practices for enhancing data sharing and access
>
> The OECD (2019a) has identified four approaches to enhancing data access and sharing, while balancing the benefits of "openness" with the risks; reinforcing trust and empowering users; and developing sustainable business models. These approaches are the following:
>
> * Open data is the most frequently used approach for public sector data, though legitimate private and public interests may justify more restrictive approaches.
> * Contractual agreements can enhance data access and sharing, especially if leveraged through data markets. Voluntary contract guidelines can reduce uncertainties and transaction costs by defining the default rights and obligations when negotiating data sharing agreements.
> * Data portability promises to empower users by giving them more control over their data, but it may also expose them to new risks, such as confidentiality breaches.
> * Restricted data-sharing arrangements are used if data are considered too confidential to be shared openly with the public or where legitimate (commercial and non-commercial) interests conflict with open sharing.
>
> There are important opportunities to use health data for improving health care quality, surveillance, management and research. But to leverage this potential while managing risks that might come from the misuse of data that are personal, appropriate governance frameworks are needed (OECD, 2017; 2019b). Poland is developing integrated patient information and e-health solutions such as e-prescriptions and e-referrals (OECD, 2019c). Yet, further efforts could boost the use of these data. For example, the French government announced the creation of a Health Data Hub in 2019, with an expanded set of information, and enhanced regulated access to the datasets. The first selected projects included public institutions, start-ups and larger firms (MSS, 2019)
>
> Source: OECD (2019a), Enhancing Access to and Sharing of Data: Reconciling Risks and Benefits for Data Re-use across Societies, OECD Publishing, Paris; OECD (2019b), Using Routinely Collected Data to Inform Pharmaceutical Policies - Analytical Report for OECD and EU countries, OECD Publishing, Paris; OECD (2019c), Health in the 21st Century: Putting Data to Work for Stronger Health Systems, OECD Health Policy Studies, OECD Publishing, Paris; OECD (2017), Recommendation of the Council on Health Data Governance, OECD/LEGAL/0433; MSS (2019), HEALTH DATA HUB - Annonce des lauréats du premier appel à projets ; Ministère des solidarités et de la santé.

Preparing SMEs for the digital transition

Promoting SMEs' participation in e-commerce would help spur their export capacity. Available evidence suggests that digital trade is becoming increasingly important, particularly for services. In this respect, SMEs are well positioned to benefit from business-to-consumer trade (OECD, 2019k). Online commerce has expanded fast in Poland, albeit the share of Polish firms participating in e-commerce is comparatively weak (PAIH, 2019; Figure 2.30). Survey-based evidence shows that, in Poland, the export participation of large firms involved in e-commerce is in line with the EU average, but lower in the case of smaller firms (Figure 2.31). This highlights the need to encourage the development of digital skills and the adoption of high-performance digital tools by SMEs (see below).

The development of e-commerce could expand the variety of inputs available to SMEs and encourage innovation in product distribution, while boosting cross-border online shopping. However, the emergence of dominant online platform operators can raise concerns about potentially anticompetitive behaviour and consumer protection. Such a situation can arise when a firm in a dominant position conducts business across multiple product segments and benefits from network effects and data collection advantages (OECD, 2018d). Poland's Office of Competition and Consumer Protection (UOKiK) is investigating a large e-commerce operator for discriminatory practices towards smaller and independent retailers. Moreover, the development of e-commerce heightens the need to safeguard privacy and personal data, and the OECD revised in 2016 its *Recommendations on Consumer Protection in E-commerce* (OECD, 2016b).

Figure 2.30. Participation in e-commerce is low

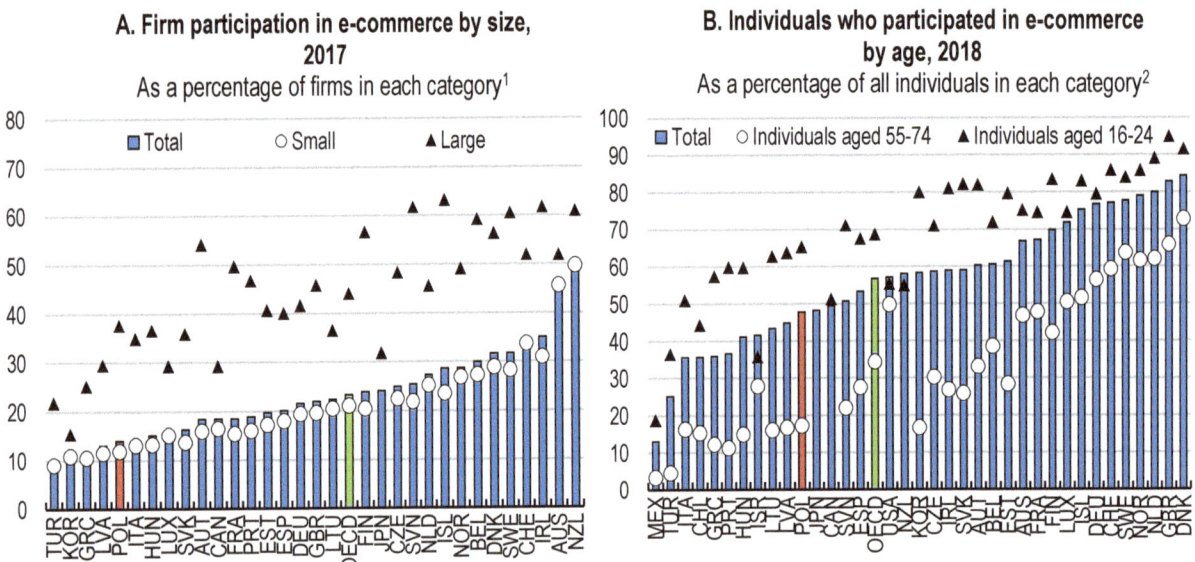

A. Firm participation in e-commerce by size, 2017
As a percentage of firms in each category[1]

B. Individuals who participated in e-commerce by age, 2018
As a percentage of all individuals in each category[2]

1. Only enterprises with 10 or more employees are considered, small firms are defined as companies with between 10 and 49 employees, and large firms as companies with 250 or more employees.
2. Data refer to the percentage of individuals that purchased online over the last 12 months.
Source: OECD (2019Unpacking), OECD calculations based on OECD (2019), *ICT Access and Usage by Businesses* and *ICT Access and Usage by Households and Individuals* (databases).

StatLink ᴹᔆᴾ https://doi.org/10.1787/888934209172

Figure 2.31. SMEs' e-commerce export participation is low

Enterprises that participated in e-commerce sales to other countries, as % of enterprises that received e-commerce orders over the last calendar year, 2016

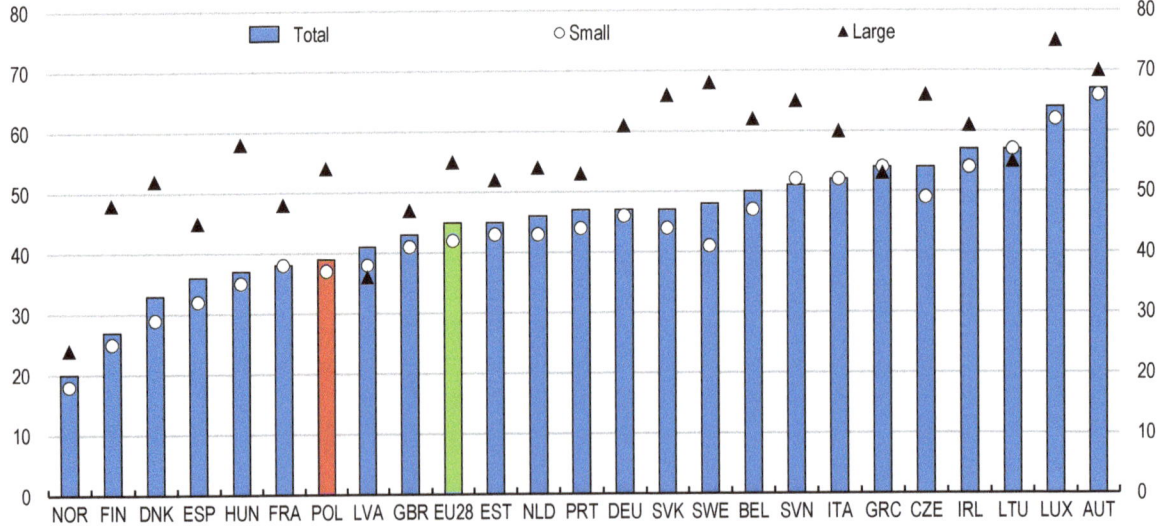

Source: OECD (2019), OECD calculations based on *Eurostat, Digital Economy and Society Statistics* (database).

StatLink ᴹᔆᴾ https://doi.org/10.1787/888934209191

Promoting digital security among SMEs would help bolstering the diffusion of digital technologies. Privacy concerns and digital security risks are often cited as barriers to the adoption of advanced digital technologies and to e-commerce participation, particularly for SMEs (OECD, 2017d). Few Polish SMEs have adopted a formally defined ICT policy (Figure 2.32, Panel A) and Poland' capacity for digital security risk management could be strengthened (Panel B). Developing reliable indicators of digital security incidents and digital risk management practice would be a good start. This would entail setting up a classification of incidents and putting in place a trusted public-private digital security incident repository (OECD, 2019l). Bolstering efforts to reach out to SMEs regarding digital security concerns would also be welcome.

Encouraging the use of ICTs by SMEs

Upgrading digital skills

Boosting workers' digital skills can help SMEs strengthen their position in global value chains (GVCs) by helping them to specialise in high-value added activities or to integrate in higher-value added segments (OECD, 2019q). Too many Poles have inadequate digital skills. According to the OECD Survey of Adult Skills, the share of adults with no computer experience is significantly above the OECD average, and Poles perform relatively poorly in ICT-related tests regardless of their educational attainment (Figure 2.33). Moreover, ICT specialists are in short supply and Polish employers face difficulties in finding ICT specialists (Cedefop, 2016).

The provision of computers per pupil is lower than in most OECD countries (OECD, 2019r) and the coronavirus epidemic has uncovered some challenges for the education system and distance learning (Gouëdard et al., 2020). Poland's National Education Network aims at connecting all schools to high-speed internet and the authorities have stepped up their efforts to increase teachers' training in ICT. In fact, developing teachers' training in ICT can encourage innovative pedagogical techniques to equip students with digital skills. Austria's "School 4.0" strategy is an example of policies aiming at developing digital competences of teachers and improving students' digital literacy (OECD, 2017e). Yet, an effective consultation with teachers is needed, since recent changes to curricula and other organisational changes to schools already require considerable efforts in teachers' training.

Boosting SMEs' involvement in the apprenticeship system, especially for professions affected by digitalisation, could help them find skilled workers. There are examples of Polish firms that strongly benefited from apprenticeship-type systems in the Łódź region or through the German-Polish Chamber of Commerce (OECD, 2018a). The authorities could build on these examples to promote the benefits from engaging into vocational education. Investing in "brokers", which aim at pooling the recruitment and placement of apprentices across SMEs, akin to Australia's Group Training Organisation, could also be helpful. Establishing training associations, as in Switzerland and Austria, would help to share the costs of organising apprenticeships among a group of SMEs (Box 2.4). The school governing authorities could consider targeted grants to encourage SMEs to offer work-based learning. The grants could vary depending on the characteristics of the learners and on their performance in final exams (OECD, 2019g).

Figure 2.32. Awareness of digital security by SMEs is weak

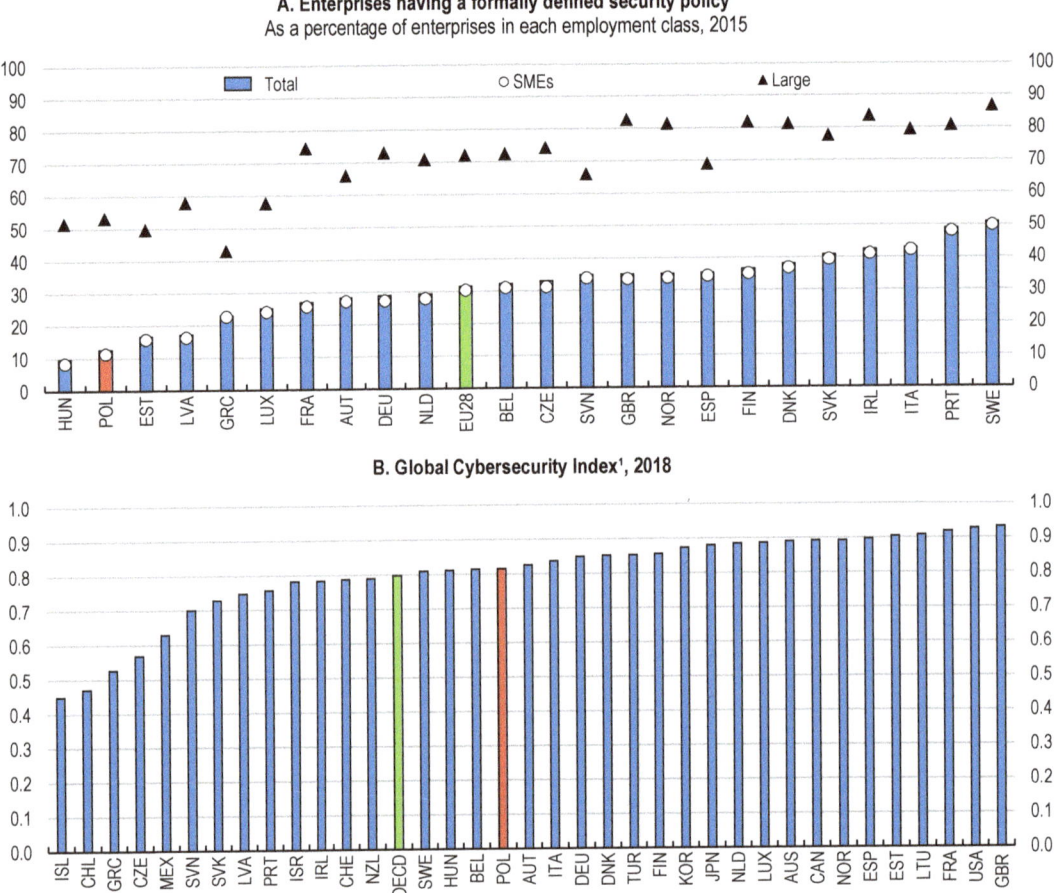

A. Enterprises having a formally defined security policy
As a percentage of enterprises in each employment class, 2015

B. Global Cybersecurity Index¹, 2018

1. The Global Cybersecurity Index is computed based on the following pillars: legal (legal institutions and frameworks dealing with cybersecurity and cybercrime); technical (technical institutions and frameworks dealing with cybersecurity); organisational (policy co-ordination institutions and strategies for cybersecurity development at the national level); capacity building (the existence of research and development, education and training programmes, as well as; certified professionals and public sector agencies fostering capacity building), and co-operation (refers to partnerships, co-operative frameworks, and information-sharing networks).
Source: OECD (2019), Measuring the Digital Transformation; and ITU (2018), Global Cybersecurity Index 2018, International Communications Unit, Geneva.

StatLink ᵐˢᵖ https://doi.org/10.1787/888934209210

SMEs' engagement in ICT training, which is among the lowest in the OECD, should also be strengthened to help lagging regions (Figure 2.34). In fact, technology-intensive firms, and the high-paying jobs that go along, are drawn to regions with high-skilled workers (OECD, 2019g). Recent initiatives include the development of sectoral skills councils to involve businesses in training institutions, including universities. The Operational Program "Digital Poland 2014-20" – with EU funds worth EUR 145 million - has helped to finance actions in these directions. The authorities are also preparing the Digital Skills Development Program 2030, with sets of actions and targets for further enhancing and developing digital skills for all firms and households. Skillsnet Ireland is an example of a training intermediary with dedicated initiatives for upskilling in the ICT sector. Providing tax credit for on-the-job training, as done in Canada (Québec), is another option. Overall, targeted public funding is likely to be necessary for the most disadvantaged groups, for example, for adults with low-incomes or recent small businesses (OECD, 2019h).

Figure 2.33. Poles lack advanced digital skills

Percentage of adults scoring high in problem solving in technology-rich environments, by educational attainment, 2015

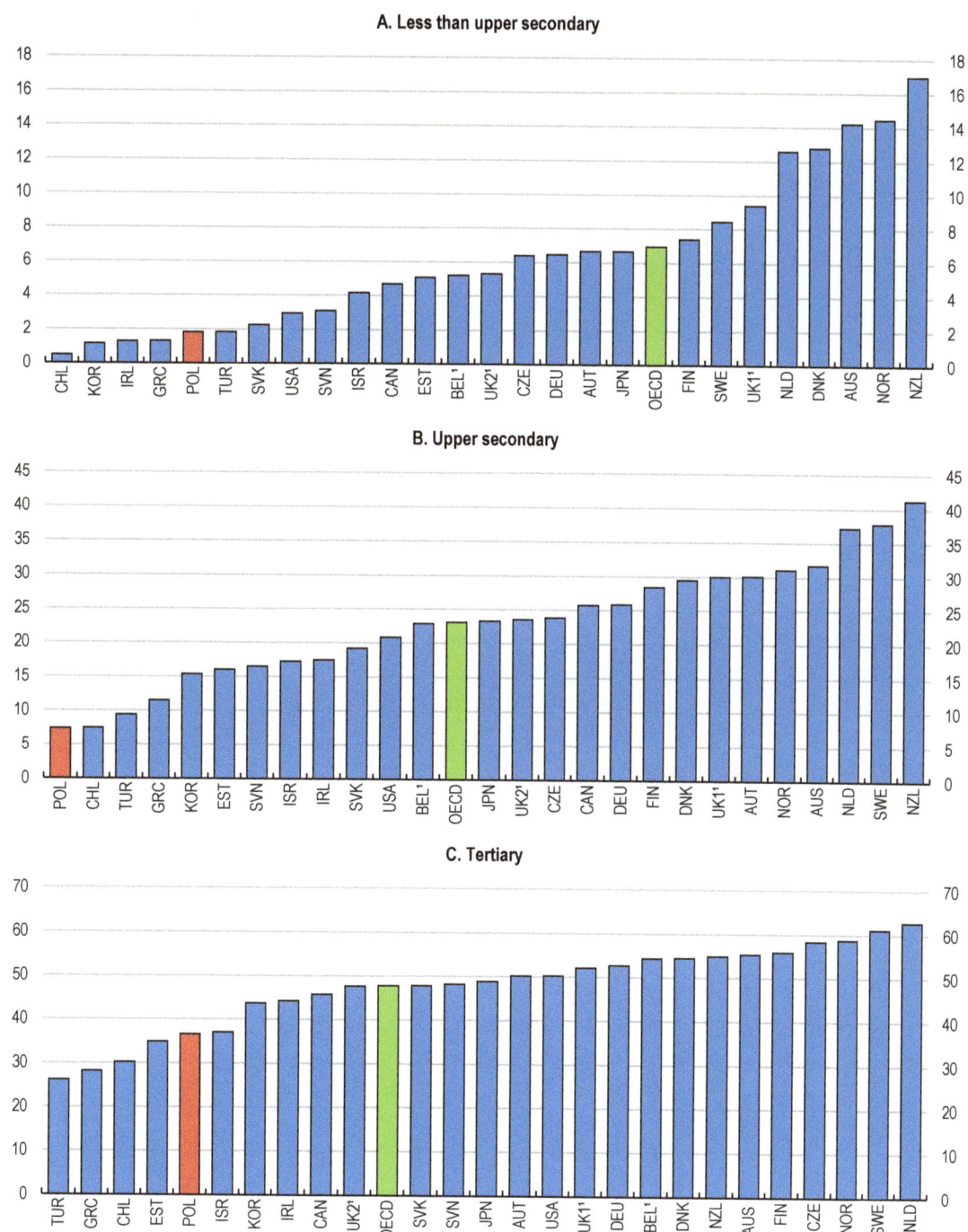

1. Flanders for Belgium (BEL), Northern Ireland (UK2) and England (UK1) for United Kingdom.
Source: OECD (2016), Survey of Adult skills (PIAAC), Table A3.2 (I) and (N).

StatLink 🔗 https://doi.org/10.1787/888934209229

104 |

Figure 2.34. Polish SMEs offer too little ICT training
Percentage of businesses providing ICT training to their employees by size class, 2018 compared to 2012

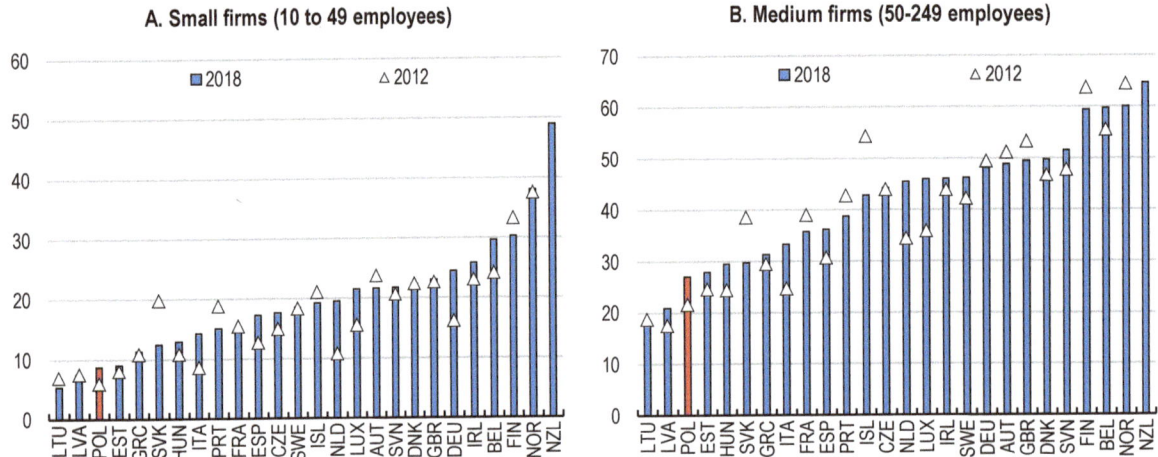

Note: Data refer to businesses with 10 or more employees that provided any type of training to develop the ICT related skills of their employees within the last 12 months. Data for New Zealand refer to 2016 and Iceland to 2014. Data for medium-sized firms in Portugal refer to 2017.
Source: OECD (2019), *ICT Access and Usage by Businesses* (database).

StatLink https://doi.org/10.1787/888934209248

Modernising SMEs' business models by promoting the diffusion of ICTs

Low managerial quality and a lack of ICT skills curb digital technology adoption with knock-on effects on productivity growth (Andrews et al., 2018). Poland's business development agency (PARP) runs different programmes for upgrading managerial skills and promoting SMEs' innovation capacity, such as the SMEs' manager academy. However, these programmes have a limited take up, reflecting a lack of awareness of existing programmes along with limited ambition from businesses. The budget available for these programmes is also low (e.g., PLN 50 million for the SMEs' manager academy programme) and is not explicitly targeted at digital technologies. Going forward, boosting efforts to raise awareness and capacity building in ICT is warranted. Germany's "trusted cloud" training is an example of a programme which helps SMEs understand the benefits of cloud computing and its possible applications.

When designing policies to encourage the adoption of advanced digital tools, the authorities should increase collaboration with firms. Strong intermediaries offering brokerage, consulting or mentoring services can help improve the take-up and effectiveness of such programmes, since complex procedures can limit take-up by SMEs (OECD, 2018a). Against this backdrop, the authorities are launching "Digital Technology Hubs" to promote digital innovation and knowledge transfer to SMEs. Previous attempts to develop clusters have been hampered by weak ties with established research and training institutions, poor governance and lack of clear objectives. To get the most of the new "Digital Technology Hubs" programme, there should be a strong focus on identifying and overcoming obstacles specific to SMEs. Examples of clusters to foster digital innovation, knowledge transfer and help firms expand into foreign markets include Estonia's ICT Cluster and Canada's Digital Technology Supercluster.

Extending the model of regulatory sandboxes to other sectors could facilitate the experimentation of new technologies and ease the diffusion of new business models. Regulatory sandboxes provide a limited form of regulatory waiver, or flexibility for firms to test new products or business models with reduced regulatory requirements, while preserving some safeguards (e.g., to ensure appropriate consumer protection) (Planes-Satorra and Paunov, 2019). Poland had launched in late 2018 a FinTech regulatory sandbox supervised by the Polish Financial Supervision Authority (KNF) to promote innovation in financial services. However, KNF managed the selection process of firms participating in that scheme, which may potentially raise conflicts of interest if companies perceive that the financial supervisor endorses specific innovations or support some companies at the expense of others. The project has been suspended and is currently being remodelled. In this process, KNF could consider following the model chosen by Sweden's financial sector regulator (Finansinspektionen). Finansinspektionen followed a model of constant dialogue and information provided to any firms willing to benefit from the regulatory sandbox, thereby circumventing the problem of selecting firms (OECD, 2018f). Moreover, extending the regulatory sandbox approach to other heavily regulated services – e.g., health care or transport – could help promote the emergence of new goods and services.

Improving transport infrastructure to boost internationalisation

The capacity and quality of transport infrastructure need to be enhanced

Efficient infrastructures are key drivers of integration in global value chains and well-being. They notably support productivity by making it easier for individuals to participate in the labour market, while strengthening business competitiveness, trade and competition, which in turn boost investment, productivity and wages. The quality of Poland's trade and transport infrastructure is comparatively low even though cost competitiveness of international shipments is high (Figure 2.35). Improving transport infrastructure could brighten export prospects, notably for SMEs in lagging regions since regional disparities in access to transport infrastructure are sizeable.

Figure 2.35. There is room to improve trade logistics
World Bank's Logistics Performance Index[1], 2018

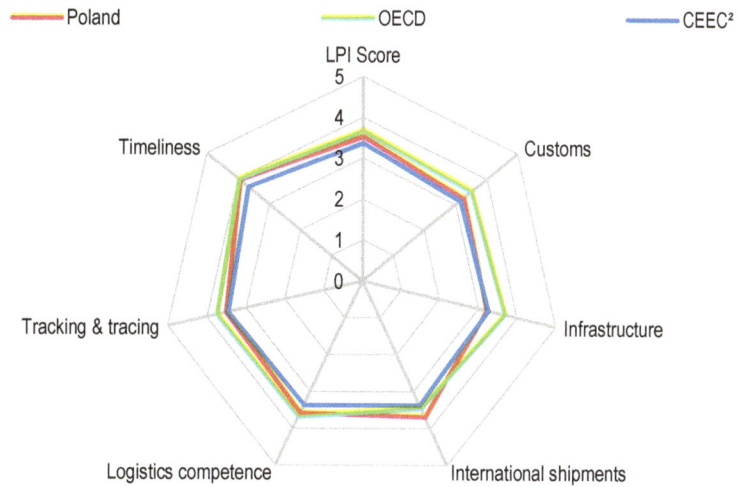

1. The logistics performance index (LPI) is a weighted average of six categories: Customs: Efficiency of the clearance process (i.e., speed, simplicity and predictability of formalities) by border control agencies, including customs; Infrastructure: Quality of trade and transport related infrastructure (e.g., ports, railroads, roads, information technology); International shipments: Ease of arranging competitively priced shipments; Logistics competence: competence and quality of logistics services (e.g., transport operators, customs brokers); Tracking and tracing: ability to track and trace consignments; Timeliness: timeliness of shipments in reaching destination within the scheduled or expected delivery time.
2. CEEC² refers to the average of Czech Republic, Hungary and the Slovak Republic.
Source: World Bank (2019), Logistics Performance Index.

StatLink ⁊⁊ISP https://doi.org/10.1787/888934209267

As in other catch-up countries, Poland makes sizeable investment in transport infrastructure, albeit it has shrunk since 2013 (Figure 2.36, Panel A) owing to the timing of disbursements of EU cohesion policy funds. The Polish expressway and motorway network remains underdeveloped compared with the average OECD country in that links to major cities have not all been completed. There are also sizeable discrepancies in transport infrastructure across regions (Panels C and D).

Figure 2.36. Investment in transport infrastructure is sizeable, but regional disparities in infrastructure are large

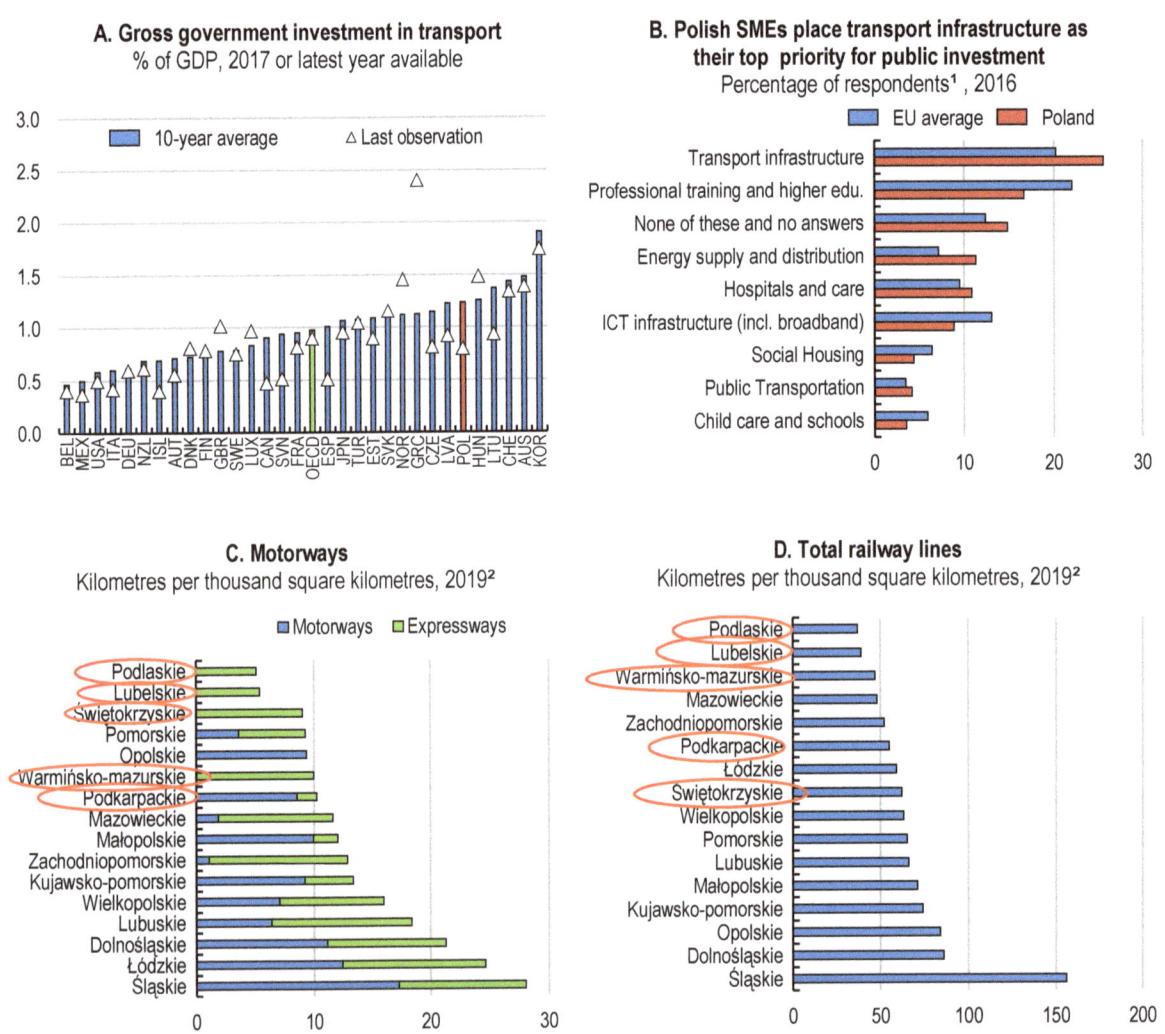

1. The question is formulated as "From your business' perspective, if you had to prioritise one area of public investment for the next 3 years, which one would it be?"
2. The five regions (voivodeships) with the lowest GDP per capita in 2017 (Podlaskie, Lubelskie, Świętokrzyskie, Warmińsko-Mazurskie, Podkarpackie) are circled in red.
Source: OECD (2019), Transport infrastructure investment and maintenance spending and National Account Statistics (databases); EIB (2017), Investment Survey, European Investment Bank, Luxembourg; and Statistics Poland (2020), Expressways and motorways per 1000 km2.

StatLink https://doi.org/10.1787/888934209286

Continuing to develop the capacity and quality of the transport network would help to reap the full benefits of Poland's participation in GVCs. Small businesses place transport as their top priority for public investment (Figure 2.36, Panel B). The coverage of public transport in large metropolitan areas is distant from the best performing European cities (ITF, 2019), pointing to investment needs in local public transport to better align the supply of labour with demand and generate sustained productivity gains. Moreover, regions (*voivodeships*) with the strongest exports as a share of GDP are clustered along the Western and South-Western Polish borders (World Bank, 2017), suggesting that enhancing transport infrastructure to lagging regions could help spur their exports. In this respect, addressing regional disparities in the access to international road connections, particularly in the north of Poland, would improve transport accessibility (EC, 2019a) with knock-on effects on the development of SMEs.

Maintenance and upgrading investments are needed to improve the quality of infrastructure

A stronger focus on the maintenance of the road network could ease internationalisation and reduce trade costs. Well-functioning logistics reduces the time, cost and uncertainty involved in importing and exporting, and Poland's trade participation would benefit from an increase in international road connections (Braconier and Pisu, 2013). The quality of Polish motorways is sound, having benefited from large investments over the last 15 years. Yet, the perceived quality of trade- and transport-related infrastructure is rather weak (Figure 2.35). This may be related to the historically low maintenance and infrastructure spending and the rapid declining of the share of maintenance spending (Figure 2.37, Panel A), as well as the road fatalities that remain high by OECD standards (Panel B; NIK, 2018b).

Figure 2.37. Increasing road maintenance spending would be a good move

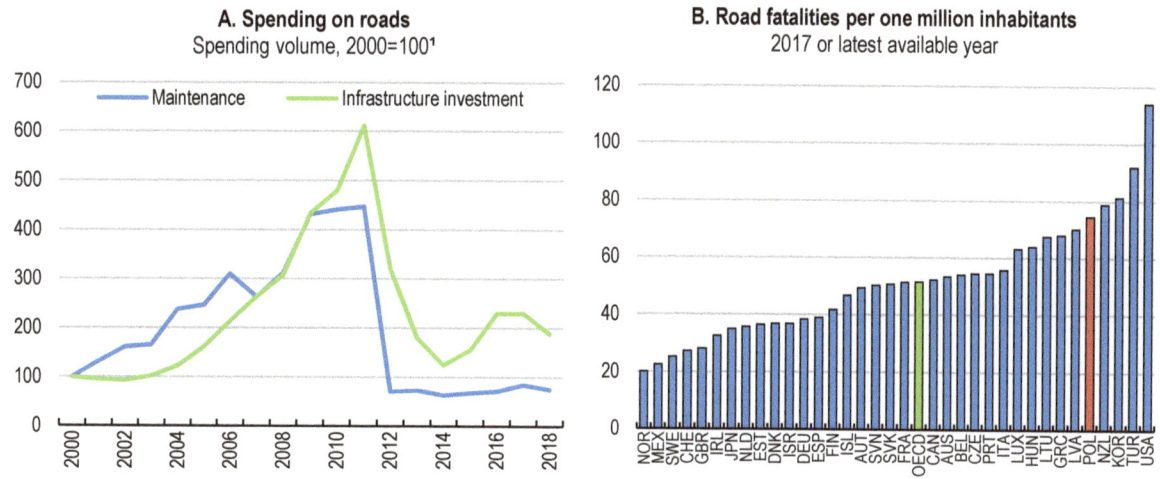

1. Deflated by the GDP deflator.
Source: OECD (2020), Transport infrastructure investment and maintenance spending (database); and OECD (2019), Transport Safety Statistics (database).

StatLink 🔗 https://doi.org/10.1787/888934209305

Tasking an agency to monitor consistently the quality of the road network, including secondary roads, would help steer maintenance spending where it is most needed. France's National Road Observatory is an example of such an institution where different stakeholders (central and local governments as well as the private sector) meet to evaluate the quality and management of the road network and share best practices. For example, Poland could task the national road authority (GDDKiA) to collect information on the state of the secondary road network, and GDDKiA could expand its efforts to reach out to local governments for transferring its expertise. Moreover, the criteria for allocating the funds from the central government to the local authorities for the construction and modernisation of the local road network (*Fundusz Dróg Samorządowych*) would benefit from being more formalised and transparent.

While in recent years the number of rail passengers has increased, there is also room to improve the quality of the rail network, notably travel times, and upgrading further the rolling stock. The density of the rail network is broadly in line with that of the average OECD country, but its quality has suffered from the priority given to road transport, hampering the efficiency of existing rail infrastructure (OECD, 2016b). Moreover, in the previous EU budgetary cycle, difficulties in the absorption of EU funds related to the weak administrative capacity of the infrastructure manager led to prioritising investments in rolling stocks rather than modernizing railway lines. Public perceptions on the quality of the rail network is low and the market share of rail in passenger transport is trending downwards even though it has increased in 2016-17.

The modernisation of railway infrastructure would benefit from a more efficient procurement process. A strong pick-up in demand for labour and raw materials towards the end of the EU cohesion funding cycle

108 |

is increasing costs in the construction sector, hampering the efficient delivery of new or modernized railway lines, and creating challenges for SMEs. To address cost overruns in the delivery of rail infrastructure, the authorities revised criteria in public procurement and the documentation of tenders. Putting in place a system similar to Norway's "quality assurance process" for large transport projects whereby external consultants are hired to assess the accuracy of cost estimates could be helpful to limit cost overruns and improve infrastructure outcomes (Odeck et al., 2015). A stronger focus on the maintenance and upgrading of rail infrastructure would also require stepping up the monitoring of the quality of the rail network to best prioritize spending (NIK, 2018c).

Investment in transport should better reflect environmental concerns

Stepping up maintenance and upgrading investment in the rail network is needed. Over recent year most of new international trade in goods occurred through roads (Statistics Poland, 2019). While international road transport of goods doubled since 2010, rail freight activity has been stagnant (Figure 2.38). The weak performance of rail freight transport reflects the insufficient adjustment of the rail infrastructure to transport needs, low speed and the low priority order granted to freight trains. Beyond investments for upgrading the quality of the network, ensuring a fair and non-discriminatory access to the rail infrastructure for the non-incumbent freight operators is also important to foster competition (European Court of Auditors, 2016). Moreover, expanding the coverage of the heavy vehicle fee for trucks – which only covers 15% of the Polish territory – would help stimulate the competitiveness of rail freight transport.

Figure 2.38. Rail freight transport needs a boost

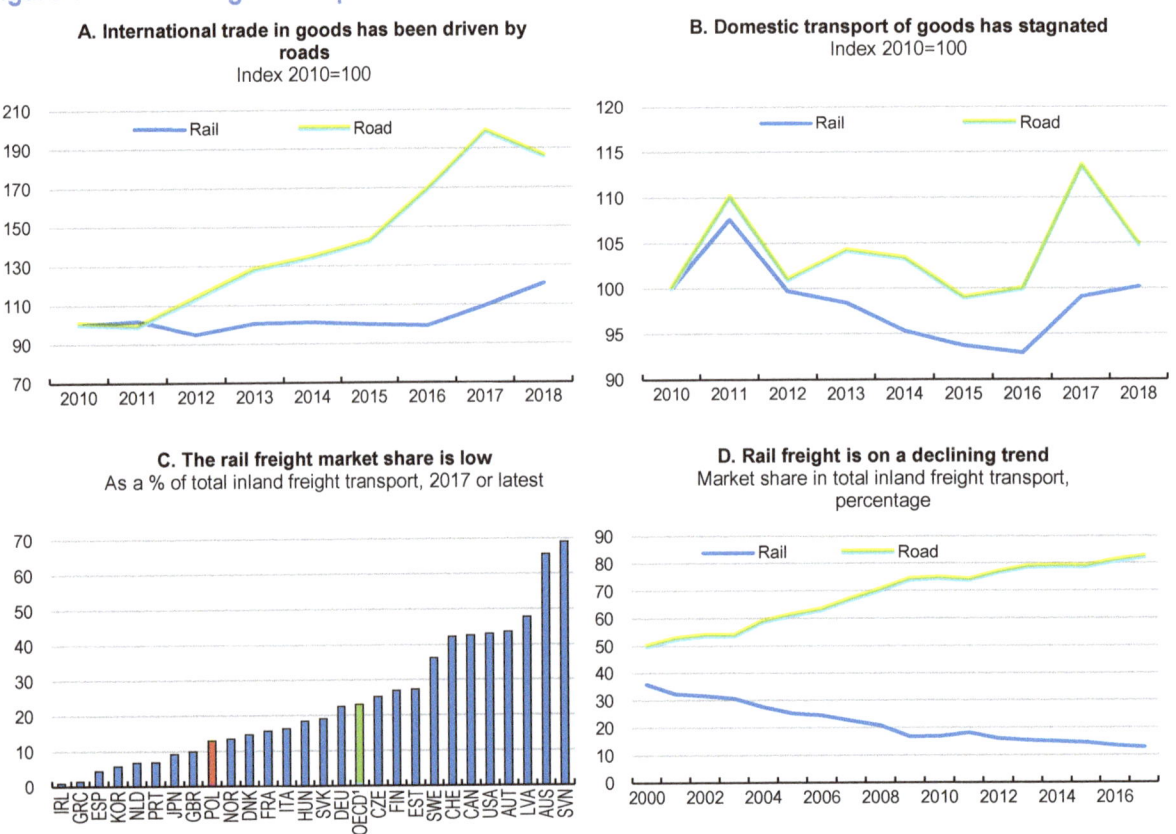

1. average for 2015, computed excluding Belgium, Iceland and Israel, for which data are unavailable or incomplete.
Source: ITF (2018), Inland Freight Transport (database), International Transport Forum, Paris.
StatLink https://doi.org/10.1787/888934209324

Investing in local public transportation could reduce congestion and enhance transport performance. Despite the use of EU Cohesion Funds for public transportation needs in 2014 – 2020, four of the five most congested small cities in the world in 2018 were located in Poland (*Łódź*, *Kraków*, *Poznań* and *Wrocław*), according to the TomTom Traffic Index . This suggests heavy investment needs in local public transportation. Better public transport services can reduce inequalities in distance-to-job opportunities and thereby have the potential to stimulate economic growth and social inclusion. Improved public transportation would also help improve air quality, since Poland's population exposure to particles is much higher than on average in the OECD. Yet, going forward, local governments will have to face the legacy of the coronavirus crisis and a tight budget constraint from ongoing personal income tax cuts (see KPI). If excessive cuts in public investment materialise, the central authorities could set up local investment grants to develop local public transports.

Developing multi-modal transport links to improve logistics' performance

Air transport for both passenger and freight expanded strongly before the coronavirus crisis (Figure 2.39). The authorities are planning the construction of a major airport between Warsaw and Łódź. This is a major undertaking with a total estimated cost – including road and rail connections – of PLN 80 bn or 3.8% of 2018 GDP. This new airport facility would help alleviate projected capacity constraints in the long-term, although traffic will not immediately return to pre-crisis levels (IATA, 2018). Regulatory measures could help develop further airfreight transport such as the implementation of paperless cargo freight formalities (e-freight) (IATA, 2018).

Seaport freight activity has also developed strongly over the past decade, but further investments to improve seaports' accessibility, notably for railways, are needed. Large investments in maritime transportation infrastructure can translate into substantial population and employment growth at a local level (Brooks et al., 2018). A concern regarding the development of Polish seaports remains their imperfect accessibility, which hinders their development and can increase congestion and pollution in the surrounding cities. Against this backdrop, substantial investments are underway to improve the rail accessibility of the Szczecin, Gdynia and Świnoujście seaports and the road and rail access to the seaport of Gdańsk. A multiannual program for the improvement of seaports and their connectivity also sets up investment targets up to 2030. Yet, the Supreme Audit Office underlined that there are concerns regarding the capacity of local authorities to finance the last-mile road facilities to seaports and that investments to improve the sea access to the seaport of Szczecin are needed to accommodate heavier maritime traffic (NIK, 2018d).

Figure 2.39. Airport traffic expanded fast before the coronavirus crisis

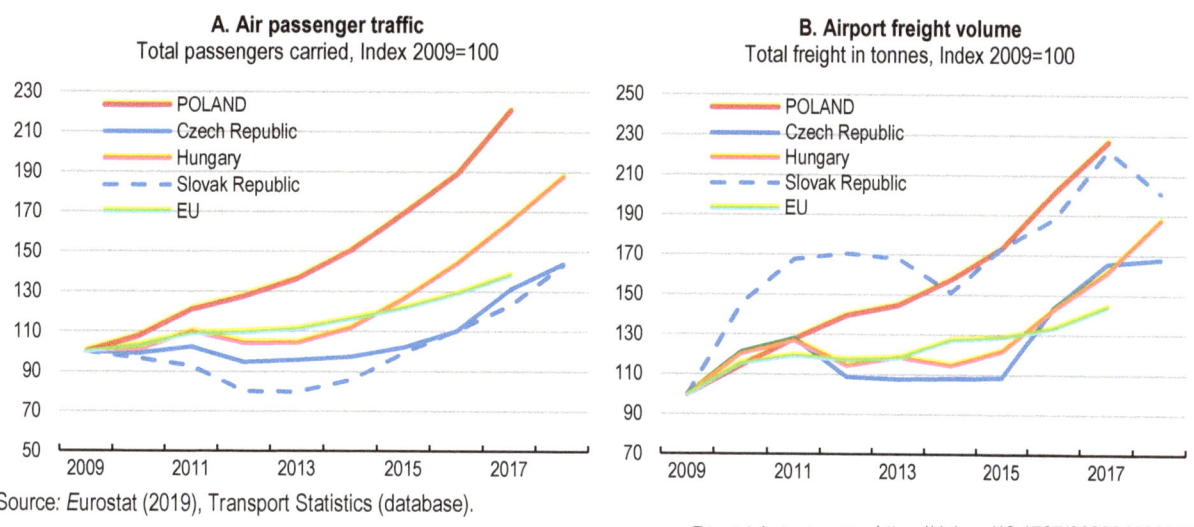

Source: Eurostat (2019), Transport Statistics (database).

StatLink https://doi.org/10.1787/888934209343

Improving the governance of infrastructure

Polish exports by mode of transport concentrate on maritime and road transport with only a small share from air transport. An international comparison of governance infrastructure indicators reveals there is room for improvement, particularly in terms of infrastructure outcomes (Hertie School of Governance, 2016). Moreover, Polish firms view adequate transport infrastructure as a barrier to long-term investment more often than on average in the European Union (EIB, 2019). Key challenges include the completion of road and railway contracts on time and within the budget envelope, since the construction industry is currently facing rising costs for both labour and construction materials due to boom-bust cycles in public investment related to the timing of disbursements of EU structural funds. Multiple estimates show significant average delay (ranging from 12 to 20 months)and increase in costs relative to initial estimates (from 50 to 89%) (reference;PNB, 2019). These implementation problems are hindering the development of infrastructure the country needs.

Putting a stronger focus on thorough cost-benefit analyses would help to better prioritise investment projects and improve their delivery. A cost-benefit analysis is mandatory for all projects benefiting from EU structural funds. However, putting in place a unified framework for project selection, with an appropriate pricing of the shadow price of carbon to reflect environmental externalities, would help rank alternative projects and competing versions of the same project. This could be done by changing the methodology of the cost-benefit analyses or introducing a new system of project selection where the result of the current methodology would be one of the factors taken into account in addition of environmental concerns and regional disparities. This would be supported by Poland's effort to develop an Integrated Traffic Model for Transport demand – including multi-modal transport flows – and the 2021-27 EU cohesion policy.

Establishing a government-commissioned committee to define and update a harmonised methodology for cost-benefit analyses and provide support to project holders would also be helpful. Australia has an agency (Infrastructure Australia) in charge of running extensive cost-benefit analyses for all large infrastructure projects, which is an example of good practice for project selection and implementation of large investment projects. Poland could also adapt Norway's transport infrastructure planning framework, including comprehensive cost-benefit analysis. Norway issued cost-benefit analyses guidelines that are embodied in an official document ("Circular R-109") and explain how to measure the benefits of a project. The guidelines also require an analysis of the environmental impact (OECD, 2019icel). Moreover, making *ex-post* evaluations mandatory for all large transport projects would also be helpful, since past experience can provide accurate estimates of engineering costs, land acquisition and maintenance costs in future years.

Spreading good practices to all relevant stakeholders, including local governments, would strengthen the influence of social and economic efficiency considerations in project selection and improve project implementation. A more efficient procurement of transport projects can encourage SMEs to update their business models with knock-on effects on their productivity and exports. Local governments are responsible for most infrastructure projects, but often lack capacity for managing larger ones (OECD, 2016b). This suggests stepping up efforts to reach out to all relevant stakeholders for project appraisal, selection and management. For example, to facilitate the use of analytical methods, Denmark set up an easy to use spreadsheet to promote the use of cost-benefit analyses. Moreover, encouraging stronger co-operation between neighbouring municipalities regarding spatial planning would help formulate an integrated development of local public transport in large urban areas (Janas and Jarczewski, 2017).

Supporting the tourism sector and its more equal regional development

The coronavirus crisis has curbed international travel. Despite government support, it hit hard Poland's most popular destinations and many SMEs that are the bulk of this industry (UNWTO, 2018). Before the pandemic, the direct contribution of tourism to the Polish economy appeared weak. It was largely linked to international visitors (OECD, 2020b), but their arrivals had lagged behind those of comparable economies

(Figure 2.40). Moreover, tourism has remained geared towards Mazowieckie, Malopoiskie, and the Zachodniopomorskie regions (Table 2.1). As the tourism recovery remains uncertain, the expectation is that domestic tourism offers the main chance for driving recovery. Special support should target these firms and regions to preserve the industry (OECD, 2020c). Recent initiatives, such as the 2020 Polish Tourist Voucher and the extended reimbursement period for tourist events not held due to the pandemic, are expected to reduce the short-term sectoral impact. Other initiatives are currently under discussion, namely the creation of a guarantee fund to reimburse customers for cancelled events.

Table 2.1. Tourism is concentrated in a few destinations

Overnight stays of foreign tourist in tourist accommodation establishments

Tourism region (voivodeship)	Share of overnight stays of foreign tourists (in percent)
West Pomerania region (Zachodniopomorskie)	21.6
Kraków region (Małopolskie)	22.0
Warsaw region (Mazowieckie)	16.8
Gdańsk region (Pomorskie)	8.9
Lower Silesia region (Dolnośląskie)	8.8
5 regions with the lowest GDP per capita[1]	6.5
Other regions[2]	15.4

1. Sum of the shares of overnight stays of foreign tourists for the five regions with the lowest GDP per capita, which are all located in Eastern Poland (Podlaskie, Lubelskie, Świętokrzyskie, Warmińsko-Mazurskie, Podkarpackie).
2. Sum of the shares of overnight stays of foreign tourists for the six remaining regions (Kujawsko-Pomorskie, Lubuskie, Łódzkie, Opolskie, Śląskie, Wielkopolskie).
Source: Statistics Poland, Tourism in 2019, Table II/14, Rzeszów 2020.

Over the long term, tourism could play a larger role in supporting small business dynamism and export revenues, while contributing to tackle regional disparities. Efforts should concentrate on strengthening infrastructure and developing a better branding as a tourist destination, as Poland's price competitiveness for tourism appears high (WEF, 2018). The Ministry of Economic Development, Labour and Technology (previously Ministry of Sport and Tourism), in charge of the tourism department, as well as the Polish Tourism Organisation, have launched several initiatives to promote Poland as a tourist destination, including the Polish Tourism Brands (Polskie Marki Turystyczne), which aims at developing a quality label system for tourist attractions. Yet, Poland's budget for tourism promotion appears small relative to other OECD countries such as Hungary (OECD, 2018h). Launching digital marketing campaigns such as Australia's "Experience Australia in 360°" or Korea's campaign to boost business tourism (meetings, incentives, conventions and exhibitions (MICE) market) could help. Additional funding could also support flagship projects and encourage SMEs to invest in tourism business akin to Austria's initiatives. This strategy could build on the promotion of the Polish UNESCO World Heritage Sites or nature-based tourism (for example, around the Great Masurian Lakes in North Eastern Poland) to attract high-spending international visitors and develop agro-tourism.

Formulating a long-term strategy and strengthening the governance structure would help to better coordinate tourism policies and develop tourism. Though such structure was adopted from 2007 to 2015, current inter-ministerial concertation and decisions on tourism bodies are on an ad-hoc basis. Poland's Strategy for Responsible Development also concentrates on health-related tourism, which is a marginal export category in most OECD countries (apart from Hungary where it represented 7% of travel exports in 2017). Such framework could be strengthened through the key existing institutions, the Ministry of Economic Development, as well as the Polish Tourism Organisation, and by involving on an ad-hoc basis other ministries and agencies, including non-government stakeholders. For example, the Tourism Policy Council of the United States is a working group of different federal agencies with the aim to promote tourism in federal decision-making Similarly, Switzerland's Tourismus Forum Schweiz is a platform for dialogue and coordination including federal and local governments as well as the private sector (OECD, 2018h).

Figure 2.40. International tourism was lagging before the coronavirus crisis

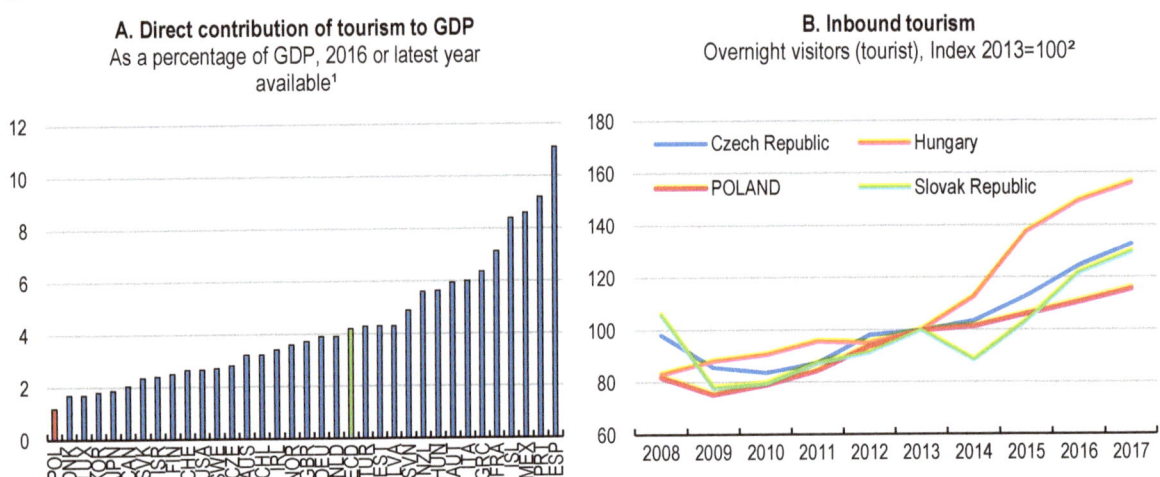

A. Direct contribution of tourism to GDP
As a percentage of GDP, 2016 or latest year available[1]

B. Inbound tourism
Overnight visitors (tourist), Index 2013=100[2]

1. Data for France refers to internal tourism consumption. Data for Germany refers to GVA. Data for Greece refers to tourism GVA of industries 55-56 or NACE Rev. 2. Data for Spain includes indirect effects.
2. Inbound tourism comprises the activities of a non-resident visitor within the country of reference.
Source: OECD (2019), Tourism Statistics (database).

StatLink https://doi.org/10.1787/888934209362

Policies should ensure a sustainable tourism development. In selected Polish cities (e.g., *Kraków),* there is some evidence that online accommodation platforms have negatively affect local residents through local housing markets (e.g., rising long-term rents). In this respect, online accommodation platforms should collect VAT on their sales (OECD, 2019r). Promoting the use of an occupancy tax – which is not commonly used by Polish municipalities – and implementing adequate regulation on urban planning and housing would be helpful. For example, Japan introduced regulations in 2018 for the owners of private lodgings used for short-term rentals and online platforms. Another example is Spain where municipalities (e.g. Madrid, Barcelona and Palma de Mallorca) enforced regulations such as the need for short-term vacation rentals to obtain a license. Moreover, developing programmes of sustainability certifications for businesses and destinations as done in Slovenia would help brand Poland as a sustainable tourist destination. Fully addressing the requests of the United Nations' World Heritage Committee regarding logging activities and other environmental concerns in the Białowieża forest – a large primary forest between Poland and Belarus – would also be a good move (UNESCO, 2019).

MAIN FINDINGS	RECOMMENDATIONS
(Key recommendations included in the Executive Summary are in bold italics)	
Easing further administrative costs and improving export procedures	
Tax procedures remain overly time consuming for SMEs. Smaller firms benefit from lower tax rates and regulatory exemptions. Yet, some regulations remain cumbersome which lower firm's ability to grow and access international markets.	Review tax expenditures and regulatory exemptions for smaller firms and envisage smoothing their effect once firms grow. Streamline administrative procedures without foregoing rules that are essential to ensure good environmental, social and economic outcomes.
Regulation and tax changes are numerous. Despite a dedicated framework for consultations, stakeholders do not perceive the existing ex-ante consultations as effective, which create higher fixed and variable costs for SMEs.	***Involve stakeholders further in the design of regulations through early consultation procedures.*** ***Conduct systematic ex-ante evaluations of regulations.***
Tourism remains underdeveloped and concentrated in a few regions and sites which are threatened by the coronavirus crisis.	In the near term, continue to support the most affected firms and workers in the tourism industry. Strengthen inter-ministerial cooperation focused on developing more sustainable and regionally balanced tourism.
Strengthening SMEs management and workers skills	
SMEs' managers appear to have significant skill gaps, which hinder internationalisation and productivity. The participation of smaller firms in lifelong learning is weak.	Provide financial support to develop workplace-based lifelong learning and the formation of training consortia by SMEs. Dedicate multi-annual co-financing schemes to build strong workplace-based vocational education programmes.
The coronavirus crisis will potentially imply strong shifts in economic structure. Vulnerable workers appear to make little use of lifelong training. Information and guidance about programmes and their effectiveness is improving but remains partly lacking.	***Strengthen lifelong learning opportunities notably for low-skilled workers, with a special focus on digital skills.*** Expand further the new system to certify training providers and the public database detailing their quality and courses.
Encouraging a better integration of foreign workers would ease SMEs' internationalisation.	Develop a migration policy strategy that better monitor work integration of foreigners while protecting migrants rights.
Encouraging the digitalisation of SMEs	
The diffusion of advanced digital technologies among Polish SMEs is weak and hinder their participation in e-commerce.	***Scale up existing programmes for SMEs with a focus on training and showcase best practices based on thorough impact analyses.***
Digitalisation remains uneven. The use of big data is constrained which may limit productivity gains and evidence-based policymaking, in particular in the healthcare sector.	***Develop data hubs providing companies and public services with access to large databases, notably in the healthcare sector, while ensuring digital security and privacy.***
Privacy concerns and digital security risks are barriers to the adoption of advanced digital technologies for SMEs.	Increase further data protection, cyber security and consumer protection, notably by improving public awareness.
The National Broadband Plan targets will not be met in 2020.	Set up a monitoring system for the deployment of high-speed broadband network, with timelines and quantitative targets.
Unduly restrictive regulations can hinder the development of the most advanced digital technologies.	Promote the use of regulatory sandboxes in other sectors than in financial services.
Easing internationalisation by improving transport infrastructure	
Despite recent progress, the quality of Polish infrastructure is low in some regions hindering firm internationalisation. Local governments are responsible for most of the infrastructure but lack information and capacity to manage large projects.	***Strengthen the role of ex ante cost-benefit analyses in project selection, for instance by establishing an independent evaluation body.*** Systematically collect information on the performance of public assets to better enable transparent, evidence-based, prioritisation of future infrastructure. Strengthen the share of maintenance in infrastructure spending.
The criteria for allocating the funds from the central government to the local authorities for the construction and modernisation of the local road network lack transparency.	Set up formal and transparent criteria in the allocation of funds to local authorities for their road network.
Congestion in Polish cities is high by international comparison which increase transport and trade costs.	Incentivise local authorities to develop public transport, for example through co-financing arrangements. Encourage neighbouring municipalities to cooperate through common urban mobility plans.
Before the coronavirus crisis, rail passenger transport growth was subdued and the market share of rail freight was declining.	Step up investment in the maintenance and upgrade of the rail network to develop more sustainable transport modes.

References

Adalet McGowan, M., D. Andrews and V. Millot (2017), "The Walking Dead? Zombie Firms and Productivity Performance in OECD Countries", OECD Economics Department Working Paper, No. 1372, OECD Publishing, Paris.

Albinowski, M., J. Hagemejer, S. Lovo, and G. Varela (2016), "The role of exchange rate and non-exchange rate related factors in polish firms' export performance," Policy Research Working Paper Series 7899, The World Bank.

Algan, Y. et al. (2018), "The Value of a Vacancy: Evidence from a Randomized Evaluation with Local Employment Agencies in France", Chaire sécurisation des parcours professionnels, No. 2018-05.

Almunia, M. and D. Lopez-Rodriguez (2013), "Firms' responses to tax enforcement strategies: Evidence from Spain", MPRA Paper, No. 44153, University Library of Munich.

Andersson, M. and H. Lööf (2009), "Learning-by-Exporting Revisited: The Role of Intensity and Persistence," Scandinavian Journal of Economics, Wiley Blackwell, vol. 111(4), pp. 893-916.

Andrews, D., Nicoletti, G. and Timiliotis, C. (2018), Going Digital: What determines technology diffusion among firms?, Background Paper 2018 Global Forum on Productivity.

Araújo, S., T. Chalaux and D. Haugh (2018), "Who's in your export market? The changing pattern of competition in world trade", OECD Economics Department Working Papers, No. 1526. OECD Publishing, Paris.

Bailin Rivares, A., Gal, P., Millot, V., and Sorbe, S. (2019), "Like it or not? The impact of online platforms on the productivity of incumbent service providers", OECD Economics Department Working Papers, No. 1548.

Braconier H. and M. Pisu (2013), Road Connectivity and the Border Effect: Evidence from Europe, OECD Economics Department Working Papers, No. 1073.

Bergner, S. et al. (2017), "The Use of SME Tax Incentives in the European Union", ZEW Discussion Paper, No. 17-006, Centre for European Economic Research, http://dx.doi.org/10.2139/ssrn.2910339.

Berthou et al. (2015), "Assessing European firms' exports and productivity distributions: the CompNet trade module", ECB working paper series 1788, May.

Bloom, N., K. Manova, J. Van Reenen, S. Teng Sun and Z. Yu (2018), "Managing Trade: Evidence from China and the US," CESifo Working Paper Series 7113, CESifo Group.

Brandt, N. (2016), "Making better use of skills and migration in Poland," OECD Economics Department Working Papers 1301, OECD Publishing, Paris.

Brooks, L., N. Gendron-Carrier, and G. Rua (2018). "The Local Impact of Containerization," Finance and Economics Discussion Series 2018-045. Washington: Board of Governors of the Federal Reserve System.

Cadestin, C., et al. (2018), "Multinational enterprises and global value chains: New Insights on the trade-investment nexus", OECD Science, Technology and Industry Working Papers, No. 2018/05, OECD Publishing, Paris.

Cadestin, C., et al. (2019), "Multinational enterprises in domestic value chains", OECD Science, Technology and Industry Policy Papers, No. 63, OECD Publishing, Paris.

Cai J. and A. Szeidl (2018), "Interfirm relationships and business performance", Quarterly Journal of Economics, Vol. 133(3), pp. 1229-1282.

Caldera Sánchez, A. (2018), "Building a stronger and more integrated Europe", OECD Economics Department Working Papers, No. 1491, OECD Publishing, Paris.

Carlino, G. and W.R. Kerr (2015), "Agglomeration and innovation" in G. Duranton, J.V. Henderson and W.C. Strange (eds.), Handbook of Regional and Urban Economics, Vol. 5, Elsevier, Amsterdam, Chap. 6, pp. 349-404.

Causa, O., M. Hermansen and N. Ruiz (2016), "The Distributional Impact of Structural Reforms", OECD Economics Department Working Papers, No. 1342, OECD Publishing, Paris.

Cdg (2018), Christian Doppler research organisation website, https://www.cdg.ac.at/en/

Cedefop (2016), Poland Mismatch priority occupations, https://skillspanorama.cedefop.europa.eu/en/analytical_highlights/poland-mismatch-priority-occupations.

CEPEJ (2016), "European judicial systems' efficiency and quality of justice", CEPEJ Studies, No. 23, European Commission for the Efficiency of Justice.

Comet (2018), "Comet K2 Digital Mobility", (Competence Centres for Excellent Technology), https://www.v2c2.at/cooperation/comet/

DeStefano, T., Kneller, R., Timmis, J. (2019), Cloud Computing and Firm Growth, University of Nottingham Research Paper Series 2019/09, https://www.nottingham.ac.uk/gep/documents/papers/2019/2019-09.pdf

Dewatripont, M. and Legros, P. (2005), Public-private partnerships: contract design and risk transfer, EIB Papers 1/2005, Vol. 10, pp. 120-145.

DFA (2015), Global Irish: Ireland's Diaspora Review, Department of Foreign Affairs.

Drozd, Maciej Adam; Kadziauskas, Giedrius; Ristic, Gordana; Zadernowski, Marek Ryszard; Vranic, Goran. 2018. Poland catching-up regions 2 - Safer food, better business in Podkarpackie and Lubelskie (Polish). Washington, D.C. : World Bank Group.

EC (2014), Good practices in the return and reintegration of irregular migrants, A study from the European Migration Network, Synthesis Report for the EMN Focussed Study, European Commission.

EC (2017), Europe's Digital Progress Report 2017 – Poland, Brussels, https://ec.europa.eu/transparency/regdoc/rep/10102/2017/EN/SWD-2017-160-F1-EN-MAIN-PART-55.PDF

EC (2018a), Annual Report on European SMEs 2017/2018, Special Background Document on the internationalisation of SMEs, European Commission.

EC (2018b), Annual Report on European SMEs 2017/2018 Growing beyond borders, European Commission.

EC (2019a), 2019 European Semester: Country Report – Poland, European Commission.

EC (2019b), Environmental Implementation Review 2019 – Poland, European Commission.

EC (2019c), Digital Economy and Society Index (DESI), Country Report, European Commission, Brussels.

EC (2020), 2020 European Semester: Country Report – Poland, European Commission.

EC (2020desi), Digital Economy and Society Index (DESI) 2020 - Poland, European Commission.

EESC (2018), Study on best practices on national export promotion activities, Europen Economic and Social Committee.

EF (2019), EF English Proficiency Index - A Ranking of 100 Countries and Regions by English Skills, Education First.

European Court of Auditors (2016), Rail freight transport in the EU: still not on the right track, Report, Luxembourg, https://www.eca.europa.eu/en/Pages/DocItem.aspx?did=36398.

EIB (2019), EIB Investment Survey: Poland Overview, European Investment Bank, Luxembourg. https://www.eib.org/attachments/efs/eibis_2017_poland_en.pdf

Eurostat (2019), "Member States (EU28) trade by BEC product group since 1999" in International trade in goods (ext_go_agg) database.

Eurostat (2020), Big data analysis database.

Fialho, P., G. Quintini and M. Vandeweyer (2019), "Returns to different forms of job related training: Factoring in informal learning", OECD Social, Employment and Migration Working Papers, No. 231, OECD Publishing, Paris.

Filippaios, F. (2018), "Cross region comparative study on the Internationalisation of Small and Medium Enterprises", *Comparative Cross-regional Study for Interreg Europe*.

Gal, P. and A. Theising (2015), "The macroeconomic impact of structural policies on labour market outcomes in OECD countries: A reassessment", OECD Economics Department Working Papers, No. 1271, OECD Publishing, Paris.

Garicano, L., C. Lelarge and J.Van Reenen (2016), "Firm size distortions and the productivity distribution: Evidence from France", American Economic Review, Vol. 106, pp. 3439-79.

Gouëdard, P., B. Pont and R. Viennet (2020), "Education responses to COVID-19: Implementing a way forward", OECD Education Working Papers, No. 224, OECD Publishing, Paris

Griffith R., S. Redding and J. Van Reenen (2004), "Mapping the Two Faces of R&D: Productivity Growth in a Panel of OECD Industries," The Review of Economics and Statistics, vol. 86(4), pages 883-895.

Growiec, J. et al. (2019), The Contribution of Immigration from Ukraine to Economic Growth in Poland, http://www.nbp.pl/badania/seminaria/31x2019.pdf

Guillou, S. and T. Treibich (2019), "Firm export diversification and change in workforce composition", Review of the World Economy, Vol. 155, pp. 645-676.

Hagemejer, J. (2018), "Trade and Growth in the New Member States: The Role of Global Value Chains", *Emerging Markets Finance and Trade*, Vol. 54:11, pp. 2630-2649.

Hagemejer, J. and M. Kolasa (2011), "Internationalisation and Economic Performance of Enterprises: Evidence from Polish Firm-level Data," The World Economy, vol. 34(1), pages 74-100.

Harding, T. and B. Javorcik (2013), "Investment Promotion and FDI Inflows: Quality Matters", CESifo Economic Studies, Vol. 59, pp. 337-59.

Harms H. (2018), "The Funding Model of the Christian Doppler Research Association", powerpoint presentation at the OECD, Paris on 14 March.

Hausmann, R., J. Hwang and D. Rodrik (2007), "What you export matters", Journal of Economic Growth, Vol. 12(1), pp. 1-25.

Hertie School of Governance (2016). The Governance Report 2016: Infrastructure Governance Indicators, Hertie School of Governance: Berlin.

Iacovone, L., W. Maloney and D. Mckenzie (2019), "Improving Management with Individual and Group-Based Consulting : Results from a Randomized Experiment in Colombia," Policy Research Working Paper Series 8854, The World Bank.

IATA (2018), Poland: Air Transport Regulatory Competitiveness Indicators, International Air Transport Association, Montréal.

ITF (2017), Strategic Infrastructure Planning: International Best Practice, International Transport Forum, Paris. https://www.itf-oecd.org/sites/default/files/docs/strategic-infrastructure-planning.pdf

ITF (2019), Benchmarking Accessibility in Cities: Measuring the Impact of Proximity and Transport Performance, International Transport Forum, Paris. https://www.itf-oecd.org/benchmarking-accessibility-cities

ITF (2020), Competition for Infrastructure Projects: Traditional Procurement and PPPs in Europe, International Transport Forum, Paris.

Janas, K., and W. Jarczewski (2017), Zarządzanie i współpraca w miejskich obszarach funkcjonalnych. Raport o stanie polskich miast, Obserwatorium Polityki Miejskiej IRM, Kraków.

Lang, V. and M. Mendes Tavares (2018), "The Distribution of Gains from Globalization," IMF Working Papers 18/54, International Monetary Fund.

Lewiatan (2019), *Jak przyspieszyć inwestycje prywatne w Polsce?,* Opracowanie zbiorowe pod redakcją dr. Grzegorza Baczewskiego.

López González, J. and S. Sorescu (2019), "Helping SMEs internationalise through trade facilitation", OECD Trade Policy Papers, No. 229, OECD Publishing, Paris.

Lorenz, E. et J. Potter (2019), « Workplace organisation and innovation in small and medium-sized enterprises », OECD SME and Entrepreneurship Papers, No. 17, OECD Publishing, Paris

Malgouyres, C., Mayer, T., Mazet, C. (2019), Technology-induced Trade Shocks ? Evidence from Broadband Expansion in France, CEPR Discussion Papers 13847, https://cepr.org/active/publications/discussion_papers/dp.php?dpno=13847

Marchese, M., et al. (2019), "Enhancing SME productivity: Policy highlights on the role of managerial skills, workforce skills and business linkages", OECD SME and Entrepreneurship Papers, No. 16, OECD Publishing, Paris.

McKinsey (2015), Poland 2025: Europe's new growth engine, https://www.mckinsey.com/~/media/mckinsey/business%20functions/economic%20studies%20temp/our%20insights/how%20poland%20can%20become%20a%20european%20growth%20engine/poland%202025_full_report.ashx

Melitz, M. and G. Ottaviano (2008), "Market Size, Trade, and Productivity", Review of Economic Studies, Vol. 75(1), pp. 295-316.

Ministerstwo Infrastruktury (2019), Projekt Strategii Zrównoważonego Rozwoju Transportu do 2030 roku, Warsaw. https://www.gov.pl/web/infrastruktura/projekt-strategii-zrownowazonego-rozwoju-transportu-do-2030-roku2

Miroudot, S. and C. Cadestin (2017a), "Services in Global Value Chains: Trade patterns and gains from specialisation", OECD Trade Policy Papers, No. 208, OECD Publishing, Paris.

Morales, E., G. Sheu and A. Zahler (2014), "Gravity and Extended Gravity: Using Moment Inequalities to Estimate a Model of Export Entry", NBER Working Paper, No. 19916.

MR (2019a), Ustawa o zatorach płatniczych z podpisem prezydenta RP, Ministerstwo Rozwoju, https://www.gov.pl/web/rozwoj/ustawa-o-zatorach-platniczych-z-podpisem-prezydenta-rp

MR (2019b), Nowy projekt wspierający eksport polskich firm, Ministerstwo Rozwoju, https://www.gov.pl/web/rozwoj/nowy-projekt-wspierajacy-eksport-polskich-firm

MR (2019c), Podsumowanie pilotażowego projektu "Centra usług biznesowych w miastach średnich", Ministerstwo Rozwoju, https://www.gov.pl/web/rozwoj/podsumowanie-pilotazu-projektu-centra-uslug-biznesowych-w-miastach-srednich.

Mrozeck, W. (2019), Geograficzne zróżnicowanie handlu zagranicznego Polski, https://www.obserwatorfinansowy.pl/tematyka/makroekonomia/geograficzne-zroznicowanie-handlu-zagranicznego-polski/.

NBP (2016), Potencjał innowacyjny gospodarki: Uwarunkowania, determinanty, perspektywy, Narodowy Bank Polski, Warsaw.

NIK (2016), Działalność Ośrodków Innowacji, Najwyżsa Izba Kontroli, Warsaw.

NIK (2018a), NIK o dokonywaniu oceny wpływu w ramach rządowego procesu legislacyjnego, Najwyższa Izba Kontroli, https://www.nik.gov.pl/aktualnosci/nik-o-dokonywaniu-oceny-wplywu-w-nbsp-ramach-rzadowego-procesu-legislacyjnego.html

NIK (2018b), Niechciane drogi, Najwyższa Izba Kontroli, Warsaw.
https://www.nik.gov.pl/aktualnosci/niechciane-drogi.html

NIK (2018c), NIK o bezpieczeństwie przewozów kolejowych, Najwyższa Izba Kontroli, Warsaw.
https://www.nik.gov.pl/aktualnosci/nik-o-bezpieczenstwie-przewozow-kolejowych.html

NIK (2018d), Porty morskie „zatoną" bez lepszej infrastruktury transportowej, Najwyższa Izba Kontroli,
Warsaw. https://www.nik.gov.pl/aktualnosci/infrastruktura/porty-morskie.html

NIK (2019), Państwo niegotowe na cudzoziemców, Najwyższa Izba Kontroli, Warsaw.

Odeck, J., Welde, M.; Volden, G. H. (2015), "The Impact of External Quality Assurance of Costs
Estimates on Cost Overruns: Empirical Evidence from the Norwegian Road Sector", European
Journal of Transport and Infrastructure Research, No. 15(3).

OECD (2010), OECD Tax Policy Studies Tax Policy Reform and Economic Growth, OECD Publishing,
Paris.

OECD (2013), Coping with Emigration in Baltic and East European Countries, OECD Publishing, Paris.

OECD (2014), "Wireless Market Structures and Network Sharing", OECD Digital Economy Papers, No.
243, OECD Publishing, Paris.

OECD (2015), Taxation of SMEs in OECD and G20 Countries, OECD Tax Policy Studies, No. 23, OECD
Publishing, Paris.

OECD (2016a), Policy Priorities for Making Poland a More Inclusive and Knowledge-Based Economy,
OECD Publishing, Paris.

OECD (2016b), OECD Economic Surveys – Poland, OECD Publishing, Paris.

OECD (2017a), "How to make trade work for all" in OECD Economic outlook, OECD Publishing, Paris.

OECD (2017b), SME and Entrepreneurship Policy in Canada, OECD Studies on SMEs and
Entrepreneurship, OECD Publishing, Paris.

OECD (2017c), Getting Skills Right: Good Practice in Adapting to Changing Skill Needs: A Perspective
on France, Italy, Spain, South Africa and the United Kingdom, OECD Publishing, Paris.

OECD (2017d), OECD Digital Economy Outlook 2017, OECD Publishing, Paris.

OECD (2017e), OECD Economic Surveys: Austria 2017, OECD Publishing, Paris.

OECD (2018a), OECD Economic Surveys: Poland 2018, OECD Publishing, Paris.

OECD (2018b), "Accounting for firm heterogeneity in global value chains: The role of Small and Medium
sized Enterprises", OECD Working Party on International Trade in Goods and Trade in Services
Statistics.

OECD (2018c), Putting a face behind the jobs at risk of automation, OECD policy brief, , OECD
Publishing, Paris.

OECD (2018d), Implications of E-commerce for Competition Policy - Background Note, Paris.
https://one.oecd.org/document/DAF/COMP(2018)3/en/pdf

OECD (2018e), OECD Reviews of Digital Transformation: Going Digital in Sweden, OECD Publishing,
Paris.

OECD (2018f), OECD Tourism Trends and Policies 2018, OECD Publishing, Paris.

OECD (2018g), Developing Robust Project Pipelines for Low-Carbon Infrastructure, Green Finance and
Investment, OECD Publishing, Paris.

OECD (2018x), Regulatory Policy: Poland, OECD Publishing, Paris.

OECD (2019a), OECD SME and Entrepreneurship Outlook 2019, OECD Publishing, Paris.

OECD (2019b), Regions in Industrial Transition: Policies for People and Places, OECD Publishing, Paris.

OECD (2019c), Country note Poland, OECD Publishing, Paris.

OECD (2019d), OECD Services Trade Restrictiveness Index (STRI): Poland 2019, OECD Publishing, Paris.

OECD (2019e), "R&D Tax Incentives: Poland 2019", OECD Publishing, Paris.

OECD (2019f), Poland Trade facilitation performance, OECD Publishing, Paris.

OECD (2019g), OECD Skills Strategy Poland: Assessment and Recommendations, OECD Skills Studies, OECD Publishing, Paris.

OECD (2019h), OECD Skills Strategy 2019: Skills to Shape a Better Future, OECD Publishing, Paris.

OECD (2019i), Individual Learning Accounts: Panacea or Pandora's Box?, OECD Publishing, Paris.

OECD (2019j), OECD Economic Surveys – Estonia, OECD Publishing, Paris.

OECD (2019k), Unpacking E-Commerce: Business Models, Trends and Policies, OECD Publishing, Paris.

OECD (2019l), Measuring the Digital Transformation: A Roadmap for the Future, OECD Publishing, Paris.

OECD (2019m), "Enhancing Access and Connectivity to Harness Digital Transformation", OECD Going Digital Policy Note, OECD, Paris.

OECD (2019n), "The road to 5G networks: Experience to date and future developments", OECD Digital Economy Papers, No. 284, OECD Publishing, Paris, https://doi.org/10.1787/2f880843-en.

OECD (2019o), Enhancing Access to and Sharing of Data: Reconciling Risks and Benefits for Data Re-use across Societies, OECD Publishing, Paris.

OECD (2019p), Government at a Glance 2019, OECD Publishing, Paris.

OECD (2019q), OECD Skills Outlook 2019 : Thriving in a Digital World, OECD Publishing, Paris.

OECD (2019r), The Role of Digital Platforms in the Collection of VAT/GST on Online Sales, OECD, Paris.

OECD (2019s), PISA 2018 Results (Volume I): What Students Know and Can Do, OECD Publishing, Paris.

OECD (2019t), SME and Entrepreneurship Policy in Ireland, OECD Studies on SMEs and Entrepreneurship, OECD Publishing, Paris, https://doi.org/10.1787/e726f46d-en.

OECD (2019icel), OECD Economic Surveys: Iceland 2019, OECD Publishing, Paris.

OECD (2020a), Corporate and personal insolvency during the COVID-19 crisis, OECD Publishing, Paris.

OECD (2020b), OECD Tourism Trends and Policies 2020, OECD Publishing, Paris.

OECD (2020c), Tourism Policy Responses to the coronavirus (COVID-19), OECD Publishing, Paris.

OECD (2020d), OECD Economic Outlook, Volume 2020 Issue 1, OECD Publishing, Paris, https://doi.org/10.1787/0d1d1e2e-en.

OECD (2020gvc), COVID-19 and global value chains: Policy options to build more resilient production networks, OECD Publishing, Paris.

Ottaviano, G., G. Peri, Giovanni and G. Wright (2018), "Immigration, trade and productivity in services: Evidence from U.K. firms," Journal of International Economics, vol. 112(C), pp. 88-108.

PAIH (2019), Analiza potencjału internacjonalizacji polskich firm oraz promocji polskich branż priorytetowych na rynkach perspektywicznych poprzez kanały elektroniczne – „E-EKSPORT" Raport końcowy 2019, https://www.trade.gov.pl/pl/niezbednik-eksportera/303217,eksport-przez-internet-raport-dla-przedsiebiorc-ow.html

PARP (2019a), Raport o stanie sektora małych i średnich przedsiębiorstw w Polsce, Polska Agencja Rozwoju Przedsiębiorczości, Warsaw, 2019.

PARP (2019b), *Aktywność zawodowa i edukacyjna dorosłych Polaków wobec wyzwań współczesnej gospodarki Raport podsumowujący VI edycję badania BKL w latach 2017–2018*, Polska Agencja Rozwoju Przedsiębiorczości, Warsaw, 2019.

PIE (2019), 15 years of Poland in the European Union, Polish Economic Institue, Warsaw.

Planes-Satorra, S. and C. Paunov (2019), "The digital innovation policy landscape in 2019", OECD Science, Technology and Industry Policy Papers, No. 71, OECD Publishing, Paris, https://doi.org/10.1787/6171f649-en.

PNB (2019), Construction Contracts Worth PLN 5 bn in Danger, Polish News Bulletin, June 19, Warsaw.

Rouzet, D., S. Benz and F. Spinelli (2017), "Trading firms and trading costs in services: Firm-level analysis", OECD Trade Policy Papers, No. 210, OECD Publishing, Paris, https://doi.org/10.1787/b1c1a0e9-en.

Slattery, S. and O. Zidar (2020), "Evaluating State and Local Business Tax Incentives", NBER Working Paper No. 26603.

Sorbe, S., P. Gal and V. Millot (2018), "Can productivity still grow in service-based economies?: Literature overview and preliminary evidence from OECD countries", OECD Economics Department Working Papers, No. 1531, OECD Publishing, Paris.

Statistics Poland (2019a),

Statistics Poland (2019b),

Szpunar, p. and J. Hagemejer (2018), "Globalisation and the Polish economy: macro and micro growth effects", BIS paper, No. 100, https://www.bis.org/publ/bppdf/bispap100_r.pdf

Thissen M., Ivanova O., Mandras G., Husby T. (2019), "European NUTS 2 regions: construction of interregional trade-linked Supply and Use tables with consistent transport flows", JRC Working Papers on Territorial Modelling and Analysis No 01/2019.

UKE (2019), Report on the activities of the President of the Office of Electronic Communications for 2018, Urząd Komunikacji Elektronicznej, Warsaw.

UN (2019), "Concluding observations on the combined twenty-second to twenty-fourth periodic reports of Poland", Committee on the Elimination of Racial Discrimination, International Convention on the Elimination of All Forms of Racial Discrimination, CERD/C/POL/CO/22-24, United Nations.

UNESCO (2019), Decisions adopted during the 43rd session of the World Heritage Committee (Baku 2019), United Nations Educational, Scientific and Cultural Organization, Paris. https://whc.unesco.org/archive/2019/whc19-43com-18-en.pdf

Unido (2005), Methodology: Development of SME Supplier Networks. Abridged Version, Unido.

UNWTO, European Union Tourism Trends, United Nations World Tourism Organization, Madrid.

WEF (2018), Travel and Tourism Competitiveness Report 2017, World Economic Forum, Geneva.

WEF (2019), *The Global Competitiveness Report 2019*, World Economic Forum.

World Bank (2013), The Status of Contract Enforcement in Poland, World Bank, Washington, DC.

World Bank (2016), Doing Business 2017: Equal Opportunity for All, World Bank, Washington, DC.

World Bank (2017), Poland Catching Up Regions Overview Report, Vol. 1, Washington, DC.

World Bank (2018), Logistics Performance Index - Country Score Card: Poland 2018, World Bank, Washington, DC.

World Bank (2019), Doing Business 2020, World Bank, Washington, DC.

Lightning Source UK Ltd.
Milton Keynes UK
UKHW020835280121
377823UK00001B/3

9 789264 632592